808

D0512456

Successful Legal Writing

AUSTRALIA
Law Book Co.
Sydney

CANADA and USA
Carswell
Toronto

HONG KONG
Sweet & Maxwell Asia

NEW ZEALAND
Brookers
Wellington

SINGAPORE and MALAYSIA
Sweet & Maxwell Asia
Singapore and Kuala Lumpur

Successful Legal Writing

by

EDWINA HIGGINS LL.B., LL.M., P.G.C.E.
Senior Learning and Teaching Fellow, School of Law,
Manchester Metropolitan University

LAURA TATHAM B.A., M.Sc., P.G.C.E.
Principal Lecturer, School of Law,
Manchester Metropolitan University

THOMSON
TM
SWEET & MAXWELL

Published in 2006 by
Sweet & Maxwell Limited of
100 Avenue Road London NW3 3PF
http:/www/sweetandmaxwell.co.uk
Typeset by Servis Filmsetting Limited, Manchester
Printed in England by Ashford Colour Press, Gosport, Hants

A CIP catalogue record for this book is available from the British Library

ISBN 0 421 96120 1 / 978 0 421 96120 3

All rights reserved. Crown copyright material is reproduced with the permission of the Controller of HMSO and the Queen's Printer for Scotland.
No part of this publication may be reproduced or transmitted, in any form or by any means, or stored in any retrieval system of any nature, without prior written permission, except for permitted fair dealing under the Copyright, Designs and Patents Act 1988, or in accordance with the terms of a licence issued by the Copyright Licensing Agency in respect of photocopying and/or reprographic reproduction. Application for permission for other use of copyright material including permission to reproduce extracts in other published works shall be made to the publishers. Full acknowledgment of author, publisher and source must be given.

No natural forests were destroyed to make this product, only farmed timber
was used and re-planted.

©
Sweet and Maxwell
2006

Contents

4. How to make your diagnosis

5. Planning and carrying out your research

6. How to use your materials in the writing process

7. The writing phase of your assignment

8. Writing in good English

9. Finishing your work and utilising feedback

Acknowledgements

The idea for this book grew from our participation in a seminar on Legal Writing organised by the UK Centre for Legal Education and the Society of Legal Scholars at Bournemouth University in March 2005, where we gave a brief presentation about the classes we run at MMU to encourage students to engage with our assessment criteria. It became apparent during the course of a very lively day that legal academics have strong feelings about the importance of good writing, and therefore how much students have to gain by working on their skills. We'd like to thank everyone at our session for their contributions.

We'd also like to thank:

Our students, who have helped us to appreciate the value of good writing, and particularly students of the LLB part time degree and the Graduate Diploma in Law at Manchester Metropolitan University for their participation and feedback on the legal writing classes we have run over the past five years.

Our colleagues in the School of Law at MMU, who have shared their tips on good writing with us, and in particular Robin Singleton and Lorraine Wrigley for their advice on tackling Tort and Contract questions. Any errors remain ours.

Our friends and family: Peter and Lena, for their hospitality and kindness in providing a haven where the bulk of the book was written; Graham, Mary and Jane, for their advice and support throughout, as well as their help with the proof-reading; Sarah, who pre-ordered a copy despite the promise of a free one; Rob, for his support, and for allowing Eddie to commandeer his PC for weeks on end when her own buckled under the strain; Dave, for his support when Laura needed to work on the book yet again; Maeve, who acted as our style consultant, and Lily, for encouraging us to get our "story" finished.

And finally Nicola Thurlow at Sweet & Maxwell needs thanks for her patience in the face of adversity when the irony of the book's title in respect of our writing methods must have dawned on her at an early stage.

How to Use this Book

Our aim is to help you become successful legal writers. We've designed this book to be flexible so you can use it in different ways according to your own particular needs. This means taking a moment to think about your purpose in selecting this book. Whatever your motivation, the advice within it will be of most value if you take some time to identify exactly what *you* need to get out of it.

Although we provide lots of advice, we can't give you a blueprint which will automatically work for you; what you must do is reflect on what *you* need to do to improve so you can target the parts of the book which will help you to write more successfully. For example perhaps:

- *You are beginning your studies and want to develop a good technique from the start.* Start with Ch.1 where we explore the qualities that your tutors will be looking for in a good piece of writing and some of the common weaknesses we've seen in student work, and then work through our suggested cycle for successful writing which we explain in Ch.2. This should help you reflect on the areas you need to focus on, and therefore which further chapters to work through, or you may prefer to read all the remaining chapters in order to maximise the benefits.
- *You already know a particular weakness in your work, perhaps from feedback, and want to tackle that.* We've used an FAQ format throughout the book, so use the contents page to find the relevant section you need.
- *You don't have a specific issue already but know you need to make some general improvements somewhere.* Again, start with Ch.1 to gain a better understanding of the qualities good writing has, identify your strengths and weaknesses and move to the right parts of the book to help you.

Completing the activities

You will be invited to work through several activities as you read, so it will be useful to have a pen and pad of paper ready. Most of the activities do not have a set "right" answer but instead will invite you to compare your views with ours to encourage reflection. We know it is tempting to miss out completing activities and skip straight to the "answers". However, we have designed the activities to help you develop your *own* writing skills—if you don't work through them, you won't get as much value from the book. You must avoid a "just give me the answer" mentality if you are serious about becoming a successful legal writer.

Appendices

In the appendices you will find examples of pro formas that you can use to help you carry out different elements of the writing cycle successfully. You may wish to copy these if you want to use them more than once. There are also sample essays and examples of assessment criteria.

And finally

We can't offer a short cut to getting better marks with less effort. There is no substitute for working hard by attending classes, doing research in the library, preparing for seminars and so on. What we can do is help you to make the *most* of the time you spend carrying out this work, by showing you how to convert all your efforts into successful legal writing.

1   Introduction

What is the purpose of this chapter?

In this chapter we will encourage you to think about the qualities which make successful writing, with **1–1** particular reference to the sort of writing you will be asked to do as part of your legal studies. This will provide a basis for you to think about how to improve your own writing, and therefore which parts of the rest of the book you will need to focus on most. By the end of this chapter you will:

- have thought about the purpose of writing in different situations and the implications of this for your academic work;
- understand the way in which your work will be judged, and in particular what is meant by assessment criteria;
- have had an opportunity to reflect on your own writing skills and make a plan to improve.

What is "successful" legal writing?

Probably the most important skill which marks out a good lawyer (whether a practising lawyer or **1–2** an academic lawyer like you, now you're a law student) is the ability to **communicate**. The most brilliant academic will be a terrible lecturer if he or she cannot get a message across in class—and similarly a barrister in court might be wonderfully well-prepared but will need to argue clearly and effectively in order to have the best chance of winning the case.

The concept of effective communication is something which we perhaps most obviously associate with communications which are made orally. If we say someone is a "good communicator", we often mean that they speak and argue well, just as in the example given above. But oral communication is only part of the story; written communication is just as important. A practising solicitor needs to be able to write appropriately to clients and other solicitors in order to advise and negotiate; a barrister must write effective advice notes and briefs.

The ability to communicate effectively in writing is vital for law students. Obviously it is important for you to understand the aspects of law you will be studying in order to succeed, but the way you demonstrate this to your tutors—which is what you need to do to get good marks—is through the work you produce. You need to be able to *show* your tutors that you understand the law. It is particularly important that you hone your skills in written communication because on law degree courses and certainly on the Graduate Diploma in Law ("CPE"), there is likely to be a much stronger emphasis on written assessments, such as essays, reports, exams and projects or dissertations, than there is on oral assessments like presentations and moots (although you may well do some of these as well). For your legal writing to be "successful", it must be an effective communication of your understanding of the law.

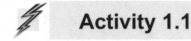 **Activity 1.1**

1–3   There are various myths and misconceptions about studying law successfully. Reflect on your own perceptions with the following exercise, which contains a number of statements about studying law and producing legal writing. Which do you think are true, and which are false? What are your reasons for thinking as you do? There are not necessarily any right and wrong answers to this, but you can compare your perceptions with our comments.

> A. The main factor in doing well is the amount of work you put in.
> B. Your level of intelligence is the key factor in how well you do.
> C. Being able to write is something you are either good at or you're not.
> D. The key to good writing is effective communication.

Compare your views:

1. The main factor in doing well is the amount of work you put in.
The amount of work you do is certainly important: if you want to do well, then you will have to put the work in. But clocking up so many hours in the law library is no guarantee of success in itself; you need to reflect on whether you are working *effectively*, and whether or not you have developed the skills to translate that effort into good marks through effective communication. You will also need to have a clear idea of the *purpose* of any particular assessment in order to complete it successfully, and we consider this further later in this chapter.

2. Your level of intelligence is the key factor in how well you do.
Well, your level of intelligence will certainly be a factor, but you may be surprised to learn that it is not necessarily the most important. The most intelligent student will lose marks if he or she has failed to put in the necessary work, or communicates poorly. That is why it is important to understand what you are being asked to do, and why, so that you can plan accordingly. (We might also argue that a student who fails to put in the necessary work without good reason is not really showing much sign of this supposed intelligence!) Students who work strategically and make the most of their skills are going to do better.

3. Being able to write is something you are either good at or you're not.
It can seem like this. Certainly some people find it easier to write effectively than others—which is great if you happen to be one of those people, and frustrating if you aren't—but most of the techniques of good legal writing can be acquired through practice. There is more detailed information on how to improve your writing throughout this book, so it is worth spending some time thinking which aspects of your work you wish to improve.

4. The key to good writing is effective communication.

Yes, in case the message hasn't come across yet, we'll say it one more time: effective communication is the   **1–4**
key to good legal writing. This might sound a bit daunting: you already know that studying law involves
learning a whole load of legal stuff, which is bad enough, and now we're saying that this isn't enough in
itself. However, remember that communication is a vital skill for a lawyer, so working to improve your
writing skills now will not only help you achieve better marks during your studies, but will also help you
in your future career (even if you do not plan to practise as a lawyer, good written communication skills
will be highly valued by any employer). And, in any case, communicating effectively isn't as difficult as
you might think. It may be helpful to think of it as a game: if you took up a new sport, then no matter
how good your basic talent, you would not expect to be successful at it without practising.

By now, you might be starting to think that the amount of work you do makes no difference.
This isn't what we're saying! Of course you will still need to put in the work to understand the sub-
stantive law, but if you get the hang of the communication game you will be able to make the most
of all those long hours in the law library. There is nothing more disheartening for us, as law tutors,
than a student who comes to us with a disappointing mark for a piece of work and says "but I worked
so hard on it—I don't understand how I could have done so badly." (And if it's disheartening for us,
imagine what it's like for the student in question). Basically that student has failed to translate all that
work into an effective piece of communication.

You won't be expected to be brilliant at this straight away, or at least not if you are a degree
student, as your work will be tied to nationally set "levels" of achievement (although the interpretation of these will vary from institution to institution). The idea is that your level of work improves
as you progress through your course, and you will get feedback on your work which will help you.
It is tempting to regard feedback on an assignment as being relevant only to that assignment, or at
least only to that subject, but in fact there will be much you can learn from feedback which will be
applicable to assignments in any subject. There is more about how to make the most of your feedback in Ch.9.

Activity 1.2

We know that good writing is based on good communication. In order to communicate effectively
you need to have a clear idea of the *purpose* of your communication, in other words, why someone   **1–5**
would read it. We're going to think about the sort of writing you might be asked to do during your
legal studies (and what your tutors are looking for when they read it) later in this chapter, but for
now, we want you to think about the purpose of various types of everyday written communication.

In this activity, consider how the purpose would relate to the way in which the author needs to
communicate in order to be successful, and complete the table overleaf.

Compare your views:

Don't worry if your ideas are not exactly the same as these—the aim is to encourage you to think
about the purpose of writing, so there are no right and wrong answers.

A detective novel—you might read this for entertainment, suspense, relaxation; therefore in order
to communicate successfully, the writer needs to make the novel exciting, interesting, a "page-turner".
If the novel was too stodgy or difficult to read, or dull, then someone reading purely for entertainment is unlikely to persevere with it.

Type of communication	The purpose of the reader in reading this would be . . .	So to communicate successfully, the writer would have to make the writing . . .
A detective novel		
A biography		
A TV listings guide		
A newspaper		
Flat pack instructions		
An advice leaflet		

A biography—the purpose of reading this is likely to be similar to the novel, in that it may be read for entertainment or relaxation (perhaps not suspense), although the motivation may also be to improve knowledge or to gain information (for example, a researcher might read a biography). If the biography contains very little about the life of the person in question, or has a number of factual errors, then it will be failing in its purpose.

A TV listings guide—you might read this either for quick information on what's on or perhaps for reviews/recommendations as to which of the forthcoming programmes are the ones to watch. Consequently, to be successful, the listings need to be clear and easy to read and the reviews need to be accurate and appropriate.

A newspaper—fairly obviously, people read a newspaper in order to get news and views (and of course the choice of paper will be influenced by the type of news and views they want to read) although of course newspapers also contain lots of other entertainment features such as TV guides, puzzles, reviews and so on.

Flat pack instructions—these are intended to give the reader the instructions needed to build, for example, a piece of furniture. So the reader reads them to learn that process. The instructions need to be clear and simple (preferably with diagrams) and well-ordered. They also need to be correct!

An advice leaflet—a reader is likely to pick up an advice leaflet with a question in mind, or a particular point on which advice is sought, and wants the leaflet to supply an answer. So, a good advice leaflet needs to be clear, written at an appropriate level for the intended audience, and give examples.

What types of writing will I be asked to do?

1–6   Now that we've considered what makes successful communication in relation to some non-law related types of writing, let's focus more on the type of writing you'll be doing on your course. Law students are asked to write in a variety of circumstances and for a variety of purposes. During your degree or graduate diploma you may be asked to submit some or all of the following: traditional essays and "problem" questions, case-notes, mock judgments, advice notes, letters, leaflets, memoranda, briefs, opinions, posters, journals, logs, diaries, portfolios, reports, literature reviews or essay plans, as well as longer projects such as a dissertation. You will be required to sit set coursework and exams. If you go on to take the Legal Practice Course or Bar Vocational Course then there will be further writing activities, designed to give you the expertise to do the kind of writing which is done by legal professionals. Additionally, you'll be expected to make lecture notes and notes on materials you've read (remember not all the writing you do will be handed in: you'll do a lot of writing which contributes to an assessment indirectly).

Although this list might look daunting, it is important to remember that you're unlikely to be starting from scratch. You'll have done writing before, perhaps for A levels, for a previous degree, writing reports for work or even helping with homework.

The most common types of legal assessment are the problem question and the traditional essay, and we're going to consider these in more detail in relation to improving your writing throughout the text (we also give further advice about dissertations in Ch.3).

Essay questions

Essay questions are common to many disciplines, and you are bound to have tackled an essay question in some sort of assessment before, although not necessarily in law. The different "types" of essay question you are likely to be asked to tackle during your legal studies are as follows:

    1. A **question** type essay is asking you provide an answer (obviously!) with reference to evidence:

Does the Practice Statement 1966 pose a threat to the stability of the doctrine of precedent?

    2. An **instruction** question is similar in type to the question essay but turns it round into an "order" which you have to carry out:

Critically assess whether the Practice Statement 1966 poses a threat to the stability of the doctrine of precedent.

    3. A **statement** type question will usually adopt a particular position on an issue, or pose a hypothesis, which you are then asked to discuss.

"The Practice Statement 1966, whilst representing an erosion of the doctrine of precedent, was a necessary development in order to allow modernisation of the law". Discuss.

Variations might include a more particular instruction, for example "Discuss with reference to the case of X" or "Discuss, illustrating your answer with recently decided cases."

Problem questions

These consist of a paragraph or so setting out a "set of facts"—in other words, a scenario where various circumstances have affected various people—and you are asked to "advise" one or more of them about particular legal issues arising out of the facts given.

An example of a problem question is as follows (we return to this one in more detail in Ch.4):

1–7

1–8

> Zebedee has been suffering from persistent headaches about which he has consulted his doctor. One morning he is driving to university when he suffers a sudden seizure and collapses at the wheel. His car veers towards Abdul who is standing on some scaffolding and jumps off it to avoid the impact of the car, suffering a broken wrist and ankle when he hits the ground. Zebedee's car ploughs into the scaffolding and on into the path of an oncoming bus. Brenda and Carl are both passengers on the bus who are standing next to each other. Carl is carrying a firework which the crash impact causes to explode, injuring Brenda. Brenda suffers severe burns. Carl suffers a minor cut on his face which activates a latent cancer condition from which he later dies. The police arrive at the scene and as the police officers are escorting people off the bus the scaffolding collapses altogether, injuring Dan, a spectator who was trying to take photographs of the incident on his mobile phone. Dan suffers injuries to his head. He has now suffered a personality change, and has attempted suicide, causing him further injury.
>   Advise Zebedee about his potential liabilities.

This is a very common type of question in legal study, and you are likely to look at a number of these scenarios in class time as well as being asked to prepare them for assessments.

Activity 1.3

1–9   You have already considered the purpose of various types of non-legal writing in Activity 1.2, and we know therefore that in order to write successfully, a writer needs a clear idea of the purpose for which he or she is writing. Now, let's apply this reasoning to your assignments.

Putting yourself in your tutor's position, take a few moments to consider why a tutor would set each of the following types of assignment:

1. An analytical essay.
2. A problem question.
3. A dissertation or research project.

What **skills** do you think a tutor is looking to test, in setting each of these? In other words, what is the purpose, or point, of each type of assignment?

Compare your views:

1. What is the purpose of an essay?

1–10   Writing an analytical essay will test whether you have a number of different skills:

- Can you work out the nuances of a particular question?
- Can you argue a reasoned position by comparing and synthesising arguments by different writers on a particular subject?
- Can you carry out research based on the particular subject matter of the essay?
- Can you write using good English?
- Can you write a coherent argument?
- Can you pursue a particular issue in depth?
- Can you write using appropriate technical legal terms?

Was one of your thoughts something like: "To see how much you know or can remember about the general topic of law mentioned in the question"? Probably not: yet this is one of the commonest complaints from tutors marking assignments: that students write a general, rather than a specific, answer.

2. What is the purpose of a problem question?

A problem question will test whether you have the following skills: 1–11

- Can you apply your understanding of the law to particular facts and people?
- Can you distinguish relevant major and minor points in relation to a given problem?
- Can you identify the relevance of particular cases to a particular set of facts?
- Can you work out the facts which are in dispute?
- Can you identify further facts which are needed to resolve areas of dispute?
- Can you provide advice to the appropriate person in the scenario?
- Can you give a balanced view which takes into account the strengths and weaknesses of a particular argument?
- Can you structure your advice appropriately and give the right weight to the major and minor points?

Again, you will note that the purpose of a problem question is never to check whether you can write generally on the topic or speculate about facts which don't exist.

3. What is the purpose of a dissertation or research project?

This is testing many of the same skills as a written essay, but in particular will test the following additional skills: 1–12

- Can you propose a suitable research hypothesis, and pose research questions?
- Can you sustain a detailed and in-depth investigation into a particular topic of your choice?
- Can you plan and carry out a more ambitious piece of work with only limited supervision?

Remember that these are not the only types of writing assessment which you will be asked to do. However, it is always going to be vital to think about the purpose, and this will help you focus on the intended audience. For example, an *advice note* is very similar to a problem question, in that it is testing your ability to apply your understanding to given facts and provide specific advice to them but is also likely to be testing whether you can write concisely and in layperson's terms; the same is going to be true if your assessment is in the form of a *leaflet* or *letter*.

> **TIP**
>
> Thinking about the purpose of the assignment and the intended audience is an important first step in tackling it appropriately.

How will my work be judged?

So far, we've emphasised that the key to success is effective communication, and therefore that it   1–13
is vital to keep in mind the purpose for which you are writing and the purpose for which the assessment was set, so that you know what you should be aiming to communicate. However, you will need a more specific idea of how your tutors will decide whether your work meets its purpose.

It seems to be a common misconception that what is being tested in legal writing assessments is how much information you can retain. *This is not the case*. **Accuracy**—in other words getting your facts right—is an important skill in academic work of course, and certainly for a lawyer. However, your tutors are looking for much more than evidence that you can retain facts and repeat them. In higher education, you are expected to make a progression from transmission of information to demonstrating that you can *use* it, *apply* it and *evaluate* it. This is sometimes described as "deep" rather than "surface" learning, or evidence of *understanding* rather than "rote learning" (which means simply memorising something, parrot fashion).

> **TIP**
>
> Use this book to work on developing your skills of *deep learning* as early as possible in your legal studies.

It can be daunting as a student to understand this distinction: it is easier (and feels safer) to repeat things rather than exploring the issues, but if you can get to grips with the concept that your tutors are looking for more than description and repetition then there will be a huge improvement in the quality of your writing. You are missing the point if you ask "how many cases do I need to learn?" or "have I learnt enough?" because this suggests you think there is a magic information "threshold" which will gain you a pass mark. There is not: because your tutors are not looking simply for information but for what you *do* with the information. It would be like an art student saying "I want to paint a brilliant picture—how much paint should I use?" It is easier in this situation to see that the student is missing the point, that it is what the student *does* with the paint which is the vital part, but exactly the same is true of the information you are going to amass as a law student (your "point") which you then need to transform into a successful piece of writing.

It is increasingly common for law schools to specify what they are looking for in relation to your written work with the use of *assessment criteria*. These will vary from institution to institution. Some institutions use generic criteria which apply, slightly adapted, to all or most written assignments; others may specify particular criteria for each specific assignment. Nevertheless, there are likely to be significant areas of overlap, in that most of your written work will require you to display certain skills (which are likely to be the same or similar for each subject) combined with evidence of knowledge and understanding (which will obviously vary from subject to subject). You may be given separate criteria are identified for answering problem questions and essay questions.

> **TIP**
>
> Earlier we compared writing successfully to playing a game; think of assessment criteria as being the "rules" of the game, so make sure you find out whether criteria are used for your assignments and if so what they are and what they mean.

You may be given details of the weight to be attached to particular criteria, for example that up to 10 per cent of the marks available are for your presentation and referencing. Where weighting is specified in this way you may also be given further information about the standard which is required to gain a particular mark against each criterion through the use of what are called "grade descriptors". For example, in order to get a high mark out of ten for presentation, you may be told that your referencing must be complete and accurate and your work must be presented well and contain no spelling or typographical errors. There is an example of a set of grade descriptors in Appendix 1 (adapted from the ones in use on the Graduate Diploma in Law at Manchester Metropolitan University). Remember that your institution may not set out the criteria in the same way as this.

Although the exact criteria used in your institution may vary, listed below are the kind of things that will, in some shape or form, be important in legal writing regardless of your institution:

• Identification of issues/diagnosis of task/analysis of task—in other words, showing you understand what you have been asked to do.

- Knowledge/accuracy—in other words, that the information you rely on to build your arguments is actually correct.
- Understanding—that you are able to show that you can select material relevant to your task, and develop your answer from it using appropriate weight.
- Application—that you can take your knowledge and work out how it would be appropriate in particular circumstances.
- Analysis or evaluation—that you can make critical judgments about your material; that your work is not just describing circumstances.
- Research—that you can find and use an appropriate range of quality materials as evidence to support your arguments and reference these correctly.
- Organisational structure/argument—that you can put together your points into a logical sequence which builds towards an appropriate conclusion.
- Presentation—that your work is written using good English grammar and spelling and in an appropriate style, and that any requirements for submission are complied with.

You may find it helpful to look for similarities between the above suggestions and any guidance your institution provides on how your work will be assessed. In other words, find out as much as you can about what your tutors are looking for before you start to plan your writing.

What common mistakes are made in legal writing and how can I avoid them?

It might seem odd, in a book called *Successful Legal Writing*, to spend time thinking about common mistakes—in other words to focus on what is, essentially, *un*successful legal writing. However, we believe it is vital that you understand the criticisms which tutors frequently make of written work, and even more importantly, what prompts these criticisms, so that you can take steps to avoid making these mistakes yourself. You may recognise these comments, or something similar, from feedback you have already received—perhaps this is what motivated you to pick up this book—and if this is the case, you will find suggestions as to which chapter or chapters will help you to tackle each mistake.

1–14

"Does not answer the question"

OK, so you are asked a question. All you have to do is answer it. Sounds easy? There are a number of things which make it hard.

Sometimes it might be that you do not have the legal knowledge to answer the question, but it is much more likely to be down to failing to show the marker that you understood what was being asked. This may have resulted in putting in irrelevant material and missing out stuff which was needed. Sometimes (especially in an exam situation) it can be due to failing to read the question properly, or wanting to include material it took hours to learn, just to show you learnt it, even though the question does not ask for it.

> **TIP**
>
> Focus on the task you have been asked to do, and then do it. We'll cover this in much more detail in Ch.4 when we explore techniques to help you make an accurate *diagnosis* of what you have been asked to do.

"Discussion of irrelevant issues"

TIP

You need to keep an imaginary bin in your mind—and you have to have the courage to put irrelevant material in that bin. Deciding whether material is relevant depends on your understanding and your task diagnosis. We'll look at this in much more detail in Ch.4.

This is sometimes called the "scattergun" or "kitchen sink" approach. This kind of comment is made on work where the student has put down so much information that there is some relevant and correct material, but it is buried in a mass of other material which is only generally related to the topic. In other words you are putting in "everything but the kitchen sink" or randomly shooting out "bullets" of law with the hope that some of the shots will hit the target. This might be because you "know" an awful lot—great—but you are failing to show that you *understand* the material. Being able to recite or regurgitate material does not, unfortunately, mean that you understand it.

Perhaps the most crucial point in writing is to remember you cannot "impress" the marker or gain marks by "putting down" material you have not been asked for, no matter how difficult the material or how laborious it was to find it and/or "learn" it. *You are wasting your own time and the marker's* and you are failing to communicate your understanding. This understanding is shown as much by what you leave out as what you put in.

Think for a moment about watching politicians being interviewed on the news or answering questions on a programme like *Question Time*. It is common practice for them to deflect a tricky question about something they do not want to talk about by changing tack and answering a different question from the one asked. A good interviewer will point this out and repeat the original question. How do you rate the politician when this happens? Do you think to yourself "Wow, what a knowledgeable person, to be able to answer on something completely different from what was asked", or do you think "Shifty guy—can't even give a straight answer to a straight question"? Your tutors aren't necessarily going to think you are being "shifty" if you fail to answer the question as asked, but they are certainly not going to pat you on the back for being able to discuss something which is not relevant.

"Misses important points"

In other words, there was important material which was not discussed. This might be due to a number of different causes, for example:

TIP

Thoroughly understanding the topic is essential before you start. Careful planning of your piece of work will be needed to make sure you are covering all the relevant issues. Where you have a tight word limit, and in an exam where you've got limited time, you may have more to say than you can, so decisions need to be made about the relative importance of points—there is more about this in Ch.4 too.

- failing to understand the topic, and therefore not realising that the missed issue was important;
- wasting too much time on irrelevant material and therefore not having the time or space to include everything you wanted to—in other words making poor choices about what to include;
- running out of time in an exam—you knew the issue was important but you just didn't have time to get it down because you'd spent too much time on a previous question.

"Where is the source?" "Authority?"

> **TIP**
>
> Always remember that every assertion of law needs to be supported by evidence. In other words, you need to prove your point by giving a case or statute where that principle of law can be found. This does not mean that you need to give lengthy explanations of the facts in the case—usually concise information is enough. There is more on using evidence appropriately in Ch.6.

Tutors write this where a student has made an assertion without providing the necessary evidence to support that assertion. This is particularly a problem in relation to assertions of law, where the evidence must be in the form of a case or statute. For example:

> There is only one ground for divorce, namely irretrievable breakdown of the marriage.

This is quite true, but it is an assertion of law (i.e. the student is stating what the law is on that point) and therefore needs to be proved by stating a legal authority (i.e. a primary source of law). The legal principle given here about divorce comes from s.1(1) of the Matrimonial Causes Act 1973.

"Insufficient application to the facts"

> **TIP**
>
> Check who you are advising about what, then make sure that as well as stating the law and providing evidence to support your statement, you then go one step further: "So in Fred's case, this means . . ." The name of the party you are advising should occur frequently throughout your work. There is more about this in Ch.3.

This is applicable to problem questions, which ask you to provide advice to a particular party or a number of parties. This mistake arises where the student writes a general essay on the area of law without saying how it affects (i.e. *applies to*) the party he or she has been asked to advise.

Application is a very important skill for a lawyer. Clients coming for legal advice do not want to pay for an hour's worth of waffle on generalities: they want to know how the law affects them, and, depending on the circumstances, whether they are likely to win in court. This is what you need to bear in mind when answering problem questions. Note that this does not mean that you give only one side of the argument—your "client" wants honest, objective advice!

"Too descriptive—lacks analysis"

> **TIP**
>
> Try asking yourself: have I explained the effect of the rule or situation, or have I just given the rule? Get into the habit of digging deeper and discussing pros and cons, weaknesses in given arguments, alternative routes for the law to take and so on, where this is relevant to the question you've been asked.

This is where a student states the law (hopefully with the right authority) but does not go on to discuss the question in enough depth. This is especially needed in essay questions. Description is important, because that is how you explain the relevant law, but in order to get good marks you need to go further than this and provide evaluation—not just what the law is, but why it is like that, what effect this has and so on. This is a skill which you will be expected to develop as you proceed with the course, and you will also learn about looking at the law from different perspectives. Try to develop a questioning or critical attitude towards the law.

"Mistakes on the law"

> **TIP**
>
> Do remember that the odd legal mistake does not ruin an otherwise good essay (although a lot of mistakes obviously do!). Consequently, it is really important to pay as much attention to what you DO with your knowledge to make sure your work pays off.

This is actually less of a problem than you might think. Yes, of course it is important to be accurate in relation to the law, as we've already said, but a student who works hard throughout the year and attends and participates in tutorials will have a very sound grounding in this. It is usually only those students who have not engaged with the course who find they are floundering in terms of their knowledge at assessment time. And you don't need to be told that students who don't do the work do badly—that is obvious.

Effective working is the key here. Attend your lectures, read around the subject appropriately, prepare and participate in your tutorials and revise carefully (and revise enough topics). Above all, if you don't understand something, ask! (Don't be shy; it's what your tutors get paid for—although they will expect you to have made an effort to help yourself first.)

How can I apply all this to myself?

1–15   In order to get the most from this book, you now need to stop and think about the steps that *you* need to take in order to improve your own writing, in the light of what you now know about what makes legal writing successful and how your tutors will judge this.

It won't help to move forward with this book with only a vague idea of your purpose. You need to work now on your specific strengths and weaknesses as so you can build on the strengths and tackle the weaknesseses. In a moment we are going to ask you to do a reflective exercise, and there will be further reflective exercises throughout this book. The purpose of reflection is to focus on issues which are particular to you: good reflective practice is about being *honest* and *specific* about how *you* measure up to whatever the reflective exercise is asking of you. Being reflective is hard—but the key is to avoid slipping into "denial": be objective. If it helps, try putting yourself in someone else's shoes and imagine what they might say about you. In this case, we're going to ask you to think about your writing skills. Remember—be specific, and be honest. You should use a pen and paper to complete this.

Activity 1.4

1–16   **Step 1: Successful writing**
What do you regard as the most successful piece of writing you have done to date? (This could be an essay you wrote at school or college, or a project you have done, or perhaps a job application or a short story or a poem.) Note this down.

Step 2: Judgment
On what basis did you make the judgment that it was successful? Was it because you got a high mark/got the job/won a prize? Now dig a little deeper and try to think about *what it was* that made

that piece of writing successful. Try to be as specific as you can—for example, was it on a topic that you were very interested in? Did you get a lot of help with writing it? Did you do it in a group? Was it with a clear goal in mind like a job or a prize? Did you do it to a tight deadline? Did you use a particular approach to the writing? Note down any factors you can think of which contributed to your success.

Your first reaction to this might be that you aren't sure, or it was "just luck" but there will have been a combination of factors which led to your success, so really try to pinpoint these. Remember that you need to think about specific factors, not vague statements like "Well, it was an English essay and I was always good at English". Try to be more focussed and specific and look for reasons and evidence to support your reflection.

Step 3: Unsuccessful writing
Now think about what you would class as one of the weakest pieces of writing you have done, and go through the same process with this as you did with your best piece, again identifying the factors which affected your writing and how you tackled it.

Step 4: Skills
Thinking back to what we suggested earlier about focussing on the purpose of different types of writing, what was the purpose of the writing you did in your most successful piece and your least successful piece? What skills were they testing? Again, note these down. If you get stuck on this, perhaps look at the list of "criteria" we gave earlier in the chapter to see if that gives you ideas for what the pieces of writing were aiming to test.

Step 5: Analysis
You should now have two lists: one relating to the factors and skills of your successful writing, and the other covering the same for your least successful writing. Can you see any *patterns* emerging as to what skills you already have, what skills you need to work on, what things help you to do well and what things hinder you?

There are not necessarily any "quick fix" solutions but if you are able to focus on what is right for you then this will help you make the most of this book. All we can do here is provide general advice and tips—we do not know you and we have not seen your work—based on the things we know about what students find difficult and what helps them to resolve these difficulties. Having a clear idea of what you need to work on and what things you are already good at will help you target the problem areas most effectively. In other words the strategy for improving your own writing has to come from you.

Summary of Chapter 1

- The key to successful legal writing is good communication, which in turn depends on having a   **1–17** clear understanding of the purpose of the writing.
- You will be expected to demonstrate that you can write in a variety of different situations.
- You need to be clear about the purpose of each different type of assessment you are set.

- Your work is likely to be judged against some form of criteria, which will vary from institution to institution.
- You will learn more about how to avoid common student mistakes in legal writing throughout the rest of the book.
- You should reflect carefully on your existing strengths and weaknesses to make the most of the advice in the rest of the book.

2   The process of writing

What is the purpose of this chapter?

When you start your university studies you will soon realise that changes are needed to the way you   2–1
have been used to studying and learning in the past. Higher education forces independence on you:
you make the decisions about where to live, when to get up, whether to attend classes and how much
time to spend studying, and how much time to spend on other things. Similarly, the way in which you
tackle your assignments is up to you. As you are reading this book, it seems likely you have already
decided that you need to make some changes in how you produce your written assignments. This
chapter won't help you with finding a place to live or help you with your washing, but it will show you
a strategy to help you tackle your assignments successfully. And if you can work more effectively on
your assignments, then this will give you more time to spend on the other parts of university life. By
the end of this chapter you will:

- have had an opportunity to reflect on your own time management skills and the implications of
  this for your academic work;
- be thinking about ways to develop your management of your studies to get the most out of your
  time;
- be encouraged to adopt a reflective approach to your writing by thinking of the writing that you
  do as a "process".

How can I manage my time more effectively?

The starting point in effective management of your writing is to look at the way in which you manage   2–2
your time, because this governs how much time you have to spend on your writing. Secondly, you need
to look at the decisions you make about what you *do* with the time you have available: in other words,
ensuring you are making the most of it by working effectively and prioritising appropriately. Deciding
what to prioritise is also part of the independence you have as a university student.

We'll start by thinking about common barriers to effective time management. Do any of the following apply to you?

- *Trying to do too much*—it often takes longer than you think to get things done. Be realistic about what you can achieve, and prioritise the things which are the most important.
- *Being too available to others*—you need to be assertive in turning people down when you need to manage your own time (for example, "today is just not going to be possible—can we get together at the weekend instead?") and manage the expectations of other people about how much time you have available for them, especially when you are coming up to an assessment deadline. Don't feel guilty about this—remember the people who care about you want you to do well on your course.
- *Being easily distracted*—for example, having MSN or your email on while you are supposedly doing some university work is an open invitation to be distracted. It is easy to drop your attention and let your mind wander, so be disciplined about avoiding distractions when you settle down to work. Having a routine and your own workspace can be a real help with maintaining your concentration.
- *Putting things off*—we all do this at some time or another. The key is to reflect on why and how it happens, to minimise the chances of it happening when you least need it to—such as when an assignment is due! Putting things off is essentially what you are doing if you've ever used the phrase "I can only work when up against a deadline" as an excuse for leaving an assignment to the last minute. What you really mean is that you don't *want* to work up until that point. Be honest with yourself—is it a strategy that works? Do you really get the marks you think you deserve? If not, then be disciplined and begin to tackle your assignments earlier.
- *Being unable to share or delegate*—for example, you agree to split the reading for an assessment task with a friend but then you still do it all yourself anyway. What was the point of this? Make realistic decisions about what work can be shared, but only do this if you are able to make use of the work of others. Similarly, you can't delegate the task of writing your assignment to anyone else, but try delegating other tasks in your life around assessment deadlines so as to free up more time to do your academic work.
- *Worrying about failing*—again, we've all been here. Try to replace negative self doubt with positive thoughts. If you find your negative thoughts are really affecting your work, then try to make a start on a small aspect of the task which you feel more comfortable with. Bear in mind that if you develop a strategy for working on assignments by following the process we suggest, this should help ease the negative feelings because you will feel you have a routine to work through rather than working in the dark.
- *Trying to be too "perfect"*—this can lead you to spend a long time getting something which isn't actually that important absolutely right, and leaving yourself less time to spend on the important things. It can help to consider the relative importance of your tasks and to appreciate that not all will need to be done to perfection.
- *Not being able to prioritise*—again, this leads to a failure to spend the appropriate amount of time on the things which are important. We look at how to acquire this skill in the context of your writing later on in this chapter. Improving your skills in prioritising may be the key to making effective changes to how you manage your time on your writing.

2–3   Making improvements to your time management will require a commitment to change. A good starting point is to look move closely at how you spend your time at the moment, by keeping a time log for a few days..

Keep a time log

Step One: On a sheet of paper record everything you do and note down when you started and when you ended each activity. For example, if it takes you 15 minutes to walk to the library then note that down. If you play football with your mates for 25 minutes in the afternoon then jot that down. Don't forget to include all your classes. Keeping this kind of log is time-consuming and you may feel a bit daft doing it, but it is really worth it—remember that the key to improvement is reflection and to reflect you need the facts. By the end of the week you will have a better idea of exactly how you spend your time.

Step Two: Now challenge your habits to establish exactly where you *could* be wasting time and effort. For example, there are obvious differences between sleeping 12 hours a night because you *need* to and sleeping 12 hours a night because you *want* to. Don't let the "because I've always done it like that" mentality cloud this radical re-assessment of your time. Ask yourself: am I normally on time for things? Do I normally manage to do all the things I need to do? Do I have to really rush to meet deadlines?

Step Three: Now think about what possible changes you can make . . . and make them! Remember this may be just as much about changing your attitude as it is about changing what, when and how you do things. If you find you simply love having too much to do, then you must make decisions about what to prioritise.

How should I prioritise?

Getting your priorities right is vital in order to make the most of the time you have available for your assignments.

Activity 2.1

Below we've drawn up a sample grid of assessments for a typical first year law student (yours might not be like this—this is just an example to get you thinking). The grid shows the assessments our student has to write during the year. We've left out the exams for now (we'll return to the question of exams in Ch.3).   2–4

Subject	Weighting (how much this assessment counts for as part of the whole grade in this subject)	Type of assignment	Group or individual	Word limit	Deadline
Contract	25%	Advice note	Individual	1,000	December 15
Legal Research	100%	Research portfolio	Group	4,000	May 20
Legal System	10%	Case analysis	Individual	500	October 25
Legal Theory	20%	Presentation	Group	n/a	May 20
Public	50%	Theoretical essay	Individual	2,000	March 15
Tort	50%	Mock judgment	Individual	2,000	January 15

If these were your assignments, how would you prioritise your work? Consider the following questions:

- Which assessment is the most important?
- Which assignments do you think are likely to be the most time-consuming?
- Which assessment should you start first?

Compare your views:

Your considerations when deciding on priorities might have included the following:

- Deadline—this helps you assess the *urgency* of any particular task.
- Percentage of overall grade—this helps you assess the *importance* of the task.
- Number of words—this may be some kind of guide (as is the weighting) of the amount of time your tutors are expecting you to spend on this task.
- Group activity or not—this helps you factor in the other members of the group and their priorities.

Did you think of any other factors to take into account?

Your considerations probably didn't include the student's personal preferences in terms of subject, because you know as a matter of reason that this shouldn't affect the prioritising of the work. However, this is a common mistake: when tackling your own assessments, the temptation may be to think "well, ok I have to do some work, I might as well make it enjoyable", and so make a start on your preferred subject. It may feel virtuous to have "got some work done" but if it was work which shouldn't have been a priority at that time then you shouldn't be patting yourself on the back quite so hard. This is true of life in general, isn't it: going out with friends is generally preferable to doing the washing up. Washing up only assumes vital importance when (a) you have no clean plates left, or (b) there is an assignment you should be preparing. If (b) this is a classic displacement activity—in other words you are doing the washing up simply to put off doing your assignment. Don't fall into this trap.

Remember, you already know that how much time you *should* spend on something isn't necessarily the same as the time you will *actually* spend on it. For example, looking at the above grid, you might find it comparatively easy to advise our imaginary student that he or she should not spend too much time on the 500 word Legal System case analysis because it only counts for 10 per cent of the whole grade for that subject. This is not to say it should be dashed off without care or attention, but simply that it should not be allowed to overshadow other activities.

In reality, however, because this *is* still an assessment (and the first one in the year at that), it is only too easy to get this out of proportion. Consequently, a student might spend a week buried in the library, reading texts and writing and re-writing draft after draft, only to find that they've produced 3,000 words worth of material which they cannot use. And now they've also missed lectures on the topic of negligence, which is what the Tort judgment assessment relates to, plus two group meetings for the Legal Research portfolio—which is 100 per cent of the assessment in that subject.

The two most common student mistakes when prioritising are:

- underestimating the amount of time an assessment will take to prepare; and
- failing to strike the correct balance between *all* types of work—assessments and other work, such as preparation for tutorials and so on—which you need to be completing.

> **TIP**
>
> Use the blank assessment grid pro forma provided in Appendix 2 to photocopy and adapt for your own schedule of assessments.

This is likely to be a real issue at the beginning of the course, because managing your own time more *independently* is one of the major differences between school and university; you will find you have less contact time and more time in which you are researching and working on your own. Make sure you develop this skill as soon as you can—and maintain it throughout. Don't think of non-class time as "free time".

A common tool to help identify priorities is a grid in which tasks are graded according to their importance and urgency. Equating importance with the weighting of the assignment, and urgency with the deadline produces a grid like this: **2–5**

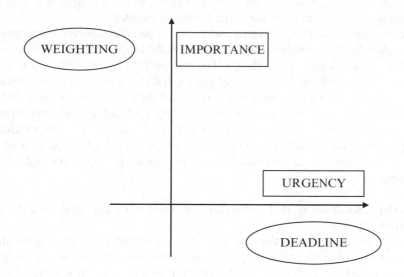

The idea is that you place tasks in the appropriate quarter of the grid to help you plan when you will tackle each task. You may find it helpful to use the grid to make a "to do" list showing the order in which you must tackle the tasks you have to do.

If you use this as a tool for planning your tasks, remember to personalise it to your own needs and skills. For example, any group working task is likely to take longer because the management of the process is more cumbersome (getting people together for meetings and so on). Or, if you know from past experience that you find answering problem questions easier than essays, you may

TIP   **2–6**

More tips for improving your time management:
- Learn how to say no.
- Manage your emails and phone calls—don't drop everything else to deal with them.
- Remember to keep your "to do" list under review.
- Keep your written notes and computer files organised to save time later.
- Try to avoid being a perfectionist!

want to give yourself a bit more time to get to grips with planning an essay.

Now that you have considered your skills at time management, we can go on to consider the process and preparation for the writing of these assessments and the actual writing itself. We have identified this process as a "cycle" which we explain below. By the end of this chapter, you should then be in a position to plan the amount of time you are going to allocate to each stage of the cycle for each of your assessments that you have already identified.

How should I manage the process of writing?

2–7   Like the way in which you learn, the exact way in which you prefer to write will be individual to you. However, in order to write successfully, you must make sure you carry out certain steps, and in a logical order. This forms what we call the "writing cycle", which we explain in more detail in this chapter. We explore each step in the cycle in the following chapters.

A major change when starting university study is that you are expected to adopt an *independent* approach to your studies. Independent learning is essentially all about responsibility. *You* are expected to be responsible for *your* learning and the quicker you can get to grips with how to do this well, the quicker you will see the results in your marks or grades. It's a bit like the first time you are out driving a car after passing your driving test. Your instructor is not there to tell you what to do; it is up to you, the driver, to take the necessary decisions, to do the driving and to eventually get there in good time. So it is with your studying at university. Just like driving, however, there are techniques to follow which will help you stay on the right track. In other words, if you adopt the pattern we suggest in this chapter, you will give yourself the best possibility of writing at the required standard.

So, in summary:

1. In order to write successfully, there are certain necessary steps, and we outline the general process which is needed below.
2. You have not necessarily found the way that is best for you *yet* (perhaps you are already only too well aware of this, as you've picked up this book) and you therefore need to reflect, in the light of what we suggest about the process of writing in this section, on whether you need to break your existing habits and start afresh with the way you tackle writing assignments.

How will the process be different from preparing A level essays?

2–8   At school or college you may well have been through a process where your tutors looked at drafts of your work and made suggestions for improvement. The main change you will face at university level is that this is a step you must learn to take for yourself. You will need to make reflection an important part of your writing at every stage of the cycle in order to produce effective work. We talked about reflection as a valuable tool for learning in Ch.1 and many of the activities you will be encouraged to undertake throughout this book use reflection in ways which will help you to consider aspects of your current practice and if and how you can improve on them.

How will the process differ from writing assignments in other disciplines?

2–9   If you are studying a law conversion case, having taken a degree in another discipline, you are likely to find that successful techniques you've developed to write well previously are likely to work here, because whatever the subject, good writing requires independent reflection, research and style. Specific differences will exist in terms of the subject matter and sources, and you may find that certain conventions are adopted which are different from your own subject (for example, in legal writing there is usually a preference for avoiding use of the first person which may have been the norm in other subjects you have previously studied). The key is therefore to adapt your existing skills rather than work on entirely new ones.

I haven't written an essay for years—how do I get back into the swing of writing?

If you are a mature student returning to education, you may be concerned that it is a long time since   **2–10** you have had to write an essay and you may have forgotten how to do it. However, this does not mean that you are totally out of practice—think about the writing you have done since, for example at work or helping with schoolwork.

Similarly, you'll have been doing other things which will help you with the process of writing, even if you don't realise it—when you read, or even when you watch the news you will have been developing skills in critical assessment. The actual writing part is only a small part of what you need to do, as we explain in this chapter. Learning how to utilise your existing skills to underpin your academic study is part of what you are coming to university for, after all.

Can other students help me with my assignments?

It makes sense to talk with your friends/colleagues about the assignments you have all been set.   **2–11** However, you may have heard the words *collaboration* and *collusion* and be confused about what is allowed and what is "cheating" when it comes to talking about your assessments with your friends.

The Oxford English Dictionary ("OED") definition of collusion is "Secret agreement or understanding for purposes of trickery or fraud; underhand scheming or working with another; deceit, fraud, trickery." So in the context of your academic work, collusion can be defined as being where two or more students work together on an individual task and hand in work which is substantially the same. On the other hand, the OED defines collaboration as: "United labour, co-operation; *esp.* in literary, artistic, or scientific work". You may well be encouraged to work collaboratively with your friends on a variety of tasks throughout your studies (indeed collaboration is at the heart of group work) as this can help you to set your assessments in context and provides a good opportunity for you to learn from others and to offer your own ideas. The key is not to cross the line from collaboration to collusion.

Universities may have their own definitions of these words, in particular of collusion as it is seen as wrongdoing, so check your student handbook or course regulations. If in any doubt, ask your tutor about what is acceptable. Generally, you will probably find that it is perfectly acceptable to brainstorm with a colleague or two and even to some extent share some of your ideas and research. However, to avoid any possible suspicion of collusion you must make sure that the work you hand in is your own, i.e. not the same as your colleague's. So do not write together and do not swap drafts.

Can my tutor help me with my assignments?

In contrast to school/college, you may not be allowed to ask your tutor for help—or if you do, then   **2–12** you may get an answer that they cannot help you with a formal assessment. If you are making the move from school/college to university then this may be one of the biggest changes you notice. In particular it is very unlikely that a tutor will be able to comment on any draft assessment. However, do remember that help is available in other ways, for example going to a tutorial or seminar on the coursework topic is bound to give you ideas.

What process do I need to adopt?

2–13   Great authors often have particular techniques or habits in relation to their writing. For example, J.K. Rowling famously wrote much of the first Harry Potter book in an Edinburgh café and Roald Dahl always used a shed at the bottom of his garden. These are writers who have found a writing technique that worked for them. It does not mean that if you write in a shed or a café you will produce successful children's books. (We pursue this idea further in the context of reading strategies in Ch.5.) It does mean that you need to find out what works for you through a process of trial and error and adaptation. We outline our suggested steps below.

However, although we are breaking this down into steps, these will tend to overlap. As you go through a particular step, issues may arise which require you to revisit a previous step. This is an important part of keeping your writing under review, so do not think of the steps as entirely separate. Nevertheless, focussing on the steps will help you to go about your writing in a logical and structured way.

Note that we've described the cycle below as it relates to coursework assignments. We explain the adjustments which are needed to the cycle for writing in exams in Ch.3.

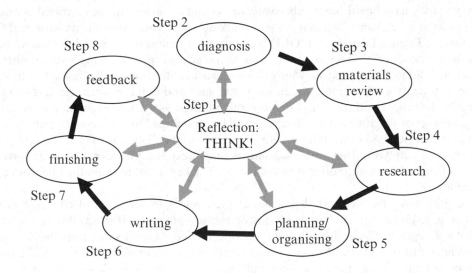

Step 1—Reflection

2–14   Successful people—whether writers or anything else—are reflective. This means that they engage in a constant process of reviewing what they are doing and what they have done in order to learn from their own experiences and improve for the future. Therefore, before even starting to write an essay or other legal assessment, you should look at your existing strengths and weaknesses when it comes to writing in order to work out the particular aspect of the writing cycle that you need to work on.

The first step is to review how you *think* you currently write and compare this to any *evidence* you have of the results this produces, for example, previous marks or grades, and feedback from tutors (or peers).

This part of the writing cycle has already been considered in detail in Ch.1 and you were given the opportunity to undertake an activity designed to do just this. As you develop your skills as a reflective practitioner (this simply means someone who always has at the back of their mind questions like *How am I doing at this? Could I be doing this better? If so, how?*) then you will find it easier to keep reflecting as you proceed with your work. Whilst you develop this habit, we've emphasised that after each phase, you reflect again: the idea of this reflection as you go along is to evaluate your progress so far and review what you need to do next.

Step 2—Diagnosis

The diagnostic phase moves you forward from the process of general reflection on your writing   **2–15** skills and abilities into the specific analysis of a particular assessment you have been given. In other words, in this phase, you work out exactly what you have to *do*. Of course, your ability to do this will be affected by the amount of understanding you already have on the topic area, and you therefore need to review your diagnosis as you carry out your research. In other words, after the diagnosis phase, you continue to reflect on whether you need to fine-tune your diagnosis.

We explore the skills you need to diagnose your task—for example, identifying key words, and instruction words, and other techniques for working out the nuances of the question—in much more detail in Ch.4. We'll look at diagnosis in the context of essay questions and problem questions, and explore how these might differ. The main point to appreciate for now, to make sense of the rest of the writing cycle, is that your diagnosis will require you to break the question down into sub-questions. The answer to each sub-question will form a part of your overall argument. As you learn more about the topic, you keep in mind whether the questions you posed were the right ones, or whether you need to adjust them.

As well as working out exactly what the question is asking you to do, and putting together your list of sub-questions, another important part of your diagnosis is looking beyond the demands of the question to any more general instructions you've been given about the assignment. Knowing the word limit, whether you are simply handing in a finished piece of work or whether it needs to be accompanied by a plan, work diary or research log and/or whether there are any other specific requirements, are all important aspects of carrying out the task effectively, so make sure that you are clear on these *from the start*. This is an essential part of understanding your *purpose* in completing this assignment.

To do this effectively, you need to check carefully any guidance you have been given about this particular piece of writing. This guidance might cover, for example, rubric (instructions or specification), presentation (e.g. word-processed, margin sizes) or style (e.g. preferred footnote scheme).

- Are there rules or instructions applicable to all pieces of work on your course? You might find instructions in your student programme/handbook or in the unit or subject manual or course guide for the individual subjects.
- Are there specific instructions for this piece of work? These might be found in the subject manuals, on your e-learning space or perhaps in a handout. Alternatively, your tutor may have gone through the instructions verbally in a class.

Remember to apply prioritising techniques to the assignment. Look at the word count. Using your completed assessment grid, check how much this assessment is worth—remember to keep things in proportion. If you are working on an assignment that is worth 25 per cent of your total mark in that subject and in order to complete it successfully you miss vital classes on a topic to be assessed in an exam worth 100 per cent of the mark in another subject, you are not working effectively.

Step 3—Review your materials

2–16   Once you have an idea of what you've been asked to do, and an idea of why you've been asked to do it, the next step is gathering your resources together in preparation. Some of these will be resources you already have and some will be resources you will need to carry out extra research to get. A *materials review* should be done to work this out.

You should start by conducting an audit of relevant materials that you already have. This might include, for example: unit manuals/subject handbooks, lecture notes, tutorial preparation notes, textbooks/cases and materials books, cases and articles. And don't forget your reading list (if you've been given one). This will give you a good idea of the sources your tutors think are important for your subject and may well include sources directly relevant to your assessment. See Ch.5 for more on this.

> **TIP**
>
> Make sure your existing materials are complete. For example, did you miss a class on the subject? If so, work out how to catch this up—can you ask a friend for their notes or perhaps the notes are available on the internet? Have you ensured that you have all the suggested readings for this topic? If not, get hold of copies.

Your purpose in assembling these materials is to help you answer the questions you have posed as part of your diagnosis. It is extremely unlikely that you will be able to find all the answers you need simply by looking at your existing work. In other words, whilst it's a great place to start, your existing work on a topic can only ever be just that—a starting point. Your lecture notes and the basic textbook are never going to be enough to get good marks in themselves, but think of them as clues—they start you off looking in the right places. If you have ever had any feedback that says more or wider reading is required, this is where you have been going wrong. You will be expected to read as widely as you can, but remember in doing so that your goal is to answer the questions you posed in your diagnosis. This is what you need to keep in mind as you move into your research phase.

Step 4—Research

2–17   The research phase of your writing is where you pursue a wider range of sources in order to find out the answers to the questions you have posed in your diagnosis. We explore how to plan and carry out your research in much more detail in Ch.5. It is really important to make sure that when carrying out your research, you remain focussed on the specific issues you need, rather than becoming side-tracked by information which is only of vague relevance to the question you have been set. Think of this as being a sifting process: you need to sift out the irrelevant or less relevant material. You cannot possibly read everything, so you will need to make selections. Doing this sifting successfully will involve learning techniques for skimming texts and articles to work out which bits are worth reading in more depth. As you make these decisions during the research phase, keep in mind the length of the piece you have been asked to write. Reading eight full-length books and six articles will yield much more than you could utilise in one 2,000 word piece of coursework. You will also need to learn how to make notes effectively from the reading material you have chosen as being the most relevant, so that you can make the most of them when you come to do your writing. Strategies for note-taking are also covered in Ch.5.

When you have completed your research, you will have found the answers to the sub-questions you have posed for yourself in your diagnosis. Perhaps we should put this the other way round: when you have found the answers you have finished your research—so *stop*. It can be very difficult to draw a line under the research phase and again there is more advice on how to do that in Ch.5. You are now in a position to start thinking about how to put your answer together, which is the next step.

Step 5—Planning and organising your answer

You now need to think about exactly how your writing will fit together. A well-written assignment will **2–18** have an organised structure which flows logically from point to point. You therefore need to spend time planning this structure. It is a mistake to jump straight into writing because you are likely to lose your focus and your assignment will end up confused. Something which students sometimes find difficult is how best to integrate the evidence they have found into their own arguments. In other words, how can other people's words and ideas become part of their own argument? What is an effective argument anyway? These matters are covered in Ch.6, which will show you how to make the most of your evidence.

There is much more general guidance on how to structure your work in Ch.7, but if you have diagnosed your task effectively, the structure should flow logically from the questions you have posed, and the answers which you have found to those questions during your research.

Once you have put your structure together, *review it*. If you write up your answer in this way, will it answer what you have been asked? When you are satisfied that the answer to this question is "yes" then you are ready to move to the writing stage.

Step 6—Writing

You are now in a position to write your answer, making sure you are still keeping the question you **2–19** have been set in mind at all times. When you are given an assignment, the writing stage is probably what you think of immediately, and yet, as you can now see, it appears comparatively late on in the cycle we are suggesting. Unless you have completed Steps 1–5 carefully first, you are not going to be in a position to start the writing phase successfully.

The writing phase is where your communication skills are at their most important, so make sure you fulfil the requirements of effective communication which we suggested in Ch.1. Chapters 6, 7 and 8 all contain material relevant to this. Remember you will need to:

- use evidence to support assertions and acknowledging those sources so as to avoid charges of plagiarism, and ensure your arguments form a logical structure (see Ch.6);
- structure your writing appropriately by writing an effective introduction, main body and conclusion (see Ch.7);
- write in good English, including use of grammar, your style, sentence construction, spelling, use of legal terminology and so on (see Ch.8).

You don't necessarily have to write your assignment from start to finish. You may find it easier to tackle some parts of the writing first and leave other areas to last. Making a success of this is going to depend on having a clear logical plan in Step 5. It is much more manageable to stick to your plan no matter in what order you actually write the essay if you use a word processor. If you don't word process at the moment, or if it is your habit to write in long hand and then type up, it is a good time to make the adjustment to writing directly into a word processor.

Once you have finished writing, it is tempting to think you've finished. Sorry, but you haven't—you now need to reflect on what you've written and make any final adjustments, in the finishing phase.

Step 7—Finishing

2–20   This stage in the cycle includes editing your work, reviewing and reflecting on your work and checking for inaccuracies or irrelevancies and presentational errors, all of which are covered in Ch.9. In addition, remember to look back at any specific requirements you've been set and make sure you comply with those. You can now submit your assignment.

Step 8—Feedback

2–21   Just when you think you have nothing else to do, remember that in order to make the most of this assignment in terms of learning for the future, you will need to reflect carefully on the mark and any other feedback you get. There is advice on how to do this in Ch.9.

Activity 2.2

2–22   Now that you have worked through our cycle of the writing process it should be easier for you to identify (now that you have been encouraged to reflect on your own practice) where in the cycle you have room for improvement. You now need to jot down some action points arising from this reflection and plan which parts of the rest of the book you are going to focus on to help you improve.

Summary of Chapter 2

2–23
- Managing your writing effectively requires you to understand the process involved and to set aside sufficient time to tackle it.
- You can do this more effectively by reflecting on how you currently manage your time and deciding what you need to change.
- Adjusting your priorities can help you manage your time better.
- To write successfully you should follow a "cycle" of reflection, diagnosis, review, research, planning, writing and finishing, with further reflection throughout.
- These stages are explained in further detail in Chs 4–9.
- Although legal writing at university level demands particular skills, you can use your existing writing skills as a starting point for improvement.

3   Strategies for different types of writing assignment

What is the purpose of this chapter?

The purpose is to highlight how you need to adapt the general advice we are giving you on how to improve your writing throughout the rest of this book to particular types of assignment. We've already discussed what makes a good piece of writing in Ch.1, and in Ch.2 we considered the "writing cycle" which takes place in successful legal writing, as follows: 3–1

Step 1: reflection.
Step 2: diagnosis.
Step 3: materials review/reflection.
Step 4: research, keeping your diagnosis under review.
Step 5: planning.
Step 6: writing.
Step 7: finishing and polishing.
Step 8: reflection on your feedback.

Advice on these steps is provided throughout the remainder of this book. By the end of this chapter, you will understand how this cycle varies in relation to particular types of legal assessment:

- answering a problem question, rather than a traditional essay;
- writing a dissertation or research project;
- writing in an exam.

What makes a problem question different?

As you are already aware from Ch.1, problem questions require **application** of the law in the context   3–2
of a specific set of **facts**. This means that the most important way in which you "hone" the advice

given in the rest of the book to problem questions is by making sure every stage of the writing process is geared towards this goal of giving specific advice. You will find, therefore, that there is less scope for flexibility, speculation and innovation when answering problem questions than essay questions. When you finish your training and are legally qualified and clients come to see you about a simple divorce, for example, they will not be that keen (or necessarily impressed) to hear your speculations on what the position might be if they had a large property abroad or had been having an affair with Tom Cruise! They want to know what you can do for them in their particular situation—on *their* facts and in *their* context. In order to provide appropriate advice, you need to be able to identify the issues which arise from their particular circumstances and avoid matters which don't. It is therefore especially vital that you keep your mental "bin" ready. There's some further advice on how to do this later on in this chapter, and we return to the idea of diagnosing your task in the context of a problem question in Ch.4. During your studies, you will find that plenty of advice is available on how to tackle problem questions, whether from books, your tutors or fellow students, and this advice is almost certain to recommend a specific technique or "blueprint" for answering these kinds of questions. The great thing about problem questions is that you're likely to get lots of opportunity to develop your technique for tackling them through preparing questions for discussion at tutorials or seminars (you may not necessarily be asked to write these up as complete answers, but you should always look on these as opportunities to practice your technique).

Making your diagnosis in a problem question

3–3   In order to make your writing successful in respect of problem questions, your diagnosis phase must have more specific elements to it. You need to do all of the following:

1. identify whom you are advising about what;
2. identify the parties, and the role of your "client" in the scenario;
3. identify the material facts;
4. identify the legal issues arising from those facts.

This is explored in detail in Ch.4.

Researching a problem question

3–4   Whatever your writing assignment, whether it is a problem or any essay style question, your research will be designed to answer "questions" which you have posed to yourself as part of your diagnosis. This is essential in order to make sure that your research is focussed. In relation to a problem question, your research may focus more specifically on primary sources of law, i.e. cases and statutes, because you are being asked to advise about how the law affects a particular person. In your research phase you must make sure that you record the *authorities* for the advice you are planning to give. Remember, however, that your research must focus not on a general answer to your questions ("what is the law on this area?") but on a specific answer as related to the facts you have been given and the "client" you are advising ("how does the law in this area affect this person?"). There is more advice on how to utilise your evidence in the context of problem questions in Ch.6.

Writing up your problem answer

There are two issues which can cause confusion about the style and content of problem questions. **3–5** The first is that "Advise Jim" may be interpreted as an instruction to give only those arguments and reasons which support Jim's case. If you stop and think about it, however, telling Jim only what he wants to hear (which is essentially what you're doing in that case) is very bad advice. Basically, what Jim needs in terms of advice is to be told the truth; the strengths and weaknesses of his case and your reasoned conclusion as to whether overall he is liable/guilty/able to claim compensation or whatever.

The second problem is in the style of the writing. "Advise Jim" is the standard way, in legal examining, of asking you to write an academic answer in which you identify the issues applicable to Jim's case and relate them to the relevant law. The emphasis here is on the words "academic answer". In general style, you are still writing in an essay format, rather than for example beginning "Dear Jim, my advice is . . .", so therefore the advice about structuring and writing which you'll find in Chs 6 and 7 is equally applicable to a problem answer as it is to an essay question: you should write in objective terms and in the third person.

A word of warning though: in order to provide more variety in legal assessment, and test your skills in different types of writing, sometimes you might be asked to put advice in the form of a letter, an advice note, or perhaps design an advice leaflet. We've already discussed the importance of identifying the purpose of a particular assessment—in these cases, hopefully you can spot that

> **TIP**
>
> Check the exact format of the assessment carefully. If in doubt, check with your tutor as to how you are expected to lay out your answer.

your tutor wants to find out whether you can write in a style appropriate for a non-legal audience (concise, straightforward language for example)—and therefore this would affect your style and tone. In the absence of a specific instruction to write your answer in the style of a letter or advice note (or whatever), however, you can assume that an academic style answer is required in response to a problem question.

At the opposite end of the scale there is a further potential problem with the writing stage of a problem answer: adopting a completely essay style answer to a problem question. Despite what we've said above about the importance of writing academically, it is still absolutely vital that you make sure that there is *application* in your answer. Remember your goal is to explain how the law on this issue affects Jim and his circumstances. A general answer explaining the law on the area without reference to Jim or the facts of the question will

> **TIP**
>
> Check how often the name of your "client" appears in your answer. If you are applying the law well, then the name should appear in every paragraph. A page without mention of the party you are advising is likely to indicate you've slipped into a generalised answer on the topic.

not score well. In relation to each issue of law which arises you must apply the law to the facts by explaining how this principle of law affects your client.

Writing a conclusion for a problem question may also differ from the process of writing one for an essay question. If you have identified the relevant legal issues and applied the appropriate law with authority to the facts then you should already have reached a series of conclusions.

> **TIP**
>
> Bear in mind that if the case actually went to court, the judges would have to find for one side or the other, even if they acknowledge that it is a close run thing. You should therefore be prepared to do the same.

Students often ask "But it could go either way—do I have to give a definitive conclusion?" It is true that many of the areas of law you will be assessed on will not be "settled"—you will be asked to provide advice on areas where there are conflicting authorities, as this is how your tutors will test whether you understand the nuances of the topic. It can therefore feel "risky" to conclude one way or the other, in case you get it "wrong", but it is a misconception to think that there is necessarily a right or a wrong answer to a legal problem. A good answer will *acknowledge* that there are conflicting authorities and that the law is doubtful on a particular point but then compare the authorities in the light of the facts of the question in order to evaluate which is the better position in relation to these facts. Your tutor is interested in your *reasoning*, and whether you can pursue this logically to a conclusion.

What makes a dissertation different?

3–6   As we discussed in Ch.1, a dissertation is an in-depth project in which you are required to research and write about an aspect of the law that you are particularly interested in. Dissertations have much in common with essays, for example:

- The same writing processes are used (see Chs 2, 4 and 7).
- The need to plan and conduct effective research and make your materials work for you (see Chs 5 and 6).
- The need for analysis and evaluation in your writing (see Ch.6).
- The same ability to write in good English is required (see Ch.8).

However, there are obviously some key ways in which dissertations differ from any other legal writing:

- You will have chosen your own topic (perhaps within certain parameters set by your institution, or perhaps with a completely free choice) and therefore essentially "set your own question" rather than responding to a question set by a tutor, which has significant implications for the diagnosis phase of the dissertation.
- You will work independently on it rather than attending lectures and seminars/tutorials, although you will be able to get guidance from one of your tutors, and you will therefore need to pay particular attention to the issue of time management and motivation.
- It will be longer than other work you write (length will vary from institution to institution, but is likely to be somewhere between 8,000 and 15,000 words). This can seem daunting at the outset and it is common to feel that you'll "never get that much written", but actually it is far more common to have too much to say than too little by the time you have finished. This will have an impact on the writing phase, which will be a longer process than with other assignments, and also on the research phase, which will need to be more extensive than for any other legal writing.

- You will also need to be particularly fastidious at keeping clear, full and accurate records of what you read in order to make sure you can reference your dissertation appropriately.

A final difference with dissertations is that the process involves use of terminology and techniques which are conventional in academic research but with which you may be unfamiliar, or at least unfamiliar in the context of your legal studies: terms like *supervisor*, *hypothesis*, *abstract*. We will explore the meaning of these terms in this section.

Completing a dissertation gives you the opportunity to explore something that you are really interested in to a greater depth, which presents an exciting challenge, but sometimes the comparative enormity of this writing task can be overwhelming. Following the advice here about the writing cycle, and how to adapt it appropriately, should help make the process more manageable. Similarly, if completing a dissertation is an optional part of your course, we hope that the advice in this chapter will help you choose whether to take this option.

The format of a dissertation

There is no single "model" for a dissertation but a common format is: title page, abstract, contents page, introductory chapter, three or four content chapters, concluding chapter, bibliography, and, where appropriate, appendices. By looking at some completed dissertations you will be able to get a good idea of the format and layout which is required, as well as a feel for topics others have chosen in the past and of the differing styles and approaches adopted.   **3–7**

Check your law library for dissertations which have been completed in the past (bear in mind that although it is usual for law libraries to archive only those dissertations which are of a certain standard—perhaps 2:1 and above—it is unlikely that the mark each dissertation received is published, so you won't know the exact standard of the work you are looking at and it will have some faults).

Managing the process of writing your dissertation

Because of the amount of work involved and the degree of independent working needed for a dissertation, managing your time effectively on a dissertation is a greater challenge than for any other piece of work you will undertake.   **3–8**

The first step is to make yourself a timetable. Working backwards from the hand-in date, list in a column all the things you can think of that you will need to do to complete your dissertation before you can hand it in, making sure you include all of the following: time for binding, final checks and amendments, last advice from supervisor on final chapters, writing up, agreeing and submitting a title, research work, planning. Now work out how many weeks there are between the date you complete the timetable and the hand-in date. Against each task you've listed in your first column, allocate an estimate of the amount of time you'll need in order to do that task effectively. This activity can be quite sobering when you realise you probably have a maximum of around six or seven months to plan, research and write up to 15,000 words as well as preparing for all your other classes, coursework and exams (and presumably wanting to have a life during this period).

Remember the hand-in requirements for your dissertation, in terms of presentation and style, are likely to be more formal than for your coursework and so will take more time. You will also probably want to make sure you consider other time constraints that may crop up like illness, breaks in the holidays and other coursework preparation.

> **TIP**
>
> It is never too early to start planning and researching your dissertation. The summer holidays prior to the year when you must complete your dissertation are a good long break when you can get started. If you are doing some legal work experience over the holidays why not see if there is anything you can be doing on your dissertation at the same time?

Your dissertation will take longer than anything else you do in that year and so you should start earlier than you would normally, and it is likely to be weighted to be worth more than anything else, so be pragmatic throughout the year in terms of how much time you allocate to it. If your dissertation is worth one taught subject, then you need to spend as much as time on it as you would spend on that taught subject: count up the number of hours you spend preparing for and attending classes in a subject each week, plus the time you'd spend preparing the coursework and/or preparing and revising for the exam. If your dissertation is "double-weighted" (i.e. takes the place of *two* taught subjects) then accordingly you need to spend twice as much time on your dissertation as on any other subject.

Carry out this calculation and you are likely to realise that you should be spending the equivalent of a day a week on your dissertation in order to do it justice. If your timetable permits, you may find it helpful to set aside a particular day for your dissertation preparation to make sure you work at it regularly and don't let things slide.

In the writing cycle in Ch.2, we suggested carrying out your research (keeping your diagnosis under review) and then writing up. Because of the length of your dissertation, you cannot adopt this approach by carrying out all your research and then trying to write it all up. There are a number of reasons why it would be a mistake to delay writing until you've finished your research, for example:

- you'll get bogged down in your research and lose your focus and there may be a temptation to prioritise other work;
- if you don't get something written early on you'll lose the benefit of the advice your supervisor can provide about your writing;
- you'll end up having to rush the writing, and trying to write a whole dissertation in a short space of time is incredibly daunting.

Therefore a better approach would be as follows:

> **TIP**
>
> To write a successful dissertation, work steadily throughout the year. Writing on computer means you can revise your work easily when you get feedback, so research a chapter, write it up, hand it in, get feedback from your supervisor, utilise those comments and use them to improve (a) that particular chapter and (b) your approach to writing a dissertation generally—remember that this is going to be the most complex piece of writing you undertake.

1. Carry out the diagnosis phase in broad terms in relation to the whole of your dissertation and make a plan of what is going to go in each chapter.
2. Then carry out Steps 2–6 of the writing cycle in relation to *each chapter* in turn—in other words, a more specific diagnosis, then carry out your research, plan your chapter, and write it.
3. Then hand your chapter in to your supervisor so that you can use their comments and advice as part of the reflection stage on that chapter, before making any adjustments which are needed.
4. Finally, once you have carried out this process in relation to each chapter, you carry out the finishing and polishing stage of the cycle in relation to the *whole*.

Carrying out your diagnosis for a dissertation

The diagnosis phase is very different in relation to a dissertation because instead of working from a **3–9** question you have been set, you have to decide on your own area of interest, and then within that area of interest, identify your particular focus. In Ch.1, we stressed that the purpose of asking you to write a dissertation is to test that you can do the following:

1. propose a suitable research hypothesis, and pose research questions;
2. sustain a detailed and in-depth investigation into a particular topic of your choice; and
3. plan and carry out a more ambitious piece of work with only limited supervision.

Keep this in mind when you are thinking about the diagnostic phase of your dissertation. A common mistake to make is to think you are simply being tested on your ability to write "on" the topic you've chosen: this shows confusion about the purpose of a dissertation, and will result in the work being descriptive. Just as we would never set you an essay title called "write everything you know about capital punishment" (or whatever your proposed area is) we don't want you to set *yourself* what would amount to such a title for your dissertation. Instead what you need to do, to make sure you adopt the right approach, is to work from a *hypothesis* and pose *research questions* (there is more about this below). Do remember it is *not* expected that you will be setting out to make a new finding or discovery about the law or conduct original research in an undergraduate dissertation.

1. Choose your general area of interest
You will already be aware how much easier something is to do if you are interested in it, so you should pick a topic which interests you for your dissertation. This is especially true given that your dissertation is going to involve more independent working than any other piece of writing you have tackled and therefore your motivation is going to be especially important. If you start out with only lukewarm enthusiasm for your subject-matter then you will find it very tough to work on it through to the finish. However, although it is important to pick something you are interested in there are some other considerations to bear in mind, for example whether the topic is going to be a suitable one for a dissertation and also whether it is a very popular topic which has already been done many times (it may be preferable to pick a topic which is a little more unusual).

Start by brainstorming an initial list of possible topics, whether this is something from your previous or current studies, or perhaps an issue or case you have seen in the quality media. If you are thinking about a subject area which is something on which you have already been assessed, you must be careful to guard against *self-plagiarism*. Carrying out the process of research for a

> **TIP**
>
> Give yourself enough time to consider lots of possible options before settling on your chosen topic—start thinking about it at an early stage.

previous coursework may give you an interest in a particular area of law, and it is fine to choose to explore this further in your dissertation, but you cannot hand in an amended version of that coursework as one of your dissertation chapters: you cannot use the same work twice for two different assessments. (In any case, why would you want to—you are expected to improve your standard of writing considerably by the time you reach your final year, so it wouldn't get a good mark anyway.) As a final note of caution, remember if you got interested in the topic through completing previous coursework on it, you will find there are many other students with the same interest—you may wish to rethink and come up with something more unusual as your area of interest.

2. Pick something specific within your general area
Once you have a list of areas of law that you are interested in you then need to conduct some initial research in the library or using the legal databases to see what is feasible. This part of the process will help you to identify an area which is not too broad (and therefore doesn't provide much scope for detail or depth) nor too narrow (which will mean there is not enough material to research and it will be difficult to reach the required word limit). Remember that, generally, what marks out a good dissertation is the quality of the analysis and argument within it. Logically, therefore, a narrow topic is preferable to a broad topic. A topic which is too broad will encourage a descriptive approach because there is too much to "cover" and therefore too many words will be wasted in basic explanations rather than in detailed evaluation. Therefore, if your initial thought is broad, you need to narrow it down. "Family Law" is much too broad, whereas "money settlements on divorce" would be more manageable. Therefore, as you are carrying out this initial research you need to be asking yourself: *What is it about the law relating to X* (e.g. capital punishment, unfair dismissal, divorce, theft or whatever your general topic area is) *that I want to consider?*

> **TIP**
>
> Think in *specific* terms about your dissertation as soon as possible. Keeping in mind a general topic like "child law" or something like that is the surest way to carry out unfocussed research.

This can be a difficult decision to make, especially if your chosen area of interest is something you do not know much about as yet (i.e. something you have not looked at in your previous studies). It is a good idea to consult a tutor about your initial ideas. If you identify a tutor with expertise in the area you are considering they will be able to help you with this issue, and will be able to suggest particular angles of appropriate depth.

3. Come up with a hypothesis and/or research question
A hypothesis is basically a theory or position on a topic, which forms the basis of your "investigation"—in other words, your research and argument is ultimately for the purpose of challenging your hypothesis: investigating the extent to which it is true. For example:

> Money settlements made on divorce discriminate against women.

Note that you are not necessarily going to argue that they do (i.e. you do not have to agree with your hypothesis): the point of the hypothesis is that it gives you, essentially, a yardstick against which to conduct your research. As you find out more on the subject, you will assess the evidence in favour of your hypothesis and the evidence against it, and so reach a position where you are able to form evaluative judgments.

Some students find it easier to do this by turning the hypothesis round into a question, for example:

> Do money settlements made on divorce discriminate against women?

This can make it easier to remember that your dissertation is about exploring both sides of the argument, although with the aim of reaching an overall conclusion. Essentially your research question and hypothesis serve the same function: they set the parameters of your research and argument.

4. Break this down into sub-questions
Once you have a hypothesis or a research question to work from, the process of diagnosing the task becomes more similar to the process explored in more detail in relation to essay questions in Ch.4. Essentially, you need to break down the question/hypothesis into a series of sub-questions which will help you to direct your research, following the advice in Ch.5. For example, suppose your research

question is to investigate whether the law in the United Kingdom on capital punishment/unfair dismissal/divorce/theft etc. needs reform. To plan your research, you can break this down logically into questions such as:

- What is the current law?
- What are the strengths and weaknesses of the current law?
- What alternative possibilities are there?
- Would these resolve the problems in the current law?
- What barriers are there to implementing reform in this way?

Researching these sub-questions, as well as providing a focus to your dissertation, will also help you structure your dissertation, as, broadly, you can explore a question per chapter (some flexibility may be required with this, depending on the nature of the questions you pose).

5. Formulate your title
We have already identified that one of the main distinctions between a dissertation and a coursework assignment is that you are not going to be given the title to your dissertation—you need to choose the title for yourself. You may have to do this at the outset, or you may only have to give a rough indication at the outset, with the opportunity for a "final" title to be submitted when you have completed more research. Either way, this is the first time you are likely to set your own title.

It is common for an analogy to be made that coming up with the title of your dissertation is like setting your own coursework title. However, this can be misleading because the kind of wording used in coursework questions is not always appropriate for a dissertation title—for example a quotation, followed by the word "discuss" is a common format for a coursework title but is not a suitable title for your dissertation. You are carrying out an investigation of an area of law and the title must reflect that investigation. For example, supposing you have decided on domestic homicide as your dissertation topic. Your initial hypothesis might be something like:

> The law on domestic homicide perpetuates gender inequalities by recognising typical male responses to violence as a defence to murder whilst not recognising a female response in the same way.

Your research question would turn the hypothesis round:

> Does the law on domestic homicide perpetuate gender inequalities by recognising typical male responses to violence as a defence to murder whilst not recognising a female response in the same way?

Or something similar. You would then pose linked sub-questions, which might be things like: What is the current law on domestic homicide? How does this affect male domestic killers? How does this affect female domestic killers? What possible reform alternatives are there? The final step would be to come up with a title which reflects the investigation you are carrying out in pursuit of the answers to your research questions. The title should indicate the specific area of law you are investigating and the perspective you are taking.

A suitable title may be, for example:

> A critical examination of the law on defences to domestic homicide with reference to gender inequality.

You may prefer to pose this as a question, such as:

> Does the law on defences to domestic homicide promote gender inequality?

Note that it is not universally accepted that posing a question is a good format for a dissertation title and you should seek the advice of your supervisor about this.

Planning and structuring your dissertation

3–10   In order to make the process of writing your dissertation more manageable you need to set out a broad overall plan before you can move into the researching and planning phase for each chapter (although you'll also need to plan each chapter individually in more detail once you've carried out the research into that chapter and understand the issues more clearly). The ordinary rules of using a good structure apply equally to the writing of a dissertation as to the writing of any piece of legal writing. Any differences arise from length and coverage, so to be readable and understandable a dissertation must be broken up into more manageable "chunks" by the use of chapters. Chapters are particularly useful for breaking up your writing and to delineate the different ideas and themes you want to explore.

You could begin by setting out a rough plan of your chapter contents. This will be based on the sub-questions you have identified when considering your main hypothesis (see above). Let's say the length of your dissertation is 10,000 words and you have decided to examine the topic of *capital punishment* your plan could look like this:

Abstract		200 words
Introductory chapter	What the law is like now	800 words
Chapter 1	Does it need reform?	2,000 words
Chapter 2	Strengths of existing position	2,000 words
Chapter 3	Weaknesses of existing position	2,000 words
Chapter 4	Possible Alternatives	2,000 words
Conclusion	Would they work?	1,000 words

Carrying out the research and writing phases

3–11

> **TIP**
>
> Before you begin writing a chapter: think—what is the purpose of this chapter? How does it fit in with what comes before and after it? How does this chapter contribute to my overall argument? Before handing in your chapter to your supervisor, check your chapter against these "goals" which you've set for it. Did you meet them? Is it clear from your writing? You may find it helpful to hand in this "statement of purpose" to your supervisor as well as the chapter, as this will help them (a) to see what you are trying to do with the chapter, and (b) to comment on whether you've achieved it successfully.

Use the advice in Chs 5, 6, 7 and 8 to help you carry out this phase, bearing in mind what we've suggested earlier about working on a chapter at a time, rather than trying to do all your research and then all your writing. In taking this chapter by chapter approach, it is important to keep a sense of how each chapter fits in to the rest of your dissertation. Plagiarism is also a particular issue with dissertations, so it is especially important to consider the advice on how to record your sources in Ch.5, and how to acknowledge where you got your ideas from and how to utilise them to help form your own arguments in Ch.6. However, if you've developed good habits in relation to your coursework then you won't find this an issue. During the process of research and writing, you'll need to work effectively with the supervisor you have been allocated, and there is more about this below.

Working with your supervisor

Another way in which a dissertation is different from other legal writing is that you will be allocated a member of staff with expertise in the area in which you are pursuing your dissertation to act as your supervisor. Essentially your supervisor is a "guide" who can provide advice on the scope of your dissertation and comment on draft chapters for example. Your supervisor is also likely to be one of the final markers of your dissertation.

3–12

Building a good relationship with your supervisor is vital. To get the most out of this relationship you will need to revisit your draft timetable and build in time to meet with your allocated tutor and get their advice at regular intervals. It is up to you to arrange these meetings and get the most out of them—don't expect your supervisor to "chase" you and don't expect them to drop all their other work to deal with you at short notice either. Use your supervisor to:

1. Check that you are on the right track at the earliest opportunity. At your first meeting (which ideally should be very early on in the academic year you are going to complete your dissertation), take along any guidance you've been given about your dissertations, your initial timetable plan, your topic ideas and a suggested hypothesis and/or research questions, so that you can find out their view on your plans, in terms of whether it is a suitable area and whether your hypothesis/research question are sufficiently focussed.
2. Discuss your research and the ideas you are forming from it. Your supervisor may also be able to suggest further reading. Remember that this is your work, so your supervisor can't do it for you but often he or she will be able to point you in useful directions for research.
3. Get feedback on draft chapters, although there are four things to bear in mind here:
   - There may be a limit to the amount of drafts your supervisor is able to look at (check this at your first meeting).
   - There is no point in handing in something which is only a collection of notes: although a draft, it should be sufficiently "finished" to make it worth your supervisor's time in reading and commenting on it.
   - Your supervisor's role is not to "correct" your work but to provide feedback to enable you to improve it yourself. It is also unlikely that your supervisor will agree to give an estimated "mark" for your work, because this can only be judged in relation to the whole, finished work.
   - When you get comments from your supervisor, remember to revise the relevant section or chapter straight away when the feedback is fresh in your mind.

One note of caution: Your supervisor will be supervising a number of other dissertations as well (and conducting their own work). The earlier you hand work in for consideration, the more of your supervisor's attention you will get. Inevitably, if five students each hand in three or four new chapters to the same supervisor close to the deadline, the amount of time the supervisor can spend looking at each piece will be correspondingly limited.

> **TIP**
>
> At your first meeting, ask to set the date **now** for your **last** meeting with your supervisor before submission to help you with your time management, and also clarify whether or not your supervisor is available to see you during university holidays (be prepared for the answer to this question to be "no").

The finishing and polishing stage

Once you have completed your chapters and acted on the advice of your supervisor to improve them, then you will need to draw the dissertation to a coherent whole. The advice contained in Ch.9 on

3–13

polishing your work is equally applicable to dissertations, but there are some additional factors involved, as the formal requirements for the presentation of your dissertation are likely to be more complex than in relation to other written work. Ensure that you comply with any rules on how you present your chapters, referencing, double spacing of text and so on. Additionally, it is likely that you will have to write an *abstract* and it may be appropriate to include *appendices*.

What is an abstract and how do I write one?

An abstract is a short factual statement which appears at the beginning of your dissertation, summarising your aims, your research hypothesis, the evidence on which you rely and your conclusions, usually on a chapter by chapter basis. It gives the reader *information* about what to expect in the dissertation and it should be concise (about 150–300 words). Although it is presented at the beginning you should leave it until the end to write because it must be an accurate reflection of what is actually in your dissertation, not a woolly statement of what you were hoping to achieve when you started.

Do I need to use appendices?

It is a common mistake to assume that the use of voluminous appendices makes the dissertation seem more weighty and intellectual. This is certainly not true. Further, appendices should not be used as a means of providing additional material over the word limit. Generally, use of an appendix is appropriate where there is source material to which you have referred which is otherwise inaccessible for the reader (raw data, for example, or unpublished or obscure material). At the level of an undergraduate dissertation you are not expected to carry out empirical research in the form of questionnaires or interviews so unless you are relying on someone else's unpublished data you would not need to use an appendix for this. If you have relied on a comparatively obscure source extensively then you might want to provide a copy in your appendix—perhaps a hard copy of a website which you have cited but which has since been changed or removed from the internet—but easily available material such as statutes or cases is inappropriate for an appendix.

> **TIP**
>
> Do not treat your dissertation as requiring a completely different technique of writing from your other work. Developing good writing skills throughout your degree will stand you in good stead when it comes to writing your dissertation, as long as you make appropriate adjustments in terms of your time management and diagnosis.

What makes exams different?

3–14   Exams are still the most popular form of assessment in the study of law. Over the course of your legal studies you may encounter different types of exam to test your writing skills. Common examples include:

> Unseen—this is the "traditional" form of exam in which you do not see the exam questions in advance.
>
> Seen—this means that the questions will be made available to you before the exam, giving you some opportunity to prepare your answers.
>
> Closed book—this means that you are not allowed to take in materials (although you may be allowed a statute book).

> Open book—this means that you can take materials in to the exam (there may be limits on the quantity and type of material which you can take in).
>
> Takeaway—this is a variation on seen and open book exams where the exam paper is released and a short period is given to complete it outside an exam room.

Despite the increasing use of a range of assessment methods, the most popular assessment in law schools remains the unseen, closed book exam, which is likely to consist partly of essay questions and partly of problem questions. Much of what we have to say about approaching essay questions and problem questions throughout the rest of this book also applies to answering these questions in exam situations, but in this section we are going to explore the aspects of writing in exams which differ from the general advice provided elsewhere.

Coursework criteria, as discussed in Ch.1, are unlikely to apply formally to traditional closed book exams, but nevertheless these criteria (other than matters of presentation, which are less significant in an exam than in coursework) represent what your tutors think makes a good piece of writing; this, after all, is what you are aiming for. So assessment criteria are likely to have some relevance to your exam work as well. Keep focussed on the purpose of your writing while you revise and don't make the mistake of *over*estimating the differences between exams and coursework: although we explore some differences below, good writing is required in an exam situation in the same way as it is for coursework.

Many students find sitting exams very stressful, and this can make it more difficult to carry out the techniques which, outside the pressured exam situations, you know perfectly well you should be applying to the writing in question. You may find it helpful to reflect on the last exams you sat. Try to identify in specific terms exactly what you found problematic so that you can take steps to counter this in your next exam by picking out the parts of this chapter which are most useful to you.

> **TIP**
>
> There are many books on the market which cover exam preparation, skills and techniques. If, having reflected on your exam performance in the past, you feel you need some extra help on this, go to the library and see what books are available. Your university may also run workshops or drop-in sessions to help students deal with exam fears, or you may wish to discuss the situation with your personal tutor.

How to adapt the writing cycle for exams

In relation to an unseen exam, the most important way in which the process differs from the writing cycle we have discussed in Ch.2 is that in an exam situation, you do not have the opportunity to carry out the research phase **after** your diagnosis. In essence, you have to *anticipate* the research which is going to be needed, and carry this out as part of the revision process. The other vital difference—in a closed book exam at least—is that you will not be able refer to your research during the exam but must rely on having it in your head. This can cause two possible problems which you must avoid: **3–15**

1. You may be tempted to prepare a **generic** answer on each topic prior to the exam and then use that generic answer regardless of the *exact* question which is asked.
2. You may tend to focus on *information* rather than *technique* or *process*. In other words, the danger is that your revision is geared towards "learning" facts and principles rather than practising what to do with them, i.e. actually answering exam questions. This mass of "knowledge" or

"information" becomes a security blanket because you feel that you have "learnt" the topic when in fact what you have actually done is *memorised* the topic—which is not the same thing at all.

> **TIP**
>
> Think of your revision as being flexible—it can "stretch" in different directions to suit the exact wording of a question, but you want your final answer to be a good fit.

Both of these problems will lead to exam answers which fall into the "common faults" we identified in Ch.1: "does not answer the question" or "write all you know". To avoid this, adapt the cycle accordingly. Break up the diagnosis phase: before the exam, carry out a general diagnosis in which you identify a *technique* for tackling questions on particular topics, and you carry out your research and revision accordingly (and practise that technique). However, what is absolutely vital is that in the exam itself, when you see the questions, you still carry out a *specific* diagnosis on the question you have been asked.

Before the exam: your general diagnosis

3–16   Here are some suggestions for the general diagnosis which you make as part of your revision:

- Make sure you are familiar with instructions as to how many questions you have to answer in the exam, and any "official" guidance about what topics will be on the paper.
- Make sure your revision is focussed on techniques for tackling questions, not simply memorising cases and facts. Remember you are making a general diagnosis about what is likely to be needed to answer a question effectively on the topics you've chosen, so look at past papers and notes from tutorials or seminars and any guidance you have been given about how to tackle a particular topic or question, so as to be able to come up with a general "plan" for tackling that question.
- During your revision, practise relevant questions: make the most of the opportunity you have to do as much as possible to prepare in advance. In practising, you are doing two things: first you are giving yourself the opportunity to write for the relevant amount of time and in similar conditions. This may sound pointless but these days we tend to be much more used to writing with a word processor than with pen and paper; so if the only time you write for an hour on a regular basis is making lecture notes then this is inadequate preparation for writing continually for an hour (or even 2 or 3 hours) in an exam under time pressure. Secondly, by practising answers you are testing out your *technique* in adapting your general "pre-prepared" diagnosis to the specific diagnosis needed for this particular question. Remember your general advance plan **will not be enough in itself** (that is the mistake poorer students make) but will need to be fine-tuned. The snag is that you are doing this without your notes and in a time-pressured environment. So you must practise how to do this.

In the exam: finalising your diagnosis

3–17   As we said above, diagnosis in an exam requires the same skills as for coursework, but what is different is:

- You have to carry it out quickly and under pressure.
- You have to rely on what you have in your head—there is no opportunity to carry out a materials review to identify any shortfalls in your understanding, for example.

It is likely that you will be given some reading time at the start of your exams (10–15 minutes is common). You should utilise this period to make your final diagnosis. During this period you may be permitted to write on your question paper only, not on your answer booklet (if you haven't taken any university exams yet, make sure you check carefully what is permitted at your institution). You will use this reading time to first, identify the various topics being assessed by the various questions and then select the questions you are going to answer. Use the same techniques of looking for key words, instruction words and so on to make sure you are really focussed on the question. You may also have time to start making a plan in rough and can also scribble down relevant authorities.

This is where you move from the general to the specific, so you need to make decisions about what to keep and what to ditch from the general plans you have devised during revision. For example, your general plan on negligence will probably have information on how to deal with issues like a rescuer, the egg-shell skull principle or damage arising from an attempted suicide. But when you move to the specific (i.e. when you come to answer a question on negligence in an exam) you must forget the aspects of that general plan that are not relevant to the *actual question* on negligence that you have been set. If there isn't an attempted suicide then do not talk about the law on that aspect. This is where your imaginary "bin" is needed. Don't forget to take it in to your exams with you (mentally!) and use it to dump the material from your general plan that is not needed for the specific question you have been asked.

From experience of marking exam papers, we know it is especially hard in an exam situation for students to risk discarding material which isn't needed for this particular question. However, in an exam just as with coursework, your diagnosis will involve making decisions about what to include and what not to include. It can feel like a "waste" to simply abandon work you have spent time on; you might feel you know everything there is to know about (and have read three erudite academic journal articles on) professional rescuers, but if there is no professional rescuer in your negligence question, there cannot be any marks for discussing it, so you would be wasting time writing on it.

If it helps, think about it this way: Imagine going on holiday to somewhere where you aren't quite sure what the weather will be like—you'd take a variety of clothes to cover the possibilities. Would you get dressed on the first day without checking what the weather is actually like? Or, having checked the weather and found out it is going to be 80 degrees, would you wear your thick sweater on the beach on the basis that you went to the trouble of packing it, so you are going to wear it? It is unlikely, but this is essentially what you would be doing if you wrote a pre-prepared answer without reference to exactly what you've been asked, or put irrelevant material in an answer just because you spent time revising it.

> **TIP**
>
> **Practice** making a "quick" diagnosis—get hold of as many old exam questions as you can and give it a go. See if you can read the question and identify what the subject area is and make a rough note of the areas it is asking you to consider. This is a good revision activity and your tutor may be happy to look over your results— if not, then trade ideas with a fellow student instead.

Choosing which questions to answer in an exam

If you have not revised sufficient topics, then you won't have the luxury of having a choice of questions. If you have, then your choice may be influenced by which you feel are your "best" topics, or—preferably—which questions you feel you can best answer, based on your fine-tuned diagnosis. Alternatively, you may find you are influenced by whether the question on each of the topics you have revised is a problem question or an essay question. In conversation with our students the majority preference seems to be for answering problem questions in exams and essay style questions for course- **3–18** work. The choice between essays and problems is therefore something which is worth exploring. Don't be tempted to "write off" essay style questions before you even start. It is especially important, if you do not know in advance which topics are going to be examined with a problem question and which with an essay, that you make sure your revision does not assume one or the other.

Activity 3.1

Think for a minute about what you consider to be the advantages and disadvantages of essays and problems in an exam situation. Do you have a preference yourself?

Compare your views:

Here are some suggestions about the advantages of essays:

- flexibility in terms of devising a structure for your answer (this is often pre-determined by the actual question with a problem question);
- the ability to adopt a more expansive reflective approach to your writing; and
- the opportunity to explore theoretical aspects in more detail.

By being positive and considering the benefits inherent in answering essay questions we are demonstrating that essay questions actually give you more freedom. This is because, whilst you are given a framework shaped in general term by the question, it is up to you how you answer it. Some of the reasons that our students give us for why they prefer to tackle problem questions in exams are as follows:

- *"I don't have enough time to answer essay questions—there is too much to say"*. This is a reasonable fear but remember everyone else is in the same position, and the question has been set to be answered in the time allocated. Plan very carefully and focus on exploring in depth a limited number of points rather than many points at a basic level.
- *"Essay questions ask me to 'critically assess' the topic. I don't know how to do this."* This is essentially a matter of confidence. If you follow the advice we provide on how to critically evaluate materials, and how to utilise this to form your own arguments, then your revision should place you in a position to tackle an analytical essay.
- *"I don't understand what the question is getting at. What if I get it wrong and everything I write is irrelevant and off the point?"* The fear here is that it is harder to make a diagnosis on an essay question than on a problem, especially under stress. However, if you follow the advice in Ch.4 and have revised the topic well, you should not have anything to fear. Use the introduction to set out what you think the question is asking and why. (But remember there is a line to be drawn here between this suggested last resort approach and writing everything you know on the topic, so make sure you know where that line is to be drawn!)

However:

- Don't do an essay question *just* because you have revised the topic (unless of course your revision has been too narrow and you don't have a choice—if that is the case reflect on this when revising for your next exam).
- Don't do an essay question because you think it gives more scope for generalities—you must focus on the question.

The point is that essay questions are not any easier or harder than problem questions—they are just *different*. As you found out in Ch.1 they assess different skills and so will naturally require a different approach when answering them. It is important to remember that each type of question offer its own challenges, so your revision should be geared to preparing you for both.

The writing phase in an exam

In an exam, you carry out the writing phase under timed conditions and under pressure. Some students find that this helps them to write more concisely; others find this problematic. In marking exam writing, there is less emphasis on the matters we have considered in Chs 7 and 8 but nevertheless if you have developed an effective writing style using those chapters then you will find this is valuable to you in an exam because it will improve the quality of your communication. There are several issues in relation to writing which are unique to exam situations:

3–19

1. Managing your writing time

We have already said that one of the key differences between writing for an exam and writing for coursework is that you are doing it under time-pressured conditions. This is a fundamental aspect of good examination technique and requires some simple mathematics *before* you go into the exam: how long is the exam? How many questions do you have to answer? Assuming the questions are equally weighted in terms of marks available, divide the writing time by the number of questions you have to complete to work out the time you have available for each question. Have this fixed in your mind before you go in to the exam; jot down the "timetable" for when you move on to each question on your paper as soon as you are allowed to start writing. Stick to these timings. Five minutes before the end of each time slot begin to draw your answer to that question to a close and be ready to move on to the next question as soon as your allocated time is up. You must be ruthless with yourself—resist the temptation to spend a few extra minutes winding up your answer as every extra second you spend on that question is one less second to spend on the next. Tutors hate to mark a paper with two good and well-prepared answers and a final short one with the words "ran out of time" scribbled hastily at the end—resolve now that you will never need to do this.

> **TIP**
>
> Remember, the first 40 marks (i.e. the pass mark) out of 100 are easier to gain than the last 40 marks, so training yourself to move on when the time is up is vital so as not to handicap yourself from the start.

2. Dealing with a mental "block"

If you get stuck while preparing a piece of coursework then you can use various strategies to get over this, such as taking a break, having a cup of tea, or whatever. As long as you haven't left it to the last minute, you can come back to it the next day. In an exam situation you don't have this luxury, so you must devise different strategies for coping with a mental block.

To start with, a mental "block" is much less likely to occur if you have revised and practised techniques and principles, as we've suggested above, rather than just lists of information. However, inevitably there will be some things you can't remember, a common example being case names (of course some rote learning is required to try and commit the case names to memory). Students often ask: does it matter if I forget the case names in an exam? This is a tricky question and you are likely to find tutors differ slightly on it. Our answer is as follows: essentially, what we are testing in an exam is your understanding and your technique rather than your ability to remember information, so forgetting the odd case name is not going to ruin an answer which displays a sound understanding of the relevant principles. However, you are writing a legal assessment, and although case names are essentially "information" they are important information because they provide the legal authority for the principles you are applying. Hence an answer with no cases in it will score poorly for lack of authority. Nevertheless fixating on whether you will struggle to remember the case names tends to indicate that you haven't yet got the right emphasis on technique in your revision, so reflect on this if you are concerned about "remembering" the cases.

> **TIP**
>
> If you do forget a case name or section number from a statute, leave a space or draw a line in your work and fill in the blank if and when it comes back to you. If you have time you could also outline a few of the important facts thereby demonstrating that it really is a mental block rather than that you never learnt the relevant authority in the first place!

Some students find that their "block" in the exam is more serious than getting confused over case names. If so, then:

- Try giving yourself a five-minute break from writing—think about something else entirely.
- Try reproducing diagrams or flowcharts from your revision notes to get your mind going again.
- Cut your losses and start a different question (this is one of several reasons why it is advisable to make sure you revise sufficient topics, and resist the temptation to revise only the exact number of topics that you have to answer questions on).

However, we would emphasise again that if you concentrate on practising your approach to answering questions in your revision, rather than trying to memorise your textbook, then this sort of thing is much less likely to happen at all.

3. Your handwriting must be legible

> **TIP**
>
> Consider writing on every other line of the answer booklet. If you find that your writing becomes more and more illegible the more you write in an exam then this can help a reader to separate words out from others and generally help their understanding of what has been written.

Remember an examination is an important form of communication from you to the marker (your final award may be at stake!) and this will obviously be much more effective if the communication is easily readable. If you know that your handwriting is hard to read you will be doing yourself a great disservice in all your examinations if you don't do something about it. Practice is the key here; don't leave this until the week of the exams to sort out.

The finishing phase in an exam

3–20   The advice given in Ch.9 on finishing your work is designed for coursework situations. In an exam you will not have the opportunity to polish your work in this way, and you won't be specifically marked on your presentation. Nevertheless, it is wise to leave five minutes at the end for a quick read through so that you can correct any obvious mistakes.

Reflecting on your exam

Don't conduct a post-mortem with your mates, as this tends to lead to confusion and anxiety. This exam is finished and there is nothing that can be done now about improving what you have just written. Besides, immediately *after* a stressful situation is usually not the best time to think about how you have done. It is likely that you will need to prepare for another exam the next day or soon after so your time is best spent looking ahead to that exam rather than dwelling on the past one. However, once your exams are over, take a few minutes just to reflect on how your planning, preparation, timing and writing actually went for each exam. Don't think about *what* you wrote but rather *how* you wrote. Were you happy with how these aspects went or do you need to consider making adjustments to these for your next exams?

> **TIP**
>
> Remember, although exams can be a stressful experience they are not meant to be full of tricks and traps, and the legal writing techniques you have practised throughout the year with your other assessments will stand you in good stead. Contrary to popular belief, exams are designed to allow you to shine, not to catch you out.

3–21

Summary of Chapter 3

- Some types of legal assessment require modification of the general process of writing identified in Ch.2.   **3–22**
- Problem questions require a greater emphasis on application of law to a set of facts.
- You will diagnose your task differently for a dissertation and apply the rest of the cycle on a chapter by chapter basis.
- In exams, you carry out your general diagnosis and research through your revision prior to a more specific diagnosis in the exam itself.

4　How to make your diagnosis

What is the purpose of this chapter?

4–1　We've already seen that it is vital to successful writing to consider why you've been set a particular assignment. Understanding what a particular type of assignment is testing is going to help you work out how to tackle it.

　　However, there is much more to identifying your purpose than this. As well as understanding generally what an essay is for, and what a problem question is for, the real key to successful writing is to understand *exactly* what you are being asked to do. This chapter will help you make this diagnosis. It may sound obvious, but this is always going to be the vital first step to producing a successful piece of work. Get this right, and you'll be well on the way to making a good job of the rest of the writing "cycle".

　　By the end of this chapter you should:

- understand what we mean by purpose and diagnosing the task;
- understand what we mean by "instruction words" and the meaning of the common instruction words used in legal assessments; and
- be starting to work out your own strategies for diagnosing the tasks you are set.

What is diagnosis of task all about?

4–2　Imagine going to a restaurant, sitting down at a table, and before you've had a chance to consider a menu or think about what to order, a plate of food arrives. The chef has thought "oh well, they've come in here for food—doesn't matter what kind". This is what you are doing to the tutor who has set your assignment if you don't take the time to diagnose your task. (And remember your tutor is allocating marks to your work: what kind of review would you write of a restaurant which tried to serve you food without reference to what you wanted to order?)

　　Essentially, diagnosing your task is all about working out *exactly* what you've been asked to do in any particular assignment or question. There are a number of different steps you can take to help you make your diagnosis. First of all, you need to spend time thinking about the question. You should already have an idea from Ch.1 about the purposes for which tutors set particular types of assessment which should help you to think in general terms about what the assignment is for. However, you need to narrow it down much more than this in order to produce an effective piece of work.

You do this by working out what issues the question is asking you to cover, and then making the correct judgment about the relative importance of these aspects so you can work out how much detail is needed on each one. In other words, good diagnosis involves making decisions in relation to two important elements:

1. coverage; and
2. depth.

You can see from this that you need to do the following (and the more of them you do, the better your work will be):

- Be clear and organised in identifying the right points.
- Work out which points are the most important (these are your major points which you will want to spend more time/words on).
- Work out which other points are relevant to the question but are not as vital as the major points (these are your minor points which will accordingly get less time/words).
- Work out whether there are any hidden issues which need discussing even though the question does not directly mention them (your examiner may have "hidden" an issue which is important to a sophisticated discussion of the subject matter of the question by not referring to it directly in the wording of the question). These are what legal examiners call oblique points, or non-explicit points, and identifying these tends to increase your marks because spotting them is difficult: you'll need to learn to distinguish between a *hidden* point and an *irrelevant* point. The former is relevant to a full discussion of the subject matter of the question even though there was no reference to it in the exact wording of the question. Only a student with a thorough grasp of the subject matter is going to be able to spot this. The latter may be peripherally related to the subject matter but is not included within the material required to answer the question.

This last point raises an important issue in relation to making an effective diagnosis, namely it is impossible to do this completely without a thorough understanding of the topic. Yet, as we've already seen, your diagnosis gives direction to the research which you carry out on the topic—and it is from that research that you get your thorough understanding. So, how can you diagnose the task beforehand? The answer is that you make a **preliminary** diagnosis and then **keep it under review**. Your preliminary diagnosis sends you off to the right places, but you then have to keep reflecting on what you find there and using this information to "fine tune" your diagnosis.

Imagine this as taking a journey from your university accommodation to your home—or if you live at home, then think about going off to see a friend in another town or city. You might catch a train to get you to the railway station nearest to your destination, then switch to a bus or tram to "fine tune" your journey to get nearer to the exact place you're aiming for. Finally, you walk from the bus or tram stop to the front door. If this is your regular journey home then you'll know the route well—you don't have to think about the "fine tuning" to get home. But if you're travelling somewhere unfamiliar,

TIP

Always keep your diagnosis under review as you learn more about your subject through your detailed research. To make sure you do this, print the question out and stick it as close as you can get it to your computer screen. Stick a copy in your wallet or purse too, or text it to yourself, so that you know you've always got it with you when needed, for example when carrying out research.

then as you change to a more "exact" form of transport you'll be checking more detailed instructions—making sure you get on the right bus, perhaps even consulting an A–Z to locate your final destination. In other words, as you move along your journey, you're constantly checking that it is still taking you where you want to go.

Finally, you need to demonstrate your good diagnosis by transforming it into an effective piece of writing. You will prove to the examiner that you have carried out an effective diagnosis in two ways:

1. By identifying what the question is asking you to do (a good introduction which pinpoints the issues and indicates their relative importance does this).
2. By then performing the tasks you have identified—in the main body of your essay, discuss the issues you indicated were relevant, weighted appropriately to their relative importance (i.e. spending more time discussing the major points than the minor points).

On the following pages, we'll work through some examples to help you understand how to do this.

Why is diagnosis important?

4–3   The sort of mistakes which result from a poor diagnosis of task include:

- Advising the wrong person in a problem question.
- Providing a general discussion of the law rather than specific advice in a problem question.
- Being too descriptive in an essay question which requires analysis.
- Including irrelevant material.
- Missing out important points.
- Writing about things you happen to know about or have revised, instead of what your tutor wanted.

If you look at the section on common student mistakes in Ch.1, you'll see that many of these result from a poor diagnosis of task. If you get comments which seem similar to any of the above, then you need to focus on this in order to improve.

A further issue to note is that students in our experience sometimes confuse diagnosing the *task* or question with diagnosing the *topic*. It is **always** a mistake to think "oh, negligence" (or whatever the topic is) and then start writing straight away. This is particularly common with exam answers, and it is something we've already discussed in Ch.3. It is extremely unlikely that you have been asked to write down anything you can remember about negligence—yet this is perhaps the commonest mistake. To improve your marks you will need to delve a bit deeper: don't think of the question as being "on" a topic, as this may lead you into a generalised approach. Instead move straight into working out exactly what **aspects** of the topic you have been asked to consider.

This is why we draw the analogy with diagnosis. The question is a bit like the symptoms of an illness—you make your diagnosis of what is needed and the "cure" is the assignment you produce. Making an incorrect diagnosis will mean that the suggested cure doesn't actually help these particular symptoms.

However, on the positive side, a student who performs a good diagnosis will find that much of the rest of the work falls into place. Diagnosing the task is a skill, not a gift. Some students find it easy from the start, but if you aren't one of the lucky ones, you can still master it through practice and by following some tips and suggestions.

How do I make a diagnosis on an essay question?

We've established that a diagnosis involves making sure you understood what the question is asking you to do. As problem questions ask you to display different skills from those which are needed for essay questions, it is logical that the techniques you use to diagnose the task are different as well. We're going to consider techniques for diagnosing essay questions first, and then later in the chapter we'll look at diagnosing problem questions.   **4–4**

Tips for diagnosing the task on an essay question include:

- "Turning round" what you've been asked to do.
- Putting the question into your own words.
- Picking out key words and instruction words.
- Producing a list of sub-questions which contribute to answering the question.

We are going to explain how to *combine* these tips into an effective diagnosis technique. As discussed in Ch.1, an essay question commonly takes one of the following forms:

1. Question:

Is X true?

2. Statement:

"X is true". Discuss.

3. Instruction:

Critically assess the extent to which X is true.

Of these, students often seem to find it easiest to diagnose the direct question format, as this makes more overt exactly what you have been asked to do. However, if you look at the statement and instruction formats, you can see that what you have to do is analyse the strengths and weaknesses of the position taken, with appropriate evidence, and this therefore involves the same skills and techniques as answering the question format. Students sometimes wrongly assume that they are expected to agree with the statement in a statement question, and this can lead to a presumption that statement questions are more "difficult" than "question" questions. However, it is comparatively easy to turn the statement into a question to get round this problem.

For example:

"The voting system used at UK General Elections requires urgent reform to reflect the values of a liberal democracy". Discuss.

This is a question which we will return to in much greater detail later in the chapter, but in very brief terms, you can see that it is asking you to say *whether* the voting system used at UK General Elections requires urgent reform to reflect the values of a liberal democracy. It would be quite easy to rephrase the assignment into a question:

> Does the voting system used at UK General Elections require urgent reform to reflect the values of a liberal democracy?

When you turn the "statement" form of question into a true "question" type of question, then it becomes clearer that what you are being asked to do is answer "yes" or "no". Of course, you won't get any marks for a one word answer—and remember that part of the skill of legal argument is the ability to acknowledge and evaluate both sides of an argument. If you are in any doubt about this, remember that the original form of the question was a statement asking for your critical assessment. We know that critical assessment involves looking at the strengths and weaknesses of any particular position. Therefore, what you have to do in this type of situation is to argue both sides but conclude which side of the argument (i.e. the "yes" side or the "no" side) is stronger. Turning the statement round is a good starting point to help you get to grips with what you have been asked to do, and can be a useful technique to try to get initial ideas flowing about what is involved in the question topic.

> **TIP**
>
> Turning a statement round into a question in this way can be a good technique to help you work out exactly what it is asking you to do, but be very careful that you do not alter the meaning in doing so.

The next step, which you will always need to do to make an effective diagnosis, is to pick out *key words* and *instruction words*. You may find that after doing this you have, in effect, put the question into your own words, but if you use the key words and instruction words as your starting point there is less danger of going off on the wrong track than if you simply try to restate the question. We'll also think about breaking the question down into a series of sub-questions later in the chapter. For now, we're going to concentrate on key words/phrases and instruction words/phrases.

Key words are words which **relate to the subject matter** and instruction words are words which tell you **what to do with the subject matter**.

For example:

> "The rule that a **third party may not sue** on a **contract which is for his or her benefit** is **outmoded**." *Discuss* this statement *with particular reference to the **Contracts (Rights of Third Parties) Act 1999**.*

The key words, which define and/or modify the subject matter, are outlined in bold. The main topic of the essay relates to third parties and enforcement of contracts (privity), and the particular focus within this topic is on whether it is "outmoded" that a third party cannot enforce the contract; this "modifies" the key subject to indicate the scope of your work, or to put it another way, the "slant" your essay has to take, rather than simply being a general discussion of privity of contract. A further key phrase is the statute which is specifically mentioned. The instruction words are highlighted in italics: you are asked to "discuss" the statement, and this is further modified by a specific instruction to make sure the 1999 Act is included within your discussion (this is something of a clue: an alternative form of the question might omit this on the basis that inclusion of detail on the recent Act is implicit in answering the question effectively).

It would therefore be a mistake—although not an uncommon one—to do any of the following in an essay on this topic:

- Discuss privity of contract generally, without reference to the specific hypothesis posed that it is "outmoded".
- Fail to discuss the content and impact of the 1999 Act.
- Merely describe the law on privity and/or the 1999 Act rather than engaging in a critical discussion of them.

All essay questions will have key words. Whether or not the essay question also has instruction words will depend on the way it is asked—if in the form of a simple question then you will have to infer the instruction word. For example, supposing you had been asked:

> Is the rule that a third party may not sue on a contract which is for his or her benefit outmoded?

Although the subject matter is the same here, there is no instruction to "Discuss" the topic. However, since it would be difficult to answer this question without entering into a discussion of the relevant issues (a simple description of the rule, for example, clearly does not answer the question because there would be no attention to the issue of whether the rule is outmoded, which of necessity demands some evaluation or discussion of the law), then the word "Discuss" or "Analyse" can be inferred as the instruction.

How to identify the instruction words

As well as *Discuss*, some more instructions words which you might come across include: **4–5**

> *Analyse*
> *Critically assess*
> *Evaluate*
> *Criticise*
> *Explain*
> *Compare and contrast*

Note that although it is possible to define these words so as to highlight different nuances, in practical terms, in legal examining the first four terms are used more or less interchangeably. So, *Analyse*, *Critically assess*, *Evaluate* and *Criticise* are all similar to *Discuss* in that they require you to examine any propositions made or implied in the question or statement given and look for the strengths and weaknesses of those propositions, relying on appropriate evidence. The key here is to explore both sides of the question but move to a conclusion which demonstrates which is the stronger.

Explain—this asks you to clarify a rule or situation, and would usually be accompanied by an instruction to do something else as well (for example, "Explain the recent reform proposals and critically assess whether they will achieve their object").

Compare and contrast—this is used in relation to two situations or positions, for example an existing law and a planned reform, or two different theories. A compare and contrast instruction requires you to take these two situations and identify similarities and differences between them.

On the other hand, you are unlikely to come across an instruction merely to *Describe*. This is because description is a lower level skill—it simply involves summarising a factual situation rather than applying any other cognitive skills to that situation. This is not to say that description is a bad skill to have. In order to explain the effect of a rule, you will certainly need to *describe* that rule. However, the trick is to be as concise as possible. A common student mistake is to focus on a lot of descriptive detail (for example, giving exhaustive accounts of the facts of a string of cases) at the expense of going on to make **judgments** about the material and draw conclusions about it. Getting this balance right is considered further in Ch.6.

Now try spotting instruction words and key words for yourself.

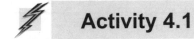 ## Activity 4.1

4–6   Consider this essay question:

> 1. Critically assess the extent to which the Practice Statement 1966 allows development of the law.

Which of the words listed below are the key words/phrases in this essay title and which are the instruction words?

Critically assess	Practice Statement 1966
Development of the law	Extent
Allows	

Compare your views:

Critically assess—this is an instruction phrase.

Extent—this is "modifying" the instruction and indicates the "slant" which is needed to your critical assessment.

Practice Statement 1966—this is a key phrase because it defines the subject matter.

Development of the law—this is a key phrase because it refines the subject matter of the essay: instead of generally looking at the pros and cons of the Practice Statement (for example) the focus must be on whether it permits change.

Allows—this is also a key word which modifies the discussion of the Practice Statement, suggesting there must be some consideration of the nature of the power granted by the Practice Statement.

We're now going to explore how to make your diagnosis further with some more activities which will help you to improve your skills in diagnosing different types of question.

Activity 4.2

4–7   We've already seen that sometimes, an essay question may be in the form of a question, in which case there is no instruction word. For example:

> 2. Does the Practice Statement 1966 allow sufficient development of the law?

However, we've also seen that within this type of question, an instruction to "discuss" or "critically assess" the issues is implicit. Would you say that this question is asking you to do the same as the question in the previous activity, or something different? As a reminder, the previous question was:

> Critically assess the extent to which the Practice Statement 1966 allows development of the law.

Compare your views:

We'd suggest the answer is yes, the two questions are asking the same thing. Our reasoning for this is:

1. both have the same key words/phrases (Practice Statement 1966, development of the law).
2. the instruction words *Critically assess* in the first question mean "examine whether the Practice Statement allows development of the law", and in the second, this is directly asked in the form of a question.
3. the word *extent* in essay 1 quantifies the "critically assess" instruction by asking **how much** the Practice Statement allows development of the law. This is matched by the word *sufficient* in question 2, which is essentially asking "is it enough?"

Now you might be thinking that the above reasoning means the questions are **different** because question 1 is asking *how much development of the law the Practice Statement allows* whereas question 2 is *asking how much development of the law the Practice Statement allows* **and** *is it enough*? This is a fair point: asking the price of something is not the same as asking whether it is good value for money, is it? It sounds like question 2 is asking you to make more of a judgment about the Practice Statement—in other words, draw some conclusions about how much development of the law is actually desirable and then compare the amount allowed by the Practice Statement with the "desirable" standard you have set.

However, if we go back to your instruction phrase in question 1: *critically assess*, we can see that this is not just asking you to *describe the amount* of development: critical assessment involves making (informed) *judgments*, so in fact, this question is *also* asking you to compare the amount of development permitted by the Practice Statement with some sort of "desirable" standard: in other words the question "is it enough?" is implied by the instruction phrase *critically assess*. Therefore, it seems these two questions are really asking you to do the same thing.

If you didn't agree, what were your reasons? Have the points above convinced you that they are the same, or have you thought of something else? It is ok to disagree, as long as you have convincing reasons to support your view (but you do need to be prepared to accept guidance and be objective in assessing whether your reasons are convincing).

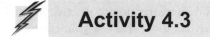 **Activity 4.3**

Now look at this question:

4–8

> 3. "The Practice Statement 1966 impedes the proper development of the law because so few cases reach the House of Lords." Discuss.

Do you think that this question is asking the same as, or something different from, the two questions we've already considered?

The two previous questions were:

---

1. Critically assess the extent to which the Practice Statement 1966 allows development of the law.

---

2. Does the Practice Statement 1966 allow sufficient development of the law?

Which of the following views comes closest to yours?

A.   It is a different question because although the subject matter is the same, the instruction word is *Discuss* rather than *Critically assess*.
B.   It is a different question because it includes reference to only a few cases reaching the House of Lords so I would have to make specific reference to that.
C.   It is the same question again because although there is a reference to cases reaching the House of Lords, this is a red herring because the Practice Statement only applies to the House of Lords anyway so this must have been implied in the other questions.

Compare your views:

If you chose answer A: We'd agree with you that it is a different question, but not because of the different instruction word: *discuss* and *critically assess* tend to be regarded as interchangeable in legal examining.

If you chose answer B: We agree. You would have been likely to discuss this particular issue in answering the other forms of this question, but here you are specifically directed to it so the issue would assume more prominence.

If you chose answer C: We can see your point about the Practice Statement only applying to the House of Lords, but actually what makes the question different is that it is asking you to concentrate on a particular "angle" of the idea of impeding the law, namely that the House of Lords can only reform the law in the few cases which come before it.

It is certainly true to say that the other questions were asking you to focus solely on the House of Lords (because the Practice Statement doesn't apply to any other court) but even so the phrase "because so few cases reach the House of Lords" add a different slant to the discussion. It does not mean you would not discuss anything else though.

Activity 4.4

4–9   Essay questions, particularly those which contain a statement and an instruction to discuss or critically analyse it, will almost invariably be based on one or more *assumptions*. Part of your diagnosis will involve spotting the assumptions so that you can research them effectively and then support or challenge them using the evidence you've collected. Let's return to this question:

"The Practice Statement 1966 impedes the proper development of the law because so few cases reach the House of Lords." Discuss.

Delving deeper into the question, essentially the statement in this essay title makes two assumptions. What do you consider these to be?

Compare your views:

In a nutshell, the two assumptions found in the statement are:

1. that the Practice Statement impedes the proper development of the law;
2. that this is because so few cases reach the House of Lords.

You are asked to "discuss" these assumptions. Therefore, you need to critically assess whether they are true. In other words, does the Practice Statement impede the development of the law? If so, is it due to the reason suggested or is it due to other reasons? You can see that the answer to the former question will bear a very strong resemblance to the answer to the question asked in the previous activity—*Does the Practice Statement allow proper development of the law?* Even the answer to the

> **TIP**
>
> You will often find that a "statement" question will make assumptions with which you have to agree or disagree, arguing your case with reference to appropriate evidence. Being able to pick out assumptions from the question is vital.

latter question will demand consideration of much of the same material as the first essay: you can see that those "other reasons" would have to be evaluated to see if they are as much/more/less to blame for the impediment as the reason given in the statement.

However, although the questions are very similar, the "slant" is still different. The current example takes the lack of cases reaching the House of Lords as a starting point: it therefore has to be front and centre in your answer. In the other answers it would have been *part of* your argument but not necessarily central to it.

We now need to move on to consider the key words and the relationship between the subject matter and the major and minor points you are looking for.

How to identify the subject matter

This is going to depend on your identification of the key words, but they are only the starting point: you will need to dig around the subject (which will depend on your understanding of it) to work out a series of points which need to be covered. You then need to classify these into "major" and "minor" points in order to work out the amount of depth you need to devote to each of them. A good technique is to pose a series of sub-questions, which you can then use as the basis for your research phase.   **4–10**

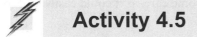 **Activity 4.5**

In this activity we are retuning to one of our Practice Statement questions: **4–11**

> Critically assess the extent to which the Practice Statement 1966 allows development of the law.

Even without any knowledge of the subject area, you can carry out a very preliminary diagnosis. To go further, you would need to have some understanding of the topic of precedent in the House of Lords. To do this exercise

> **TIP**
>
> To diagnose your task effectively on an essay question, break the question down into a series of sub-questions.

properly, you are therefore recommended to refer to your own notes on this topic, if you have covered it in Legal Method, Legal System, or a similar subject.[1]

We're going to look at how posing sub-questions can help you get to grips with what a question is asking for. You'll see some suggested questions below. Have a look at these questions, which are all related in one way or another to the doctrine of precedent, and try to pick out the ones which help answer this particular assignment title.

- What was the Practice Statement about?
- What difference did the Practice Statement make?
- What are the advantages of the Practice Statement?
- What are the disadvantages of the Practice Statement?
- What was the position before the Practice Statement?
- How much development of the law is a good thing?
- What has happened to precedent since the Practice Statement?
- What has happened to precedent in the Court of Appeal?
- What are the dangers of allowing development of the law?
- What are the dangers of impeding development of the law?

At this stage we're just brain-storming: this is not yet an essay plan and we aren't yet trying to classify these into major and minor points—we're just trying out a few preliminary ideas. Brainstorming is a useful technique to consider when trying to diagnose your task. Once you've narrowed it down to the questions you think are relevant, then the next step is to rank the relative importance of the questions.

Compare your views:

Here are our thoughts about the brainstorming questions on the previous page:

- *What was the Practice Statement about?*
  This is factual information and as such should be given briefly, but it is important information to inform the reader before you can explore the intricacies of the question.
- *What difference did the Practice Statement make?*
  This is a vital question to consider as it is directly relevant to the idea of the extent to which it has allowed development of the law. Essentially, it involves comparing the respective positions before and after the Practice Statement.
- *What are the advantages/disadvantages of the Practice Statement?*
  Although this has some relevance—you might for example be planning to argue that allowing or failing to allow development of the law is an advantage or disadvantage of the Practice Statement—this very general brainstorming question needs some care, as it could easily lead to a "write all you know" approach.
- *What was the position before the Practice Statement?*
  This is an essential requirement preparatory to thinking about what change it has achieved. Caution is always needed with historical background but here it is necessary: remember the purpose of the Practice Statement was to allow some flexibility in development of the law, so here the "history" has direct relevance to the question.

---

[1] A good introduction can be found in the following texts: ZANDER, M. *The law-making process*, 6th edn, Cambridge: Cambridge University Press, 2004, Ch.4; HOLLAND J. and WEBB, J. *Learning legal rules*, 6th edn, Oxford: Oxford University Press, 2006, Ch.5. Try reading these chapters with the essay title in mind (this will help you develop the skills we're going to be talking about further in Ch.5).

- *How much development of the law is a good thing?*
  This is implied within the idea of critically assessing how much development is permitted. We've already discussed that you need to conclude whether there is sufficient development, and you can only evaluate this if you have an idea of how much flexibility there should be. What makes this more difficult is that this is a matter of debate. You therefore need to take a position on the flexibility/certainty debate, backed up, of course, by suitable evidence.
- *What has happened to precedent since the Practice Statement?*
  Yes, this is vital factual information to underpin discussion of whether it has allowed sufficient development of the law. Note that a comparison of your answers to this question and the "position before" question provides the answer to the question what difference did the Practice Statement make, so essentially that question has been broken down further into these two "before" and "since" questions.
- *What has happened to precedent in the Court of Appeal?*
  Absolutely not! The question is asking you to consider events in the House of Lords only (although you might draw on arguments used by Lord Denning in the Court of Appeal, who had much to say on the subject. It is acceptable to use the *argument*, because that could have happened anywhere).
- *What are the dangers of allowing/impeding development of the law?*
  This is an excellent evaluative question. The answer should help you take a position in relation to the question considered above—how much development of the law is a good thing.

So, this leads us to the following sub-questions:

- What was the Practice Statement about?
- What was the position before the Practice Statement?
- What has happened to precedent since the Practice Statement?
- What are the advantages/disadvantages of the Practice Statement?
- What are the dangers of allowing/impeding development of the law?
- How much development of the law is a good thing?

Producing a list of sub-questions in this way will help focus your research, and will also assist you with structuring your arguments later.

Keeping your diagnosis under review

What can be daunting about the idea of diagnosing a task is if you don't feel that you know enough about the subject in order to do it effectively. The temptation is therefore to think "I'll read around the subject first and then come back to the question later". This is a fatal error, because your research will be unfocussed and you will therefore waste a lot of time; you may become expert in an area not specifically required, which then leads to the further mistake that rather than waste all that work, you think of a way to "get it in somewhere". You're now well on the way to writing the essay you *wish* you'd been asked to write, rather than the one you *have* been asked to write.   **4–12**

So, even if you don't feel very confident about the subject matter at least **have a go at some kind of basic diagnosis**. If we're back to the medical analogy, think of this as being a "preliminary" diagnosis, which will then be followed by various tests (i.e. your more detailed research on the topic), so that the original diagnosis can be confirmed or refined. In fact, making a preliminary diagnosis is a skill which can be learned, regardless of how much you currently know about the subject matter of the essay. To some extent, making your diagnosis is about your skills in interpretation—although your understanding of the topic will be vital to refine your diagnosis (which is why we're so keen for you to keep your diagnosis under review as you carry out your research).

So far, we've spent a lot of time looking at examples of different essay titles in Legal Method/System, which is an area you are likely to have studied at an early stage in your course and will therefore be familiar with. To improve your skills in making a preliminary diagnosis, try the following example, which is drawn from another subject area which tends to have a strong emphasis on essay writing skills, Public Law (Constitutional and Administrative Law). Even if you have not yet covered this subject, attempt this as it should improve your confidence that there is a certain level of diagnosis you can make even without a detailed knowledge of the subject matter.

Activity 4.6

4–13   Consider this essay title:

> "The voting system used at UK General Elections requires urgent reform to reflect the values of a liberal democracy". Discuss.

We're going to use this essay title as a worked example.

Our starting point is to note first that it is an essay, so therefore we know that the sort of things our examiner is wanting to test are those listed in Ch.1. We can further note that this is a *statement* kind of question. The instruction word here is *Discuss*. We know that a legal examiner will use the word discuss to require a critical assessment of the position taken in the statement. It is vital to present both sides of the argument; in other words, you have to demonstrate the extent to which the proposition (that the voting system at UK general elections needs urgent reform to reflect the values of a liberal democracy) is true, and the extent to which it is false. It can help to turn the statement into a question, as we saw earlier, for example, *Does the voting system used at UK General Elections require reform in order to reflect the values of a liberal democracy*?

This makes it easier to see that this question is asking you to argue: does the voting system used at UK general elections demand reform or doesn't it?

Try picking out the key words and instruction words.

Compare your views:

"Voting system at UK general elections"—this is your general subject matter: the topic involved.

"reform"—this shows a particular element which you are required to discuss—in other words, you need to think not just about the strengths and weaknesses of the existing law but propose solutions to any problems you identify, to indicate how the law could be improved in the future. It is common for legal examiners to include some reference to the prospect of reform. Reform questions always involve a **comparison** between the current system and possible alternatives.

"values of a liberal democracy"—you can see that an explanation of principles is going to be involved and this therefore makes it clear that this is a theoretical essay. These "values" are going to be the measuring stick against which you evaluate the current system and any proposed reform.

From your key words, you can begin to identify the knowledge and understanding you are going to need in order to tackle the question by breaking the question into sub-questions. Try this yourself, and then read on to compare your suggestions with the ones below.

Compare your views:

Consider the following questions:

- What are the values of a liberal democracy?
- What are the issues which influence judgments about voting systems?
- What is the current voting system in UK General Elections?
- What alternative systems could be used instead?
- Would the alternative systems be "better" than the existing system in relation to the values identified?

These are the issues which you can see are required simply from looking at the title, with no knowledge of the subject whatsoever. When you start to learn about the topics you'll be able to make a more detailed list. Everything on the list should be *relevant*. You can use your sub-questions to form a research grid (see below) where you jot down the question in one colum and note the basic gist of the answer to it in the next column (of course you won't be able to make full notes—just the bare outline: you may also find you discover conflicting information in answer to the questions you have posed, in which case, note that down too). Note down the evidence which supports your answer (i.e. the source you have used) in the third column. The next step, and again this will go hand in hand with completion of your research, is to *rank your points*—in other words, to work out which are the most important and therefore require the most depth. Remember as well that some of your questions will be factual/knowledge based questions, where others will be more evaluative ones. When answering a factual question be clear but as concise as possible.

You can put this into practice as follows: against each knowledge point, write down whether you consider it a major or a minor point—is it vital to your argument or a more subtle point? When planning your essay, you must cover all the major points; incorporate as many minor ones as you have room for, keeping the fundamental issue of relevance in mind. Ideas for the evaluation of a question include strengths and weaknesses of a legal rule/academic argument/case etc. Here, what are you being asked to consider the strengths and weaknesses of? It is the voting system at UK general elections, obviously, but because you are considering *reform*, we've already identified that you need also to compare alternative systems, so you need the strengths and weaknesses of alternative systems as well. Therefore you need to note that this is an area where evaluation is needed.

The next logical question is **how** do you evaluate strengths and weaknesses? In order to evaluate, you need a yardstick to measure against. This may be implied rather than specifically stated: you might have to evaluate against generic yardsticks for the law—justice, consistency, fairness, human rights, efficiency, and logic for example. But in this case, we are given a specific yardstick: "values of liberal democracy" so you need to relate your evaluation to that.

Sub-question	Basic answer	Evidence (sources)
What are the values of a liberal democracy?		
What are the issues which influence judgments about voting systems?		
What is the current voting system in UK General Elections?		
What alternative systems could be used instead?		
Would the alternative systems be better than the existing system?		

By this stage you are in a position to carry out your research, remembering to keep your diagnosis under review. Your diagnosis and your list of sub-questions will also help you to make an essay plan when you move to that stage of your writing. There's more on how to do this, and we return to this particular question, in Ch.6.

How do I make a diagnosis on a problem question?

In a problem question, you will be given a set of circumstances in the form of a case study involving a number of people, and asked to advise one or more of them about how the law applies to them. The vital word here is "**applies**". The aim of your diagnosis in a problem question is to relate your understanding of the area of law in question specifically to the circumstances and the people who are involved in the scenario you have been given.

As discussed in Ch.3, the diagnosis phase for a problem question contains the following elements:

4–14

- identify whom you are advising about what;
- identify the parties, and the role of your client in the scenario;
- identify the material facts;
- identify the legal issues arising from those facts.

For example, suppose you are given the following problem question:

> David's unusual hand-moulded canoe is stolen from his back garden. He places an advertisement in *The Herald*, his local free newspaper, advertising a reward of £50 to the person who finds it. Jim, who never saw the advertisement, finds the canoe on the riverbank, puts it on the roof of his car and takes it home. His wife, Dorothy, recognises it as the canoe in the advertisement and shows Jim the paper. Jim drives straight round to David's and returns his canoe but David refuses to pay Jim the £50 claiming that the offer has been withdrawn.
>   Advise Jim.

A. Identify whom you are advising about what:

In this example, we are advising Jim about whether he has a contract (i.e. whether, applying the facts of this question, the necessary elements for forming a valid contract are satisfied—this is your *core issue*). Always check this first, so that you read the rest of the question with this in mind, looking for the facts and law that specifically affect Jim's position. However, do remember what we discussed in Ch.3 about the meaning of "Advise Jim"—you must identify the strengths and weaknesses of Jim's case.

B. Identify the parties and the role of your client in the scenario:

In the example, the other parties are David and Dorothy (as you explore the legal issues and material facts in this question, you will decide whether all your parties are legally relevant to the scenario) and Jim is in the position of claimant—i.e. he needs advice on whether he can make David give him the promised reward, which, as identified above, involves working out whether there is an enforceable contract between them.

> David's unusual hand-moulded canoe is stolen from his back garden. He places an advertisement in *The Herald*, his local free newspaper, advertising a reward of £50 to the person who finds it. Jim, who never saw the advertisement, finds the canoe on the riverbank, puts it on the roof of his car and takes it home. His wife, Dorothy, recognises it as the canoe in the advertisement and shows Jim the paper. Jim drives straight round to Davids and returns his canoe but David refuses to pay Jim the £50 claiming that the offer has been withdrawn.
>   Advise Jim.

These two points are quick to identify, but you need to make sure you do it before trying to analyse the question any further.

C. Identify the material facts:

From your first reading of the scenario, you need to identify the *material facts*, i.e. the ones that you consider are of importance and/or of particular relevance to this question. This will help you diagnose your task and identify the area(s) of law which need to be discussed. A good technique is to read through the question scenario carefully underlining the words and facts that you consider might later prove to be relevant. Keep these under review: remember they are only material if they make a difference. So, for example, it might well be material that the advertisement was placed in the local free paper, but the name of the paper is unlikely to be relevant.

You might come up with the following (these are just indicative of the process: we aren't trying to produce a model answer here):

- unusual hand-moulded canoe: this suggests that the subject of the reward is something unusual and/or valuable;
- advertisement in the free local paper: the offer was made in a widely circulated newspaper;
- reward of £50: the amount of the reward is comparatively low;
- reward is for the person who finds the canoe: the wording does not offer the reward for returning the canoe;
- Jim never saw the advertisement: so he doesn't know about the reward offer when he finds the canoe;
- Dorothy shows Jim the advertisement before Jim returns the canoe: so he knows about the offer before returning the canoe;
- David refuses to pay: Jim will not get a reward as things stand.

D: Identify the legal issues

From your identification of the material facts you go on to the next step of classifying the legal issues arising from these facts. Remember that your diagnosis of the core legal issue (what you are advising Jim about) sets the basic legal framework which will always be required on a question on a particular topic. Here, it is the general principle that in order to form a valid contract, offer and acceptance are required. This principle forms the framework of any similar contract question. However, to make sure your answer is specific rather than general, you must say whether, *in these particular circumstances*, these requirements are satisfied. Here we return to the idea of posing sub-questions to help make your diagnosis.

To do this, the factual points must be generalised into legal issues, on which your sub-questions will be based. Finding the answers to these sub-questions, as in an essay question, will form the basis for your research. Initial sub-questions, from the material facts we identified, could be as follows:

- Does the value or uniqueness of the subject matter of a reward affect its validity?
- Can a valid offer be made via a newspaper advert?
- If so, does it make a difference that the newspaper is a widely circulated one?
- Does the amount of the reward make any difference to the issue of whether a contract is formed?
- Does the offeree need to know about the offer in order to accept it?
- At what point does acceptance take place where a reward is offered via an advert?

Of course, as you research more about the law on this area, you will be able to work out whether these questions are major points, minor points, or not at issue at all (even posing the questions in this way may help you to eliminate irrelevancies; sometimes your tutors will include matters as deliberate "red herrings" and you need to be on the lookout for these). Keeping your diagnosis under review, which is just as important on a problem question as on an essay question, will also help you identify whether there are any questions (i.e. legal issues) which you have missed.

You then relate the legal issues back to the material facts through your *application* when you write your answer. Setting these out as a grid is helpful, just as it is on an essay question, with the relevant material facts in an additional column, to remind you to apply them later. Of course, generating questions in this way will not produce the logical order for you to discuss the issues in your final answer—that will be something for you to work on when you consider how to structure your answer (see Chs 6 and 7), and of course to some extent will depend on the "basic" law of the subject under consideration (here, we know an explanation of the basic rules of offer and acceptance would be needed).

CORE ISSUE: IS THERE AN ENFORCEABLE CONTRACT IN TERMS OF OFFER AND ACCEPTANCE?

Relevant material fact	Legal issue	Answer (in the form of a legal principle)	Authority (case or statute)
David's canoe is unusual	Does the value or uniqueness of the subject matter of a reward affect its validity?		
David makes his offer in a newspaper	Can a valid offer be made via a newspaper advert?		
The newspaper is a free local one	If so, does it make a difference that the newspaper is a widely circulated one?		
The amount of the reward here is £50	Does the amount of the reward make any difference to the issue of whether a contract is formed?		
The reward was for finding the canoe not for returning it	How crucial is the exact wording of the offer?		
Jim did not know about the offer when he found the canoe but he did when he returned it	Does the offeree need to know about the offer in order to accept it?		

You would then focus on completing the final two columns during your research phase, just as with an essay question. Because you are seeking the answers to legal questions, your answer will be propositions of law, and whenever you assert a principle of law then you also need to use authority or evidence to back up your assertion. So, for example in the question above, you might contrast the case of *Partridge v Crittenden* [1968] 2 All E.R. 421 on invitations to treat with the famous case of *Carlill v Carbolic Smoke Ball Co* [1893] 1 Q.B. 256 on offers in advertisements. Your overall goal with your research (and with your writing later) is to make sure you have provided an answer to your core issue, with answers to the sub-questions which, following your research, you decided were relevant along the way, leading to that final conclusion. For example:

> In light of the relevant authorities, particularly *Gibbons v Proctor* (1891) and *R. v Clarke* (1927), Jim can be advised that he is fully entitled to the £50 on the basis that there is an enforceable contract.

Activity 4.7

4–15   Consider the following problem question, which concerns the text of negligence:

> Zebedee has been suffering from persistent headaches about which he has consulted his doctor. One morning he is driving to university when he suffers a sudden seizure and collapses at the wheel. His car veers towards Abdul who is standing on some scaffolding and jumps off it to avoid the impact of the car, suffering a broken wrist and ankle when he hits the ground. Zebedee's car ploughs into the scaffolding and on into the path of an oncoming bus. Brenda and Carl are both passengers on the bus who are standing next to each other. Carl is carrying a firework which the crash impact causes to explode, injuring Brenda. Brenda suffers severe burns. Carl suffers a minor cut on his face which activates a latent cancer condition from which he later dies. The police arrive at the scene and as the police officers are escorting people off the bus the scaffolding collapses altogether, injuring Dan, a spectator who was trying to take photographs of the incident on his mobile phone. Dan suffers injuries to his head. He has now suffered a personality change, and has attempted suicide, causing him further injury.
>   Advise Zebedee about his potential liabilities.

How could you apply the above approach to this question? Remember to try the four steps we have identified above, and put together a grid which you could use to research this question.

Compare your views:

> Zebedee has been *suffering from persistent headaches* about which he has *consulted his doctor*. One morning he is *driving* to university when he *suffers a sudden seizure* and collapses at the wheel. His car veers towards Abdul who is *standing on some scaffolding and jumps off it to avoid the impact of the car*, suffering a *broken wrist and ankle* when he hits the ground. Zebedee's car ploughs into the scaffolding and on into the path of an oncoming bus. Brenda and Carl are both *passengers on the bus* who are standing next to each other. *Carl is carrying a firework* which the crash impact causes to *explode, injuring Brenda*. Brenda suffers *severe burns*. Carl suffers a *minor cut* on his face which *activates a latent cancer condition from which he later dies*. The police arrive at the scene and as the police officers are escorting people off the bus the scaffolding collapses altogether, injuring Dan, a *spectator* who was trying to take photographs of the incident on his mobile phone. Dan suffers *injuries to his head*. He has now suffered a personality change, and has attempted *suicide, causing him further injury*.
>   Advise Zebedee about his potential liabilities.

A. We're advising Zebedee, about his liability in the tort of *negligence*.

B. Zebedee is the defendant in this situation and the other parties involved are Abdul, Brenda, Carl and Dan. Our overall goal is to establish whether Zebedee is liable to these other parties. The basic principles of our core legal issue are that negligence is established through four essential components: duty of care (in law and in fact), breach of that duty, causation of damage which is not too remote, plus the consideration of the availability of any defences (see the spider diagram in Ch.5 for an outline of the topic of negligence).

C. Identification of the material facts could include the following (note that this is not intended as an exhaustive list):

- Zebedee has been suffering from headaches;
- Zebedee knew he had some kind of health problem;
- Zebedee is a driver;
- Zebedee has collapsed at the wheel;
- Abdul is on scaffolding at the side of the road;
- Abdul suffers injuries jumping off the scaffold;
- Brenda and Carl are road users;
- Brenda sustains injuries from an exploding firework;
- Carl is carrying the firework;
- the firework explodes because of the impact with Zebedee's car;
- Dan is a spectator;
- Dan suffered head injuries;
- Dan has suffered a personality change;
- Dan has sustained further injuries after attempting suicide.

D. Identification of the legal issues involves generalising the facts we've identified to pose legal questions about the law of negligence, which would form the basis of the research phase.

For example:

- *Zebedee has been suffering from headaches* could become the question: *does a pre-existing medical condition affect the liability of a driver in negligence?*
- *Zebedee is a driver*: becomes *does a driver owe a duty of care to other road users?*
- *Zebedee has collapsed at the wheel*: becomes *does collapsing at the wheel constitute breach of any existing duty?*

The grid which you would take into your research phase might look something like this (again, not necessarily exhaustive):

4–16

CORE ISSUE: IS THERE LIABILITY IN NEGLIGENCE IN THIS SITUATION?

Relevant material fact	Legal issue	Answer (in the form of a legal principle)	Authority (case or statute)
Zebedee has been suffering from headaches	Does a pre-existing medical condition affect the liability of a driver in negligence?		
Zebedee is a driver	Does a driver owe a duty of care to other road users?		
Zebedee has collapsed at the wheel	Does collapsing at the wheel constitute breach of any existing duty?		
Abdul is on scaffolding at the side of the road	Does a driver owe a duty to people at the side of the road?		
Abdul suffers injuries jumping off the scaffold	Is the damage sustained of a type for which a claim can be made?		
Brenda and Carl are road users	Does a driver owe a duty of care to other road users?		
Brenda sustains injuries from an exploding firework	Is the damage sustained of a type for which a claim can be made?		
Carl is carrying the firework	Does this constitute an intervening act?		

CORE ISSUE (continued)

Relevant material fact	Legal issue	Answer (in the form of a legal principle)	Authority (case or statute)
The firework explodes because of the impact with Zebedee's car	How does this relate to the chain of causation?		
Dan is a spectator	Is there a duty of care to a spectator?		
Dan suffered head injuries	Is the damage sustained of a type for which a claim can be made?		
Dan has suffered a personality change	Is a personality change following an incident within the boundaries of remoteness?		
Dan has sustained further injuries after attempting suicide.	Is the damage sustained of a type for which a claim can be made?		

There are some further issues to bear in mind when diagnosing a problem question.

The limits of acceptable speculation

Students sometimes comment that they find it difficult to identify the "answer" to the core legal question posed in a problem question because of a lack of sufficient facts. The temptation here is to invent facts to fill these gaps, but this is not appropriate; instead, comment on the fact that an informed opinion cannot be reached because of the facts that you do not know and briefly mention the alternatives. Remember, if there is an ambiguity in a question it is deliberate, so don't go behind the facts you have been given. Essentially this involves drawing a distinction between

4–17

acceptable speculation and making up facts to suit your interpretation. It is vital that you do not make up facts.

Example:

> Supposing the facts you are given are that X and Y are married with two children. Your answer needs to advise about something to do with the children, and two possible variants on your answer relate to (a) the age of the children, and (b) the marital status of the parents.

Here, we are not told the age of the children, but we are told the marital status of the parents.

If your answer gives the position about the children "supposing the couple weren't married" then this is going too far because you are told they *are* married—this is re-inventing the facts and is therefore *un*acceptable speculation. On the other hand, we are not told the age of the children and therefore if it would make a difference if they are aged A rather than aged B, then it is acceptable to speculate. What you should do in this situation is cover both bases: state the position *if* the children are aged A and *if* the children are aged B, because you are not told whether they are A or B.

It would be wrong to do either of the following:

1. ignore the importance of the age issue altogether on the basis that you haven't been told the ages—state that you would need to know more and explain how; or
2. plump for the children being *either* A *or* B and answer accordingly—here, you are inventing facts which would make your advice incomplete: you must acknowledge the gap in the facts and provide advice accordingly.

It can be difficult to get the balance right in relation to speculation because you see the judges speculating in their judgments—it is where we get *obiter* from—but in a problem question answer you are not expected to give *obiter*. This is not the same as refusing to give a position at all, however. What makes this different from the second point above is that either of those positions (A or B) *would* be *ratio*, if we knew the facts: it is just that you don't know which because you have not been given the information you need to decide.

Adapting the facts of a well-known case

4–18   Your tutors may well set a question which uses facts of well-known cases in their invented scenario but with a few important material facts changed. Your identification of the material facts is going to be vital to make sure you do not get caught out by this. You would need, in this situation, to highlight the material facts which make your facts different from the facts of the case in question, so that you can then go on to argue that the *ratio* of the case is not binding.

Addition of a "compare and contrast" to the advice you are giving

4–19   Just as we've seen that you might be asked to compare and contrast on an essay question, you might be asked to do the same in a problem question. However, be alert that the *words* "compare and contrast" might not be used.

Two common ways in which a compare and contrast angle can be added to a problem question are as follows:

1. How would your answer differ if the facts were slightly different, for example *Would it have made a difference if Jim had only returned the canoe because a policemen saw him find it and put it on his car?*
2. How would your answer differ if new legal reforms had been brought into force, for example *Would it make a difference to your answer if the Bill on X, Y and Z 2006 was in force?*

In both of these situations, what is being asked is that you compare and contrast the facts as given, or the law as it stands, with the alternative facts given or the new law. In both cases, the question will have been asked for a reason—in other words, it is likely that there are significant differences for you to identify which would have an important effect on your answer. However, this is not an automatic rule: sometimes this compare and contrast would be set simply to test that you understand that in this particular case, there would be no difference (as in the first question above).

Dealing with conflicting evidence

It is extremely likely that your research into your sub-questions will produce sources which conflict. You will find the answer to each legal sub-question will be either settled law (i.e. all the authorities point in one direction) or at issue (i.e. there are conflicting authorities). Areas of settled law will be minor points; where the law is at issue it will require more detailed treatment as a major point. We return to this theme in Ch.6.   **4–20**

Summary of Chapter 4

- Diagnosis of task is all about working out exactly what the question is asking you to do.   **4–21**
- A correct diagnosis is vital to tackling the question in the right way.
- In an essay question, a good starting point is to put the title in the form of a question, and then work on breaking this down into sub-questions.
- In a problem question, you need to identify the material facts and from these work on a series of legal questions.
- In both cases, these questions will form the basis of your research and it is helpful to put these questions in a grid format.
- You need to keep your diagnosis under review as you learn more about the subject area.

5   Planning and carrying out your research

What is the purpose of this chapter?

5–1   Once you have diagnosed your task, and worked out what you need to do to complete your assignment, you will know from Ch.2 that the next stage is to carry out a review of your existing materials. Carrying out this exercise, together with the questions you have posed in your diagnosis, helps you to define the scope of the research which you need to do. Remember that you must not assume that you can complete your assignment from your existing materials: you will always need to carry out additional research.

Finding relevant cases, books and articles for your research can be a challenge and this chapter will help you do the following things:

- Review the materials which you already have at your disposal and consider how these will help you write your assignment.
- Understand the difference between the various types of source material and how you can use each type (use of evidence in your writing is also considered further in Ch.6).
- Identify gaps in your research material, find new sources, and how to evaluate the quality and relevance of what you find (your tutors will have helped you with this stage when providing you with recommended reading, but it is a vital stage when you are searching yourself).

By the end of this chapter you should:

- understand the importance of planning your research;
- understand the importance of organising your sources;
- be beginning to develop ways of logging/recording your research; and
- be considering the best way for you to organise your information and thoughts before starting to write.

What is a materials review and how do I do it?

By the time you begin to carry out your materials review, you should already have made your diag-   **5–2**
nosis of the task you have been set. As you know, you have to keep this under review as you learn
more about the topic and improve your understanding, so that you can pick up any additional
nuances to the question which passed you by at the first stage. However, to get to this improved understanding, you have to carry out some research. Before you do the research, you should review the
materials you already have on this topic.

To carry out your materials review, gather together all the material you have relating to the
subject matter of the assignment you have been set. This is likely to consist of all or some of the following: notes made in a lecture, notes made from your textbook in preparation for a tutorial or
seminar, notes made during the tutorial or seminar, copies of articles or further reading recommended by your lecturer or tutor (perhaps with your own notes on them, or perhaps highlighted
photocopies), a reading list specific to this assignment. If you are working on a dissertation, then
we've discussed in Ch.3 how your diagnosis of task differs from a traditional essay or problem question, but you may still have some general notes on the topic (picking an area for your dissertation
which has already captured your interest in class and on which you have some basic understanding—albeit not yet at the level or depth needed for a dissertation—is usually a wise move). Similarly,
you may find that (particularly at the later stages of your degree) you are set assignments on topics
which have not been "done" in class, so that you are expected to do more research yourself.

This can be daunting, but think of your essay preparation as a fitness campaign. Imagine you are
trying to improve your fitness by replacing some of your daily bus journey home from university with
a walk. The bus part of the journey is the guidance you get from your tutor about your assignment,
and the walking part of the journey is the research you do independently. When you first start, you go
most of the way on the bus and just get off a stop or two before home, but as you get fitter (i.e. as you
progress with your studies and get better at researching and writing your assignments) you get off the
bus at an earlier and earlier stop. You can imagine that if you were really trying to get fit then by the
end of your fitness drive you could walk the whole way. In these terms your materials review is working
out how far along the bus route home you have got with the materials you have already amassed.

Note that your purpose in carrying out a materials review is **not** to amass a huge pile of paper
and therefore feel proud of yourself—it may give you a sense of having "got on" with your essay, but
a false sense, because all you have done is compile information, when the marks are available for what
you *do* with the information—but rather to gauge how much and what you need to do in terms of
the next step of your writing, which is the **research** stage. By the end of your diagnosis of task, you
should have posed a number of questions to yourself which you need to research in order to tackle
the question you have been set. So, review the materials you have *critically* in order to work out what
gaps you have and work out a strategy to tackle those gaps. Your materials review is therefore about
rating the materials you already have against the materials you need in order to carry out the task you
have diagnosed.

When you have identified the gaps in your materials you will have to carry out research to fill   **5–3**
them.

Most research involves a combination of two different "levels" of reading:

1. General readings—which help you gain an understanding of the topic and help you hone your
   diagnosis and therefore your essay plan.

TIP

Before you go any further, ask yourself: how good is my general understanding of this topic already? This will help you get the balance right between general sources and particular sources.

2. Particular readings—once you have carried out the general research so that you understand the topic, you are in a position to review your diagnosis from a more "educated" and sophisticated position. At this stage you will be able to fine-tune your diagnosis, to identify more specific questions which you need to address, and therefore by implication, more specific sources which you need to find. Of course, as already explained, the provision of a suggested reading list will help you with this—the specific sources you need (probably articles) may be on it—but keeping your diagnosis under review is vital to help you work this out for yourself in relation to any given question.

How can I find materials to supplement my reading list?

5–4   We don't have scope within this text to provide detailed advice on legal research skills.[1] However, here are a few basic tips:

- Follow any advice you have been given, in a student handbook or guidance pack, as to how to get the best from your university's law library. Most universities have a specialist law librarian and there is likely to be some formal class contact—perhaps a demonstration in a lecture theatre or smaller workshops in computer labs, or a combination of both—as part of your induction or as part of a skills or research methods course. It can be tempting for busy students not to give "research training" the priority it deserves, dismissing it as "not a real subject" or "not something we get assessed on". This is completely missing the point—research training is a skill which underpins **all** your assessments, so it is vital you make the most of any training or advice you are offered.
- Learn how to use both paper and electronic sources. Electronic sources are easier to access, as you don't have to trek to the library and you can download them to read later if you like, but there will be various materials which are available only in print form.

TIP

Searching on Google for the answers to assignment questions is the internet equivalent of wandering up to a random person at a bus stop and asking them to explain Contract Law to you, in preference to going along to your Contract Law lecture.

- Start from the right place: a quality resource. Steer clear of Google, at least until you have more confidence in how to evaluate sources for quality and relevance (see below). These days, we are used to thinking of Google or other similar search engines as the quick way to find the answer to almost anything, but remember that in academic work, you are not looking for a quick answer to a factual question—you are presenting an argument based on evidence. Use of Google Scholar or similar filters will help to some extent, but it is much better to utilise the specialist legal databases your university has paid vast licence fees to bring you, as you are immediately then ensuring some measure of quality

---

[1] See KNOWLES, J. and THOMAS, P. *Effective Legal Research*. London: Sweet & Maxwell, 2006, for a detailed discussion.

(academic articles go through a review process before they are published; anyone can put anything on the worldwide web).
- Make sure your sources cover the right legal jurisdiction—in other words if you are writing an assignment on English law, make sure your sources relate to English law. As more materials become available electronically it is easy to make a mistake here and find yourself reading an Australian judgment avidly without realising its jurisdiction.
- Learn more about research terms and how to link them, for example by use of what are called Boolean search terms. Again, you will find more detail on this in a legal research text but there is a basic summary below.

Boolean search terms

These are words and characters which can help you search the web more effectively by allowing you to specify which words and letters are included in or excluded from the search. These searches are carried out using linking words or "operators", as they are sometimes called, such as AND, OR, NOT which determine how the search terms are treated.   **5–5**

1. If you use AND between search terms then this means that both terms must appear somewhere in the entry text.

   > A Boolean search for *legal* AND *writing* is a narrow search that will find entries containing both the words legal and writing, thus avoiding any legal material which is unrelated to writing, and material related to writing which is not legal.

2. Using OR between two or more search terms means that either or both of the terms can appear in the entry text.

   > A Boolean search for legal OR writing is a much wider search and will find entries containing either or both of these search terms. (You might be reading all day!)

3. Using NOT before a search term will mean that that term must not appear anywhere in the entry text.

   > A Boolean search for *legal* AND NOT *writing* is a slightly narrower search that will find entries containing the word legal, but will exclude any entries which contain the word writing, even if they do mention legal.

4. It is also possible to use truncation or wild cards when searching. For example: the * asterisk symbol can be used as a wildcard, taking the place of several unspecified characters. This allows you to broaden a search.

   > A search on *leg** will enable you to find material including *legal* and *legality* (as well as, potentially, material on *legumes* and *legwarmers*).

You can only use the wildcard symbol to represent letters at the end of a word, not the beginning.

TIP

If your initial search generates a lot of results, don't just start reading them one by one: **narrow your search down** before proceeding.

However you conduct your search, the vital thing is that your search terms are related to your diagnosis of what the question is asking for. Sometimes a student will do a reasonably effective diagnosis of task but then ruin it with a general search on "consideration" or "negligence". This will generate a lot of material and if you do something like that you will get so bogged down that you will find it difficult to get started on your writing.

How do I know that I'm not missing something?

5–6   By definition, you will be missing a lot. This is an entirely good thing, because you cannot possibly read everything there is on a particular topic. Having bundles of photocopied sheets or printouts may well have a "security blanket" effect but it will not help you write effectively. If you have been honest and reflective about your general level of understanding so that your diagnosis is accurate, and then by use of effective techniques you have designed searches to answer the questions you posed in your diagnosis, then you should be confident that all you have missed out on are irrelevancies, poor quality materials and wasting your own time.

Before you start your research phase, set yourself a time-limit when you will stop looking for further materials. Again, this is a matter of confidence—it is tempting to carry on to make sure you don't miss anything. But if you think this way, you are still falling into the trap of thinking that you are being assessed solely on your ability to *find information*. In other words, this assumes that there is a Holy Grail in the form of the "right" answer out there somewhere, and the research phase is some kind of treasure hunt in which lucky students (or those which spend the longest time searching) are rewarded. *This is not the case*. The "answer" is not hidden in some remote part of the library waiting to be liberated; to the extent that an answer can be said to exist, it comes from what you *do* with the material: you have to process the information from your different sources and utilise it to form arguments which answer the question set.

TIP

Don't adopt a "just in case" attitude to your reading by reading something on the off-chance it may contain something useful. This is simply putting off making an effective diagnosis of what is relevant to your assignment.

Imagine setting out to cook a gourmet dinner to impress a new girlfriend or boyfriend. The length of time you spend merely buying the ingredients is no guarantee whatsoever of the quality of the final meal. The quality of the ingredients you choose is obviously going to be a factor, but it is the recipe and the cooking skills which really make the difference.

How do I evaluate sources?

5–7   There are really two levels of evaluation which you need to carry out. First of all, you need to do a "preliminary" evaluation, in which you are checking the material for its **quality** and that it is **relevant** to the assignment you are working on. Secondly, for those materials which pass the preliminary test, a more detailed evaluation is needed in order to glean information and analysis which will help you form the arguments you need for your assignment.

Stage 1 is a form of "quality control" which we're going to call the *filtering stage*. Where you have been given a reading list, then this stage has been done for you, in respect of the suggestions on that list. However, it is a skill which it is still vital for you to develop for two reasons:

1. You will not always be given a set reading list for your assignment (it is reasonably common practice to reduce the level of "set" assignment preparation given out in a list as a course progresses, on the basis that the students are expected to develop their skills in finding information—think of this as your tutors encouraging you in your fitness campaign by forcing you off the bus earlier). In particular, where you are writing a dissertation or research project, then one of the things on which you are being assessed is your ability to effectively locate materials.

2. Even if you are given a reading list, you may well be expected to go beyond it. Again, this is increasingly likely

> **TIP**
>
> Check any coursework guidance you have been given—where you have been given a reading list, see whether the list is meant to be exhaustive or just designed to get you started. If there is no guidance on this point, then use your common sense and compare the reading list to your diagnosis. A recommendation with a couple of textbooks on it is likely to be meant as a starting point, whereas a tutor who gives you a list with forty lengthy articles on it may well be expecting you to narrow this down to a relevant selection.

as the course proceeds, especially if you are an undergraduate. (CPE students are more likely to be expected to work independently from the start.)

Stage 2 of your evaluation is when, having decided that a particular piece of writing is something which can contribute to your research for a particular assignment (i.e. it has passed your filtering test), then you read the material in more depth, and make notes on it in order to utilise the ideas (properly acknowledged and referenced of course) in your own work. It can be tempting to use your sources simply as a source of *information*: in other words you accept the facts and arguments within them at face value and replicate them in your own work. This will tend to result in tutor comments on your writing like "too descriptive" or "insufficient analysis". What you therefore need to do is take your reading a step further and carry out a **critical** evaluation.

In a critical evaluation you are not simply summarising the position of the writer, but going on to identify strengths and weaknesses in the arguments and positions adopted. You can then begin to develop a much more sophisticated writing style in which you compare the arguments and positions of different writers and make critical **judgments** about the material. We're therefore going to call this the *critical phase* of the research process, which we discuss in more detail at the end of this chapter.

Essentially, you are moving from saying "A says X" and "B says Y" into "A says X, but this position can be criticised as illogical, and incompatible with Y, the view put forward by B, which is a stronger argument, as it reflects . . ." and so on. There is more on how to construct a logical argument in Ch.6.

We go into more detail on how to conduct an effective "filtering process" and how to critically evaluate materials which you are sure are worth the effort in the next section.

How should I filter out the sources I don't need?

This will be a task proportional to the effectiveness of your search techniques: for example, a search in the Legal Journals Index section of Westlaw using key search terms is going to produce a narrower field than typing random words from the assignment title into Google, and those sources which are   **5–8** generated are much more likely to be of good quality. So, improving your search technique is the key here, as we've already explained.

Always keep in mind the *purpose* for which you are compiling resources. You want **quality** sources which are **relevant** to the question. We have also seen that you will need some sort of balance between general and specific sources, depending on how good your general understanding of the topic already is, and you will need sufficient **coverage** to meet the requirement of your diagnosis (i.e. to help you answer the questions you have posed), which is something you will have addressed in your materials review.

When you get more confident about using sources, you will carry out this filtering process as a matter of course, particularly in respect of quality. You will spend more time checking for relevance. However, for the time being we will look at both issues, starting with quality.

How to rate the quality of a source

5–9   Rate your proposed source against the following questions:

1. *Where did you get it?* Is it published by some reputable source, or it is just the views of someone on the internet? Of course there are quality sources available on the internet, but you have to be cautious. Similarly be cautious with newspapers: tabloid newspapers (or what used to be called tabloid newspapers, like the *Sun*, the *Mirror* and the *Mail*) should **not** be used as a source (unless your assignment is on misrepresentation of the law in the tabloid press or similar); even quality papers like *The Times* and *The Guardian* have a reputation for some degree of political bias which you should bear in mind, although it should not prevent you from using them as a source where appropriate.
2. *Who wrote it?* Is it someone you would expect to have knowledge and understanding of the issues involved, for example a legal academic, practitioner or judge? Is the author even named? Be careful with anonymous pieces unless you are confident of the source, such as the editorial of a quality newspaper. Is the author someone who might be biased or have an axe to grind, for example, a member of a pressure group or an aggrieved claimant?

Note that being a reputable author in a reputable journal does not mean that the article will automatically be good, but answering these questions is a vital first step in evaluating material: if the quality looks suspect you will be wasting your time even reading it. Once you have done a quick quality check, then the second part of the filtering process is to check for relevance.

How to rate the relevance of a source

5–10

> **TIP**
>
> Rate the relevance of the material with reference to your diagnosis, and remember that you determine whether to include some general material to improve your basic grasp of the topic by reference to your materials review.

If you are working from a reading list, then your tutor has already carried out this part of the exercise for you. If not, you will have to learn to do it yourself. When checking for relevancy you should:

- check the title of books;
- check the contents and/or index pages of books;

- read the abstract or summary provided at the start of articles;
- scan headings of chapters or sections.

Finally, once you've amassed your materials, revisit your diagnosis. Have you got sources to help you answer each question you have posed? If not, then carry out further searches to find the gaps. You are now ready to begin reading in more depth, but remember to keep reflecting as you do so on whether you need to fine-tune your initial diagnosis.

> **TIP**
>
> If you find yourself checking out a lot of sources which turn out to be irrelevant, then reflect on your search techniques—revisit any guidance you've received on this and if necessary seek further help from a research methods text or the law librarian on narrowing your research.

How can I read effectively?

At first glance it may sound strange to include reference to reading as part of a book on writing. However, reading quality material is an essential part of improving your writing skills. It will help you in two ways: **5–11**

1. the more "reading around" a subject you do, the more chance you give yourself of improving your understanding of it; and
2. reading quality materials will familiarise you with what good writing is like; you will begin to absorb its qualities.

Reading legal material can be a time-consuming business. Even when you are familiar with the constituent parts of a statute and a case, it is still an effort to wade through the material itself. You will also have to read a lot of secondary material—textbooks and articles—which may also be long-winded. Reconcile yourself now to the fact that you will **not** be able to read everything—every case, every book, every article—in detail.   **5–12**

However, don't use this as an excuse to throw up your hands before you start. To be successful, you have to make a commitment to doing as much as you can. You then have to make a judgment call as to where your time would be most effectively employed and how.

Remember: you are *reading* for a qualification and to succeed, effective reading is a vital skill—you must be prepared to devote considerable time to your reading. Generally speaking, the old adage "practice makes perfect" is true here. The more reading you do, the better you will become at it. In order to develop your skills in reading effectively there are a number of techniques you can adopt.

You will already be aware that you will need to read a variety of different sources as part of your studies. Here are some examples: **5–13**

> Textbooks
> Law reports
> Statutes/statutory instruments
> Journal articles
> Dictionaries
> Email, websites, CD Roms

By the time you begin your law course you will have developed reading strategies already, even if you don't realise it. However, students often comment on the challenge reading legal material presents and you may need to adapt your current strategies.

5–14 Some of the issues that our students have commented on when reading legal material are as follows:

- Having to re-read pages as the words don't seem to go in the first or even the second time. (This might be especially true when you first start to read law books).
- That reading legal material takes too long.
- Not "getting it"!
- Finding the language used too complex.
- Not being sure what the point of making notes is and how many to take and of what.

Do these seem familiar? Here are five top tips to help you improve the effectiveness of your reading:

1. **Prioritise**
   You will need to make decisions about what you'll read (and when). Prioritise the key cases or materials and rank them—tackle them in order of importance. To do this, try the following ideas:

   (a) Use your diagnosis of task: which are the most relevant resources to your diagnosis? Which are going to be helpful to you in getting a general understanding of the topic? (Read these first because the better you understand the topic, the easier it is to make informed decisions about which of the more specific resources are the most relevant to the particular question you've been set).
   (b) Review your lecture notes: picking up hints in lectures as to what sources are the most significant on any topic is vital.
   (c) Look at reading lists for tutorials as well: these are likely to indicate key cases or materials for that topic, even if they do not give guidance specific to the assignment title (and of course this is essential where you are reading in order to help your revision for an exam).
   (d) What part of the textbook have you been referred to on this topic? If you haven't been specifically referred to a particular section, then don't assume it means you don't have to read the textbook: use your initiative! Look at the chapter headings and/or the index to work out what parts to read. The author will have done his or her prioritising too, and you can compare this with your own ideas and the indications from lectures and reading lists.
   (e) Ask! Seek clarification from your tutor if you're not sure, but remember your tutors expect you to try and find out information for yourself first. Asking which is the most important case when it has been clearly highlighted in a handout or in a lecture is a waste of both yours and your tutor's time. Additionally, you may find your tutor is unwilling to give you much extra assistance with the subject matter of a piece of assessed work, because it is important that all students are treated fairly.

2. **Get to the end of the material you are reading**
   When we learn to read we are conditioned to read in sequence from the beginning—skipping to the end would "spoil" it. The problem with this is that when time is precious, you end up making notes only on the first page or two of the material. If you find it difficult to get to the end, there are several possible explanations. Whatever it is you are reading might be pretty boring or it might

be that you are spending too much time agonising over the detail instead of being more selective. It is more important to get all the way through the key material, even if it is not in quite as much depth as you would like, than making copious notes on only the first page of a couple of items. Learn to skim read—but relate this to the decisions you made about what was the most import-ant. Most of all, get right through it! It is better to skim read paragraphs and get some idea of the relevant arguments than to give up. Vital conclusions are likely to be towards the end. Try the fol-lowing techniques:

(a) Get the idea that looking at the end "spoils the story" right out of your head in university studies. We are not story-telling here, we're drawing reasoned conclusions on the basis of evidence. Cut to the chase and look at the conclusion first. Doing this will help you estab-lish how much of your time the material is worth. Do the conclusions the author draws add to your understanding of the particular issues you're investigating? If so, then go back to the beginning and have a look at the opening sentences of the paragraphs—these should help you isolate the really important points and therefore help you to work out which para-graphs you need to spend your time on. Don't assume that important points will necessar-ily be near the beginning of the material.

(b) You need to have a clear purpose and read to that purpose: *why* are you reading any par-ticular material? Are you trying to answer a particular question you've been set or advise a particular "client"? You will not want to use the same reading technique you'd use for reading the latest Booker Prize winner or Harry Potter. Look for key points and skip over material which is not relevant.

(c) Set a time target to complete outline notes, and stick to it.

3. **Look for signposts**

Good writers indicate the direction of their arguments by using "signpost" words such as "addi-tionally", "further", "however", "in contrast". Recognising these words helps you skim or speed read because you can identify when the writer is continuing to advance an argument, and when the writer is changing tack. (This is also something to bear in mind when you start writing, as you can use signposts effectively yourself.)

 ## Activity 5.1

Match the following terms to the meaning intended by the author.   **5–15**

1 Additionally	A This example is the opposite of what I've previously explored
2 Further	B I am extending my argument
3 In contrast	C I am adding further examples to my argument
4 However	D I'm now going to argue a different angle to the same argument
5 Alternatively	E I'm now going to present an alternative point of view

Compare your views:

Our suggestions are as follows:

1–C, 2–B, 3–A, 4–E, 5–D. These are to some extent a matter of personal style, so don't worry if your judgment was different on the distinction between "additionally" and "further" as long as you got the essential point that they both indicate a *continuation* of the same argument—by means of further views, examples, or evidence. Likewise, "in contrast", "alternatively" and "however" all indicate that the author is now offering an opposite or conflicting perspective. You may not have chosen exactly the same nuance of meaning as we did but the main thing is that you understand that all these terms point to a shift in direction.

So, as long as you matched 1 and 2 to B and C (whichever way round), and 3, 4 and 5 to A, D an E (whichever way round) then you have got the hang of signposts. We'll return to this in Ch.7, as signposts are important in your writing as well as in your reading.

4. **Don't just make copies of things**
   When you are given a reading list, it can be a satisfactory feeling to spend an hour in the library on the photocopier or alternatively searching electronically and printing materials out, and think that you "got" everything. A common mistake is therefore to be lulled into a false sense of security that sticking something in your file somehow means you have absorbed the material. Of course it doesn't—you just have a full file!

5. **Don't just read things**
   Most people do not learn effectively simply by reading material through in detail—once you have made your decision about which parts of which material you need to prioritise, then tackle them either by highlighting or underlining points (on your own copies only, of course!) or making separate brief notes. You may find it helpful to write down the purpose you've identified for your reading at the top of the page to help you stay focused. There are further suggestions for making effective notes and recording what you've read below.

How can I improve my note-taking strategies?

5–16

> **TIP**
>
> If your experience of taking notes is that you end up with a lot of paper but no idea how to incorporate it into your assignment then you need to review your approach: notes should help you rather than hinder you.

Notes can take many forms—scribbles, line drawings, bulleted lists, notes on index cards, spider diagrams and so on. Some of our students find the idea of making notes daunting: they don't know why, how or when they should make notes. It is important to remember that the goal in taking notes is to help you utilise the information later, so whatever technique you currently use for your note-taking, use this section to reflect on whether you can improve on it. If you are new to university study then you are likely to find that the amount of note-taking which is needed at university level is significantly more than you have been used to—again, this is part of the process of adapting to independent study.

The purpose of note-taking

5–17   The primary reason for taking notes is "to help me remember".
Other reasons include:

- To help you understand—you can go back over your notes to check your knowledge and understanding.

- To make connections between differing ideas, themes and debates.
- To act as a record of your reading/research.
- To distil down large amounts of material into more manageable chunks.

How to practice note-taking

We're going to divide this into two steps—the first is making general notes on a reading and the second is making more focused notes.   **5–18**

1. *General reading*

   Find a piece of writing that you need to read for an assignment. Don't overwhelm yourself by picking something complex for the purposes of this exercise—aim to pick something more straightforward. You are the best judge of what is manageable for you.

   Then break the piece into definable "chunks" of text, which might be sections or paragraphs. Read to the end of the first one. When you finish reading that chunk, write down in your own words one sentence which sums up the content. Then repeat this for each successive "chunk" until you have reached the end of the text.

   You may find this hard to do—especially if you are new to reading academic texts—but persevering with this method will really help you to tackle complex texts in an organised way. You will end up with essentially a précis, or brief summary, of the entire text. This will not necessarily be enough to inform the writing of your assignment but will give you a clear sense of the overall content, which in turn provides the basis for a more detailed, focused reading of the same text and for taking helpful and informative notes on the exact areas most relevant to your assignment. You won't have to do this task every time you take notes. Once you have mastered the skill of taking effective notes from focused reading (see below) then this generalised approach to reading may not be needed.

2. *Focused reading*

   A blank sheet of paper with a vertical line drawn down it about one third of the way across can be used to make more in-depth notes. Look back over the same text as you used for the previous activity and use the space to the right hand side of the line to set out these notes. Remember what you are trying to do is to make a compact and correct record of the information you have read. You might choose to include your own comments in the space to the left-hand side of the line by way of brief notes or sub-headings but the important thing is that your notes reflect what you have read and the views contained within those texts.

   Some people take so many notes that they are soon drowning in paper and can't work out which to use when it comes to sitting down and doing the writing. This is usually caused by two common errors when note-taking. Either you have written down too much of the original or you haven't been discriminating enough when it comes to choosing topics to take notes on. To fix these problems you need to be more selective. This is the first step in only using the *relevant* in your writing. You need to think more and write less. Be ruthless—less descriptive and more analytical. In addition, you must stay focused on the question you are reading for. If you write out the question on a piece of paper and pin it up over your desk when you are reading, it should stay clearly in your mind and this may help you to stick to the directly relevant material when note-taking.

Tips for note-taking

5–19
- Before you start, make a note of the title, author, and other essential information.
- Write clearly, leaving spaces between each note/comment, and write on only one side of the page.
- Don't try to write complete sentences. You will find that as you progress through your studies you will devise relevant legal abbreviations that will help you to be brief and concise in your note-taking.

> **TIP**
>
> Keep a "key" to your abbreviations—it's no good if you suddenly think of an abbreviation at the start of your note-taking and go on to use it extensively if when you come to review your notes you have no idea what it means!

- Using legal abbreviations in your notes such as AC for Appeal Cases, HL for House of Lords, CA for Court of Appeal and LQR for Law Quarterly Review will help you in your note-taking. As well as these recognised abbreviations you will develop your own shorthand as you go through your course which will help your note-taking, for example Ct for court, Cl for claimant, D for defendant, J for judgment and so on.
- Devise a logical layout like the one suggested above. Headings, sub-headings and numbering help you to take in the information and to remember it when needed.

Here's an example of notes taken from Chapter 18 of *Davies on Contract*.[2]

Davies on Contract—9th edition Upex and Bennett

Chapter 18 Breach:	"A br of c occurs where a pty fails to perform or evinces an intention not to perform, one or more of the obligations laid upon him by the contract.
Forms of breach	e.g. *actual* (non-performance or defective performance or non-truth of a statement that is a term of the c)
	or *anticipatory* i.e. occurs before the date of performance (explicit and implicit)
Effects of breach	can sue for damages. Plus may be extra right to treat yourself as discharged if you wish NB NOT rescind see Johnson v Agnew (1980) HL so C still valid.
Anticipatory breach	Used to b: always = contract discharged BUT see Decro-Wall (1971) CA = same test as for actual breach . . . *innocent pty must act so as to make plain that he claims to treat the contract as at an end.*

(See also: Frost v Knight (1872) on repuidatory breach and The Mihalis Angelos (1971) CA)

Alternatives to linear notes

5–20   Notes do not just have to be in a linear form. For example, if you are a visual learner, you may prefer to utilise a spider diagram or mind map to set out your notes. Here is one we prepared on the topic of negligence in Tort giving a broad overview of the topic.

---

2   UPEX, R., BENNETT, G. and CHNAH, J. *Davies on Contract*, 9th edn, London: Sweet & Maxwell, 2004.

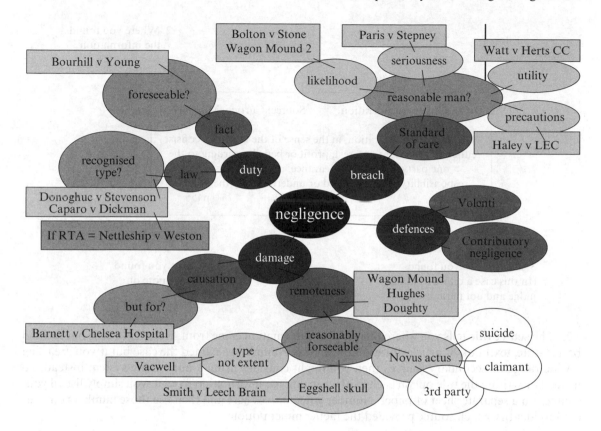

You may find it helpful to use a combination of linear and spider diagram notes—perhaps a spider diagram to help you get an overall sense of the text, or for revision notes, but with linear notes for closer analytical reading.

Other alternatives to linear notes include underlining or highlighting a text (as long as it is not a library copy!) or flow diagrams. If you have yet to find an approach to note-taking that works for you, now is the time to try out some alternatives.

Organising your sources

In order to ensure you can keep track of your notes as you move from researching your assignment into planning the writing, you need to devise a system for summarising and recording your sources.　**5–21**

One possible approach to summarising that you could adopt is a **note card** system. In this approach each sentence, idea or quote from a judgment that you find in your sources is paraphrased in your own words and written down, in brief note form.

See for example (figure on next page):

1.　The **card topic** is the title or name of the card. Here it is "Definitions of consideration" but it could be "Cases on mistake" or "Comment on privity". What you are trying to do when you give a piece of information a title or topic name is to categorise it. This will help you focus on the relevant aspects.

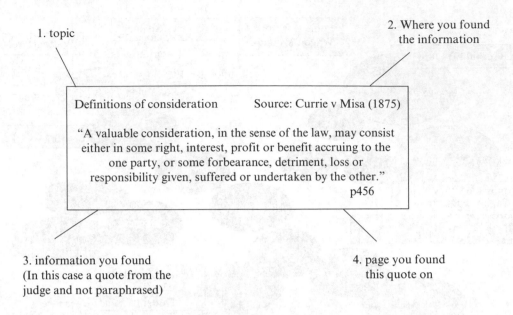

1. topic

2. Where you found
the information

Definitions of consideration   Source: Currie v Misa (1875)

"A valuable consideration, in the sense of the law, may consist
either in some right, interest, profit or benefit accruing to the
one party, or some forbearance, detriment, loss or
responsibility given, suffered or undertaken by the other."
p456

3. information you found
(In this case a quote from the
judge and not paraphrased)

4. page you found
this quote on

2. The **source title** tells you where this piece of information came from. Here it is a case but it could be a statute, textbook or article, for example. In this example, we named the case but if you are using a wide range of secondary sources then you might consider using a numbering system instead. So instead of writing the title out on each card when you use information from it, you simply list all your sources on a separate sheet of paper. Number your sources here and then use those numbers on your card to identify which source provided the fact/comment/quote.

Example Source List

1. Davies on Contract: Upex & Bennett
2. The Law of Contract: J C Smith
3. Smith & Thomas: A Casebook on Contract: J C Smith
4. Exclusion Clauses and Unfair Contract Terms: Richard Lawson
5. Damages for Breach of Contract: Jill Poole
6. Contract Law: Anne Ruff.

Remember: this is not a complete works, cited bibliography or reference page. You will need to add the publication information and use the correct citation form when referencing your actual answer (see Ch.6 for referencing and Ch.9 for how to set out a bibliography).

3. This is the **paraphrased information** or brief quotation that you discovered in your research. You might actually find it easier to do this summarising while you are taking notes from your research. What should be clear is that if you paraphrase reliably at this early stage then you run a lower risk of plagiarising someone else's work by chance and being penalised because of an accident.

4. Being accurate with the precise location (**page/paragraph numbers**) of your item of information, fact or quotation is obviously very important as this will help you to find the correct citations which you will need when starting to reference your work correctly. So, you are keeping track of all your sources to save time later and to avoid any charge of plagiarism. "EndNote" is a software package which helps you to manage your sources by creating bibliographies for your work automatically. Many universities have site licenses for EndNote and training may also be available through your

university library. It is worth familiarising yourself with this package, if it's available, as early on in your university career as possible. The time spent now (before you have any assignments to submit) will pay dividends as a deadline fast approaches. If you do not have access to EndNote, open a document on your computer to manage your references instead. As you are reading and making notes from your sources, you must also ensure, as well as just summarising information, that you carry out a critical evaluation of your sources in order to make use of them in your own arguments later. This is considered in the next section.

How can I develop critical skills in relation to my reading?

The purpose of critical evaluation is to form judgments about the material you have read so that you can then utilise it effectively as part of your own work (with appropriate acknowledgement). Basically, this means taking a questioning approach to what you read. Being *critical*, in an academic sense, is not just about being negative: essentially you are evaluating the strengths and weaknesses of the material. By developing your skills in this area, you will also develop your ability to evaluate your *own* work.

5–22

Activity 5.2

The purpose of this exercise is to test what you understand by critical assessment or critical evaluation. What sort of questions would you ask yourself if you were critically evaluating an article or text? If it helps, think about something about which you have to make critical judgements in your work or home life. How do you decide if a TV programme is any good? How do you judge whether your football team played well at the weekend?

5–23

You won't use the same criteria for legal materials, but it may help you to think about how to develop a critical *attitude*. It may help you to think of this as "marking" the material you are reading. If there are a number of good points, then you will want to use these, perhaps by using a quotation or paraphrase. But be ready to spot any weaknesses in the arguments as well, so that you can make an appropriate judgment about whether the author's conclusions are valid. This is the same process that your tutors will go through when they look at your assignment, looking for the strengths and weaknesses.

Write down three questions you could pose yourself about the material you read, which you think would help you **critically evaluate** it. Your questions should be capable of acknowledging strengths as well as weaknesses (remember that critical assessment in this sense does not just mean finding things wrong with the piece you are reading). You may find it helpful to reflect back to the exercise in Ch.1 where you considered what makes a good piece of writing.

Compare your views:

Paul and Elder suggest a number of different questions which you could pose in order to critically evaluate an article or text. The following questions are loosely based on Paul and Elder's suggestions, but you may wish to look at their comments in full for further ideas.[3]

[3]   PAUL, R. and ELDER, L. *The Miniature Guide to Critical Thinking*, 4th edn, Dillon Beach: Foundation for Critical Thinking, 2004.

- Why do you think the author wrote this material?
- What is the key question the author is trying to answer in this article or text?
- What is the author's conclusion?
- What evidence is advanced to support the conclusion?
- Does the author make any assumptions? If so, what are they?
- What is the opposite point of view from the one the author is advancing, and do you know of anything from your reading which supports this opposite point of view? Has the author acknowledged the opposite point of view?

Activity 5.3

5–24 Consider the following statements and judge whether each could form part of academic criticism of a piece of writing:

Statement	Possible academic criticism—yes or no
A. There is little or no evidence presented	
B. The argument is logical	
C. The piece is mainly descriptive	
D. The piece is largely anecdotal	
E. There are spelling and grammatical errors	
F. The piece is from a reputable source	
G. The author is well-respected in the field	
H. The piece is boring	
I. The print is too small	
J. The author seems to have an axe to grind	
K. The author of the piece is not identified	
L. The piece uses emotive language	
M. I do not agree with the writer	
N. Unjustified assumptions are made	
O. The piece is factually accurate	
P. The piece challenges the established thinking in the field	
Q. The piece is vague in its conclusions	

Compare your views:

A. There is little or no evidence presented—yes: looking at the quality of evidence is a vital part of critical assessment.

B. The argument is logical—yes: although it is a favourable comment (which might lead some to conclude that it is not critical) analysing the logic of an argument is a vital part of critical assessment.

C. The piece is mainly descriptive—yes: this is basically saying that there is not enough analysis in the piece.

D. The piece is largely anecdotal—yes: again this is criticising the text for being lacking in evidence, or the right kind of evidence to justify its conclusions.

E. There are spelling and grammatical errors—this is probably a "maybe" as it might indicate that there has been no editing process and that therefore the quality of the source might be questionable. However, it isn't something you would actually use as a critique in an essay.

F. The piece is from a reputable source—yes: this would tend to add weight, but does not automatically guarantee its quality.

G. The author is well-respected in the field—yes: as above.

H. The piece is boring—no: this is just opinion and not very constructive at that!

I. The print is too small—no: this is nothing to do with the quality of the piece as an academic authority.

J. The author seems to have an axe to grind—yes and no: noting the possible bias is a relevant issue but the informal phrase "axe to grind" should not be used to express it. Bias is a better word.

K. The author of the piece is not identified—yes, potentially, if it is some random piece off the internet, but there are some situations in which you would not expect an author to be identified, for example a newspaper editorial.

L. The piece uses emotive language—yes: this may indicate an overly journalistic approach rather than an academic approach. Why is the author relying on emotion rather than logic to sway the audience? Is it because there are faults in the logic or evidence being presented?

M. I do not agree with the writer—another yes and no: you can certainly be critical of the author's position, but you would need to express this in objective terms and with supporting evidence ("The author's position can be criticised because . . ."). You should not use the statement in the form given here.

N. Unjustified assumptions are made—yes: identifying where the author is leaping to conclusions is an important part of critical analysis.

O. The piece is factually accurate—yes: assessing the accuracy is an important starting point in critical analysis.

P. The piece challenges the established thinking in the field—yes: this is higher level critical analysis because it involves having an understanding of the literature on an area **and** being able to draw parallels between the arguments of different authors on the same subject.

Q. The piece is vague in its conclusions—yes: if the piece is not specific in what it is saying, why is this? Is it because the author has failed to make a case by appropriate use of evidence?

There is more about logic in relation to your own writing in Ch.6—as we have seen before, the skills needed for reading are very closely linked to the skills needed for writing.

How does critical evaluation work within a problem question?

It is easier to relate the idea of critical assessment to an essay question than to a problem question. **5–25** Our students sometimes ask us what we mean by critical evaluation in the context of a problem question where we have asked them to "advise Jim": does it mean advise Jim and critically evaluate the law in this area, as an essay question requires?

   The answer to this question, as with so much in relation to legal writing, is really "it depends" and it is worth checking this with the tutor who set you the assignment (if the issue has not already been clarified in any written or oral instructions you have received about the task). Generally, critical evaluation in relation to a problem question means in the context of the advice you are providing to Jim: usually in a problem question much of Jim's case will be "on the edge"; therefore your critical evaluation is of the alternative positions which are possible. In other words, supposing there are two conflicting authorities which are both similar to Jim's circumstances. Case A, if followed, would help Jim's case but Case B goes against him. Your critical evaluation comes into the answer by comparing these two cases and forming an argument as to which one is the better authority, in order to advise Jim whether he is likely to succeed or fail.

Summary of Chapter 5

5–26
- A materials review will enable you to plan the research you need to do to answer the questions you have posed as part of your diagnosis.
- Effective reading is a vital component of good research.
- You should ensure that the materials you read are good quality and relevant.
- There are different approaches to note-taking and you should experiment to find what works for you.
- You should adopt a critically evaluative approach to your reading.

6 How to use your materials in the writing process

What is the purpose of this chapter?

The purpose of this chapter is to show you how to make the most of the research you have carried out in the research phase by utilising the material you have read and using it to construct your own arguments. This is a particularly challenging part of the writing process, because it is moving on from the stage of posing questions and finding things, to starting to really *think* about what your answer is going to be like; in other words, this is the stage at which you have to start drawing conclusions about the questions you have posed yourself, drawing on the research you have carried out.

6–1

> **TIP**
>
> What is said in this chapter about logical argument in your writing is equally applicable to the sources you read—using the same techniques will help you to evaluate your sources as well as improve your own writing.

Nevertheless, although it is a skill which comes more naturally to some people than others, it is still one which can be learned. The more you have taken on board the skill of critically evaluating other people's work, through your reading skills (as explored in Ch.5), then the more naturally this will come to you. Your goal is to *utilise the sources* you have read as *evidence* to *help you answer the question*, whilst fully *acknowledging* where you have drawn on the views of others by appropriate *referencing*.

More specifically, by working through this chapter you will learn:

- What makes a good argument and the concept of logical progression of ideas.
- How to use evidence to support the assertions you make.
- How to draw on your reading through paraphrasing and quoting the arguments of others.
- How to acknowledge the sources you have used through appropriate referencing and so avoid the academic offence of plagiarism.

It might be helpful, before we go any further, to outline two common student mistakes in relation to using research material in the writing process:

6–2

1. *Failing to acknowledge your sources in the mistaken belief that you will get more marks if you can fool your tutors into thinking you thought of all this yourself.* This is a mistake for two

reasons—first (and most obviously), this is *plagiarism* (there is much more detail about this later in the chapter). Secondly, it shows you do not understand what academic work is about, which is essentially taking other materials and analysing them. The starting point is the primary source (e.g. a case); a writer writes about the source, thereby making a secondary source. The next person comes along and looks at the primary source *and* the secondary source, and produces a further secondary source. Somewhere later in the chain, you come along and look at the primary source and all the various secondary sources you have found and draw on them to produce your own work on the subject (in the context of your particular question).

It may help you to get your head round this to think of these other secondary sources becoming something a little like "precedents" in a case. Just as you cannot walk into court and say "I think the law on this area should be as follows . . ."—you need evidence in the form of existing precedents—existing academic views on a topic are the *evidence* on which you base your own arguments.

Therefore there is nothing to gain by pretending that the views of others are actually your own, but much to gain by showing (through appropriate acknowledgement) that you can work with these materials: in doing this you are working *academically,* as the previous writers on the topic have done.

2.   *Production of an essay which is a collection of quotes or a collection of paragraphs merely* **describing** *the academic views which have emerged from your reading*. These may be linked together something like "Smith says . . . And Khan suggests . . . And McAllister says . . .". The student in question may be quite pleased with the end result, because, after all, it demonstrates that he or she has "done a lot of reading", and this is true, it does. However, simply providing a collection of quotes or summaries is not going to gain the best marks, because it is essentially descriptive. To make the most of the time spent researching all this material you need to make more *judgments* about the material: in other words, did Khan's view conflict with Smith's? If so, which is the better view in the context of the specific question or circumstances? As is more likely, perhaps Khan and Smith had some areas of agreement, and some areas of disagreement; being able to highlight these more subtle implications of their arguments—a process sometimes called *synthesising* their views—and turn them into effective arguments of your own is going to demonstrate your understanding of the topic at the highest level.

There is more about how to avoid both these mistakes in this chapter. To begin with, as this chapter is all about using your materials to support your arguments in your writing, we'll start by exploring the concept of an argument.

What is an argument?

6–3   The term "argument" means something different in academic writing than it does in ordinary language. In ordinary language, an "argument" means a disagreement or a row, whereas in academic writing, what is meant by an argument is taking a *position* (essentially making a conclusion, or a series of them) by making an *assertion* of some kind (i.e. a point) and backing this up with *reasons* to justify that point, and *evidence* to support the reasons. To form arguments in your writing, you work **backwards** from the evidence you have read to formulate the reasons for your overall conclusions or position. This will be much easier if you have diagnosed the task properly because you will be looking at the relevant evidence and, more importantly, looking at it from the right perspective in order to utilise it in an argument.

This is the process to follow:

1. You diagnose the task and set yourself sub-questions which inform your research.
2. You then carry out research to find out the answer to the questions you have posed.
3. You review the answers you have found to the questions (and of course, bearing in mind that you keep your diagnosis under review, as you research further into the subject you keep checking that you asked the *right* questions) to form a conclusion.
4. When you write this up by putting it together as an argument, your answers to your sub-questions form the reasons for the conclusions you have reached, and the material you have researched provides the evidence for those reasons.

This may be easier to understand in the context of an example. Look back at the problem question on negligence at the end of Ch.4. In diagnosing that task, various sub-questions emerged for consideration, one of which was, *does Zebedee owe a duty of care to the people in the scenario?* If you were really completing this as an assignment, then you would have carried out your research in order to provide the answers to all these sub-questions, and we're going to take this particular one about the duty of care to the other road users as an illustration.

Let's suppose that you have carried out a relevant search, or perhaps looked at lecture or textbook notes, and from this you have identified that *Nettleship v Weston* [1971] 2 Q.B. 691 is the crucial case on this point (see the spider diagram notes in Ch.5), because it establishes the legal principle that a driver owes a duty of care to other road users. Because this is a problem question, you then need to *apply* this to the case in point: from the general (a driver owes a duty of care to other road users) to the particular (*this* driver, Zebedee, owes a duty of care to *these* road users A, B and C). This becomes your *conclusion* on this point, your *reason* being that a driver owes a duty of care to other road users (which is an assertion of law) and your *evidence* (or authority) being the case of *Nettleship v Weston* (the evidence for a proposition of law must always be a case or a statute).

In other words:

This is what is known as a *syllogism*, which is a form of logical reasoning. In a syllogism, the

A driver owes a duty of care to other road users	PRINCIPLE / RULE
Zebedee is a driver, and A, B and C are other road users	APPLICATION
Zebedee owes a duty of care to A, B and C	CONCLUSION

principle or rule would be identified as a *major premise* and the application as a *minor premise*, but in terms of your legal study, it is probably more helpful to stick with thinking of these as *principle* and *application*, as this is more likely to keep you on track with your writing. The process of translating your diagnosis and research into your writing can be represented as follows (still using the negligence case as an example):

TIP

Whenever you state a legal principle, you are making an assertion of law, which must be supported by legal authority. There is more on this later in the chapter.

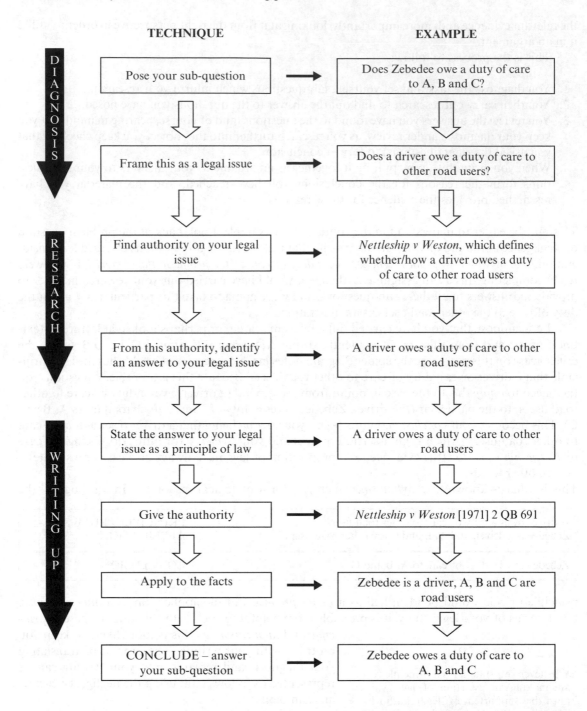

This diagram represents the *broad process*. When you "write up" your answer there is some scope for flexibility: for example, as a matter of style you may give your conclusion, then your reasons (the principle of law) and authority, rather than (as represented in the diagram) stating the principle and authority and then moving to the conclusion. Similarly, it is often unnecessary to separate the application stage from the conclusion, where the facts are straightforward. In other words, you do not necessarily need to spell out the "Zebedee is a driver" part—where the facts are sufficiently simple (as here) you could simply move from the principle and authority to concluding that this means Zebedee owes a duty of care to A, B and C. However, we've specified the application stage as separate from the conclusion in the diagram to help you understand the process. As you become more practised at legal analysis and problem solving you will find it easier to make judgment calls about which parts of the process need to be spelt out more clearly.

Bear in mind also that as you complete the research to inform the questions you have posed as part of your diagnosis, you need to keep in mind the issue of the *ranking* of the issues into major and minor issues. Research into this particular issue (i.e. a driver's duty of care to other road users) should confirm that the example we've chosen here is one which is uncontroversial: it is "settled law" (i.e. a confirmed legal principle with very little or no room for doubt) that a driver owes a duty of care to other road users. This is therefore a comparatively minor point: it is an important preliminary step to the establishment of Zebedee's liabilities (which is what you have been asked to do) because of the nature of the particular topic of negligence (and so **must** be included in your answer), but not one on which you would spend a lot of time. Of course, in relation to much of your writing, you will be asked to explore issues which are *not* settled; in other words the evidence is *conflicting*. This would be the case if your research had revealed some authorities stating a driver owes a duty of care to other road users, and some stating that a driver does not owe such a duty. How to deal with conflicting evidence is pursued further later in this chapter.

We now need to think in more detail about the process of using evidence to form arguments. The following activity will help you do this.

Activity 6.1

Consider the following question: 6–4

> Which is the best football team?

Compare your views:

If you are a supporter of football, then an instinctive answer may spring to mind; in other words what you are giving is your *opinion*, based on the team you support. In order to develop an argument, you must be able to specify *reasons* to support this opinion. In other words *why* are Manchester United/Chelsea/Liverpool (or whoever) the best football team? Again, the football supporter's answer might be "because they are" but this kind of "it's obvious" reason is not an argument at all. In order to be an effective reason, it must be based on *evidence*.

If you are not a supporter of football, then you are much more likely to have given an answer which is based on evidence, as you are not starting from a position of *bias*. This is important in developing your skills in making an academic argument, where objectivity is crucial: instead of giving opinions or "gut reactions" you form arguments on the basis of evidence—and the evidence is the material you have gathered as part of the research stage of your work in coursework, or the material you have revised for an examination.

In order to evaluate this question of "which is the best football team" in a more reasoned way, you would need to find some sort of "yardstick" or criteria to measure what makes a good football team (you would also need to set the parameters of the question—is this the best team in the world?

The United Kingdom? England and Wales? Professional teams only or amateur? Men's football, women's football or both? National sides or club sides?). The criteria you set would form the basis of your sub-questions, which might relate to number of competitions won, or loyalty inspired in their supporters, or good play or whatever (of course, with a subject like football, this would be a matter of some controversy!). According to what we already know, having posed the sub-questions, you would then carry out your research, to find out the answers to them, remembering to keep your diagnosis under review (in case, when finding out more about football, you discover that a key issue in how to rank football teams is something you had not included in your original list of sub-questions).

Of course, it is unlikely with a question like this one, which particularly appeals to a "gut reaction" answer, that you would have delved so deeply. However, we're going to stick with this example for some further exercises to show you how to develop effective arguments.

How do I develop effective arguments?

6–5   In order to help you develop your argument, you must have supporting reasons for your conclusions. Effective reasons are those which are:

- accurate; and
- relevant; and
- based on evidence.

The final issue is that the source of the evidence must be acknowledged by use of proper referencing, which is something we'll pursue later in this chapter.

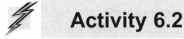

Activity 6.2

6–6

> **TIP**
>
> Remember your goal is to be objective: so ignore your own *opinions* about Chelsea for the time being.

For example, let's return to the football question. Supposing you wanted to argue, in answer to the question posed, that Chelsea is the best football team. Have a look at the following statements and decide which of them are effective arguments in this respect:

Chelsea is the best football team.

Chelsea is the best football team because they just are.

Chelsea is the best football team because I've always supported them.

Compare your views:

We already know that in order to argue, you need supporting reasons, which in turn must be based on evidence. Simply stating *Chelsea is the best football team* is not an argument—it is an opinion, and one which is not supported by any reasons.

Chelsea is the best football team because they just are—again, this is an opinion, supposedly supported by a reason, but "they are" is not really a reason at all, it is simply a restatement of the position that they are the best (this might be described as a circular argument). You will note that there is no evidence presented and therefore no objective basis for the opinion.

Chelsea is the best football team because I've always supported them. Again, this is simply a restatement of the opinion, represented as the reason.

Conclusion: None of these statements represents a valid academic argument.

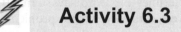 ## Activity 6.3

What about these statements—are they any better?

Chelsea is the best football team because the team has won the European Cup five times.

6–7

Chelsea is the best football team because the team is based in London.

Chelsea is the best team because everyone thinks so.

Chelsea is the best football team because the team won the Premiership in 2005 and 2006.

If you are not very familiar with football, then in order to carry this activity out, it will help you to know that the European Cup (also known in recent years as the Champions League) features the best teams from across Europe, culminating in a knock-out competition, and the Premiership is the most prestigious league in England and Wales.

Compare your views:

Chelsea is the best football team because the team has won the European Cup five times.

Your view on this one will depend on whether football is something you know very much about. On the face of it, this looks like a valid argument, because it is based on a reason, namely success in the European Cup, and this sounds like a valid "yardstick" in ranking football teams, so it seems to be a *relevant* reason. However, if you know something of football, you may have stopped short when reading this argument: because in fact Chelsea has not won the European Cup five times. This is therefore not an effective argument because the evidence on which it is based is not true. To be an effective argument, your reasons must be *accurate*.

Chelsea is the best football team because the team is based in London.

Bearing in mind what we've just said about accuracy, your first thought should be whether this statement is accurate (and just in case football geography is not your strong point, it is). However, accuracy in itself is not enough to justify an argument—looking at this statement, do you think it is based on a relevant reason? In other words, is location of the team essential to rating its quality? In order to make sure that you are relying on reasons which are relevant, you should refer back to the sub-questions which you have set yourself following your diagnosis. In relation to the football example, these were questions setting possible criteria for rating the quality of a team, for example relating to competitions won and so on. Is location of the club an appropriate criterion? If not, then this is not a relevant argument.

> Chelsea is the best team because everyone thinks so.

There are several problems with this one. First of all, your first reaction (particularly if you are not a Chelsea supporter) might have been something along the lines of "who says?" In other words, you are challenging the accuracy of the reason. And more specifically, what is problematic about this statement is that there is no evidence to support it—where are the opinion polls indicating that everyone thinks Chelsea is the best team? If such evidence had been provided, then the reader could at least acknowledge that the reason is accurate—without it, this is not an adequate argument.

Supposing that this statement did offer some evidence in support (maybe a survey that 100 per cent of people think Chelsea is the best team—unlikely though this might be), then although the statement is then *accurate*, you might again question whether public opinion is necessarily the best evidence to put forward in response to an evaluation of who is the best football team. Again, this comes down to whether *who is popularly rated as the best team?* was one of the questions you set yourself to help you evaluate who the best football team is. Do you consider this to be relevant?

We asked you to think about this particular statement for two reasons: first, to illustrate that statements like "everyone thinks so" tend to be indicative of poor argument—they are what is called *sweeping statements*, i.e. broad assumptions made without evidence in support. Essentially, what the writer is arguing in this situation is that it "goes without saying" that a particular position is right or correct. In fact, in academic writing, anything which forms part of your argument needs to be articulated and evidence needs to be supplied: it does not "go without saying". It's a common political ploy to begin statements with phrases like "All right-thinking people agree we need this reform

TIP

Avoid sweeping statements which over-state your case without accompanying evidence in support. It is a good idea to check your work through very carefully for this specific fault.

. . ." in order to deflect attention away from tricky questions about the real motive for the reform. "Everyone says . . .", "It is commonly accepted that . . ." and "It is a well-known fact . . ." are similar statements which will set off alarm bells in a critical reader, who will immediately be thinking *who says*?

The second reason for including this example is to encourage you to reflect on the appropriateness of using *popular opinion* as evidence in support of your arguments: even if you can prove what popular opinion is on a particular point, it is not necessarily appropriate evi-

TIP

Be cautious with the use of popular opinion to justify your position.

dence in an academic essay (unless perhaps your essay is something to do with the nature of democracy, or the role of public opinion in influencing law reform, for example).

> Chelsea is the best football team because the team won the Premiership in 2005 and 2006.

Here we have a reason which would certainly seem to be relevant, as long as it is true (which it is, therefore this reason can be said to be accurate). We could criticise this statement for a lack of authority—there is no evidence given to prove that Chelsea won the Premiership in the years given—but this could be argued to be *common knowledge*, more about which later, in which case authority is not required. Apart from this point, we seem to have a good argument here.

So we now know that the reasons which support your arguments must be *relevant*, *accurate* and based on *evidence*. This is all very well in the context of football, but we need to think about this in the context of law and legal writing.

What evidence do I need to use in my arguments?

In academic writing, it is essential to use evidence to support any points you make. As a law student you are expected to back up the points you make by reference to **authority**. In other words you cannot simply make claims without having reasons and evidence. This evidence might be a primary source of law (i.e. a case or a statute) where you are making a point about the law. Alternatively you may refer to a secondary source, such as a textbook or a journal article, to support an argument about the law or about a particular legal theory.

6–8

The basic rule about providing evidence or authority for your reasons is as follows:

- An **assertion of law** needs a case or statute (i.e. a primary source) as authority;
- An **assertion of fact** needs a secondary source (wherever you found the fact) as authority;
- An assertion which is **common knowledge** or **common legal knowledge** does not need authority.

Assertions of law

Many of the assertions which you make in legal writing will be assertions of law—essentially where you state what the law actually is on a particular point, in other words where you are stating a legal rule. These are also sometimes referred to as statements of legal principle.

6–9

> The courts can use *Hansard* as an aid to statutory interpretation providing certain criteria are satisfied.

This is an assertion of law, because it states what the law is on this issue. Assertions of law must always have a primary source as evidence (a primary source, in legal terms, means either a case or a piece of legislation). The source for the assertion of law given above is the case of *Pepper (Inspector of Taxes) v Hart* [1993] A.C. 593; this information could be included within the text or added via a footnote, depending on the referencing system you are using for your assignment.

TIP

Whenever you state a legal rule, you **must** cite where that rule comes from. There is more information on **how** to cite your evidence later in this chapter.

Assertions of fact

You may in the course of legal writing find yourself making certain assertions of fact, for example: "The number of contact orders granted by the courts has risen from 40,000 to 60,000 in the last five

6–10

years" or "The Government has stated that it is committed to reform of this area". Alternatively your assertion of fact might be summarising the position of an academic writer, for example: "Ahmed argues that . . ." or "In Thompson's view, this is correct . . ."

You must provide evidence for any assertions of fact which you make, unless the fact can be considered to be one of "common knowledge" (see below). Where your assertion relates to summarising the view of a writer, then of course, your secondary source will be the work by this writer from which you obtained these views. Note that you provide this evidence regardless of whether you have quoted directly from the work. Other possible sources for assertions of fact in a legal context could include judicial statistics, Law Commission reports, official inquires, or perhaps *Hansard*.

Matters of common knowledge or common legal knowledge

6–11   You do not have to provide evidence of matters of *common knowledge* (e.g. you do not need evidence for an assertion that the Battle of Hastings was in 1066) or within the general sphere of legal knowledge. (It's the "It's obvious!" factor.) However, be careful with this: just because something is obvious to you, having researched it, it is not necessarily obvious to your reader. Similarly, this is linked to the idea of writing for a particular audience: when writing a legal assignment, you are writing for an intelligent reader who understands all the general issues of law but is ignorant of the particular subject matter of your assignment. Suppose you were answering a problem question which involved looking at a House of Lords decision. In this context, it is a matter of common legal knowledge that this is a strong precedent, although the House of Lords could use its power under the Practice Statement 1966 to depart from it if it wished to do so, and you would not therefore have to take time out in your assignment to explain this. However, supposing the subject matter of your assignment was directly related to matters of precedent in the House of Lords, then the ability of the House of Lords to depart from its own previous rulings could no longer be regarded as a matter of common legal knowledge. You would be expected to explain this rule and give its source (i.e. the Practice Statement 1966).

 **Activity 6.4**

6–12   Which of the following statements would need evidence?

> The House of Lords will only use the Practice Statement rarely.

> There are three main exceptions to the principle that the Court of Appeal is bound by its own previous rulings.

> The Lord Chancellor, Lord Falconer of Thoroton . . .

> Zander asserts that the literal rule is "defeatist and lazy."

> The literal translation of the phrase *stare decisis* is "let the decision stand."

Compare your views:

> The House of Lords will use the Practice Statement only rarely.

Although this might seem an obvious statement, it is not so "obvious" that it could be considered common knowledge, even for a law student. This is a statement of fact, so you would need to provide authority, such as statistical information or point to a text where the use of the Practice Statement is discussed.

> There are three main exceptions to the principle that the Court of Appeal is bound by its own previous rulings.

This is an assertion of law and therefore must be supported by evidence (here, the authority is the case of *Young v Bristol Aeroplane Co Ltd* [1944] K.B. 718.)

> The Lord Chancellor, Lord Falconer of Thoroton ...

This does not need a reference. It is a statement of fact, but it is one which counts as within the sphere of legal knowledge: in other words, to a lawyer, the fact that the Lord Chancellor is Lord Falconer (as at August 2006) is as much "common knowledge" as the fact that Tony Blair is the Prime Minister would be to anyone else.

> Zander asserts that the literal rule is "defeatist and lazy".

This is an assertion of fact, because it is stating what the views of the writer Michael Zander are. This therefore needs evidence, in the form of a reference to the work where Zander makes this statement (which is *The Law-Making Process*, 6th edn, Cambridge: Cambridge University Press, 2004, p.145). Note that giving Zander's name, and therefore acknowledging that this is his idea, not yours, is not enough in itself: you have to give exact details. Your goal should be that your readers can find this quote for themselves.

> The literal translation of the phrase stare decisis is "let the decision stand."

This is a statement of fact, but one which counts as common knowledge for a lawyer.

Although we can be categorical about the need to reference assertions of law, and about the need to acknowledge the words or ideas of others, learning to recognise matters of "common knowledge" is less easy to provide clear-cut advice on: it really is a matter of experience, so generally speaking, if in doubt give your evidence.

TIP

If you fail to reference your sources properly, at best your arguments are weakened, because you have not given your evidence, and at worst you may commit plagiarism. In particular, if you are new to university study, you may find that the stress placed on giving your evidence, acknowledging your sources and avoiding plagiarism is very different from what you have been used to previously, so you need to get yourself into a new way of thinking and new habits straight away. There is more guidance on plagiarism later in the chapter.

How do I integrate evidence from other sources into my own writing?

There are two ways of doing this: **6–13**

1. by paraphrasing (or summarising); or
2. by quoting from the work directly.

Paraphrasing

6–14   This means taking someone else's idea or theory and including it on your own essay, but instead of doing this by use of a direct quotation in quotation marks, you integrate it into your own argument by putting it into your own words. It is easy to get confused (especially in the light of warnings about plagiarism) about whether paraphrasing is "allowed" or a "good idea" but do not be afraid to do it providing you give the appropriate references: paraphrasing positions taken by other authors is a good way of demonstrating that you have understood those positions. So, the rule is that it is good to paraphrase as long as you reference properly.

> **TIP**
>
> What you are doing when you paraphrase is making a statement of fact (about the author's view or position) so cite the evidence accordingly.

Effectively, when you paraphrase, your goal is to sum up the position of the author on that particular point. In doing this, you should be looking to identify the core point that the author is making on a particular issue: if you paraphrase a side issue or an illustration, then you run the risk of taking comments out of context.

 Activity 6.5

6–15   Have a look at this quote from Lord Denning's book, *The Discipline of Law*,[1] and then consider what you think the main position in this section is:

> In almost every case in which you have to advise you will have to interpret a statute. There are stacks and stacks of them. Far worse for you than for me. When I was called in 1923 there was one volume of 500 pages. Now in 1978 there are three volumes of more than 3,000 pages. Not a single page but it can give rise to argument. Not a single page but the client will turn to you and say: "What does it mean?" The trouble lies with our method of drafting. The principal object of the draftsman is to achieve certainty—a laudable object in itself. But in pursuit of it, he loses sight of the equally important object—clarity. The draftsman—or draftswoman—has conceived certainty: but has brought forth obscurity; sometimes even absurdity.

Which of the following do you think is an effective paraphrase of Lord Denning's *position*, as evidenced by this quotation?

A. Lawyers today have to work much harder than Lord Denning did to interpret statutes.
B. The number of reported cases rose from enough to fill 500 pages in 1923 to 9,000 pages in 1978.
C. Certainty is incompatible with clarity but both are equally important objects.
D. Problems with the methods of drafting statutes have caused a huge rise in the number of cases in which statutory interpretation is an issue.

Compare your views:

A. Lord Denning does allude to the fact that the volume of cases has made the position of the lawyer today more difficult (assuming that this is who he is addressing when he says "you"—from this quote, it isn't entirely clear). However, do you think it really sums up the core point Lord

---

[1] DENNING, *The discipline of law*. London: Butterworths, 1979, p.9.

Denning is making? It would not be wrong to include this kind of statement within a lengthier paraphrase of Lord Denning's work, as long as that core point was also clearly represented.

B. Again, Lord Denning does imply this in his discussion of the number of pages which are found in law reports these days. However, there are a couple of reasons why this would not make an effective paraphrase: this is simply an illustration which Lord Denning is giving as he moves towards his core point and in any case this is a simple question of fact. Lord Denning's statements are hardly the best evidence of how many pages there are in law reports.

C. This would need a little work to be an effective paraphrase. Yes, Lord Denning does say that certainty has come at the expense of clarity and he does say that clarity and certainty are "equally important". However, his comments are clearly made in the context of statutory interpretation and the drafting of statutes in recent years, and therefore as it stands C is not an accurate paraphrase because it does not specify this context. Simply adding "In statutory interpretation" brings this much closer to representing Lord Denning's position.

D. This comes closest to being an effective paraphrase because it gets to the core point which Lord Denning is making about the nature of legislative drafting. However, although accurate, this particular statement does illustrate one of the difficulties with paraphrasing, which is striking the right balance between summarising the position concisely, and yet giving sufficient detail to be of value. Arguably here, although the position is accurately summarised, the flavour of Lord Denning's argument does not really come across.

A really effective paraphrase might therefore need a little more detail. Suppose a student had written the following:

> Lord Denning pointed out in his book about the discipline of law that statutory interpretation has become a much more significant issue for today's lawyers; there has been a huge rise in the number of cases in which statutory interpretation is an issue, which he argues is because the drafting process prioritises certainty (which he acknowledges is important) over clarity (which in his view is equally important).

A student writing a paragraph like the one above has represented Lord Denning's position accurately, and has therefore shown that he or she is getting to grips with what Lord Denning is getting at. However, there are two things missing here, both of which are covered in more detail later in this chapter:

1. a reference is needed to Lord Denning's book, and exactly where within it this paraphrase is located;
2. the student needs to add his or her own judgment on Lord Denning's position in order to move from *describing* what Lord Denning said to *evaluating* what he said.

Using quotations

Quoting from a work can be a good way of integrating your research into your own arguments.   **6–16**
However, there are several things to bear in mind with quotations:

1. Quotations are someone else's words, not your own, and the marker will award marks only for your *own* words. Yes, you can gain marks for your *choice* of quotations, and what you do with them, but not for the quote itself. Despite this, it is likely that quotes will count towards your allowed word limit on an assignment, so every time you include one you are using up your word count with material which cannot contribute directly to your mark. This is not to say that you should avoid quotes,

> **TIP**
>
> Before including a quote, ask yourself "Could I paraphrase this instead?"

but you should certainly be sparing with them, and keep them as short as possible. This is especially true with secondary sources—unless the author's position can be summed up in a short, punchy quote, then a paraphrase is usually better.

2. Learning to paraphrase the ideas in secondary sources rather than quoting directly from them can be a challenge, because of course a learned author is likely to have made their point particularly well, and you may well feel that you cannot improve on it. However, you *can* usually improve on it because the author was not writing in response to the specific assignment you have been set, whereas you are. On the other hand, if the quote perfectly encapsulates what you want to say, and is short, then by all means use it—but remember to explain why it is relevant to your argument (see below).

> **TIP**
>
> In your assignment, show clearly when you are using someone else's words by indenting a quotation, using italics or inverted commas. Check whether your institution has any particular specifications on how to delineate quotes.

3. One area where a quote can be particularly useful is where you are quoting from a primary source, in the form of a case (direct quotes from statutes are rarely needed), particularly in order to explore the implications of the case with reference to the facts you are considering. Again, however, keep your quotes as short as possible.

Making the most of paraphrasing and quotes

6–17   Remember that just paraphrasing or quoting from the source is not enough in itself to get you really high marks: you also need to make *judgments* about the material. This is the difference between the following types of statement:

A. *this is Smith's position* (which is **describing** Smith's position); and
B. *this is the implication of Smith's position for my argument* (which is **evaluating** Smith's position in the context of your assignment).

A weaker essay will contain only statements of type A. Descriptive statements are certainly needed (if you want to use Smith's position in your argument, then clearly you need to say what it is) but should be as concise as possible (and of course accurate). However, such statements show only that you have been able to *find* relevant material: they do not show that you have *understood* the material fully and can really use it as part of your own arguments. To show this, you need statements of type B.

So a good essay will have a balance of A type statements and B type statements, with the A statements presented concisely and as *evidence* for the B statements; in other words, a B statement about the implications of Smith's views is illustrated by an A statement of what those views are. You should do the same with case law: A statements will be a concise representation of the relevant point decided in the case, and B statements will critique the decision, or explain how the legal position taken by the court affects your argument through application to the facts of a problem question.

Always remember that a quote or paraphrase only **illustrates** the point you are making; it is up to you to **make** the point. If you find this difficult, try asking yourself why you want to include this quote or paraphrase in your assignment. Articulating the reason for your choice to yourself should help you move towards an appropriate evaluative statement and help you to get your point across.

> **TIP**
>
> Even though you are building your own arguments by reference to the evidence, keep your language objective—avoid writing in the first person (in other words, don't say "I think . . ." or "In my opinion . . .").

How do I use a source within another source in my writing?

By this we mean the sort of situation where you read a book or an article by author X and it gives you a reference to another source by author Y, which you want to use. This is something which occurs frequently in research, and it can cause confusion.   **6–18**

The starting point is that if you want to make a significant use of the "source within a source" (i.e. the material written by author Y) then you should find it and read it for yourself, rather than relying on second-hand information about it (i.e. the views of author X). However, where you are only going to make a minor use of the text then you may not, realistically, have the chance to chase up every reference which is thrown up in your research. Therefore, it is acceptable to make use of a "source within a source" provided that you acknowledge both the original author, and the author who found that source for you. In your research, you always need to acknowledge the ideas of others, and the "idea" of using the source within a source came from author X, not from you. It is a common mistake to think that you only need to reference author Y in this situation.

For example, supposing as part of researching material for an essay about the interpretation of *ratio decidendi*, you wish to draw on the work of Holland and Webb in *Learning Legal Rules* (their references omitted)[2]:

> There is no set single test for defining what is meant by ratio or for establishing the ratio of a particular case. As Cross stated: "It is impossible to devise formulae for determining the ratio decidendi of a case." But before you lose heart altogether, Cross also stated that "this does not mean it is impossible to give a tolerably accurate description of what lawyers mean when they use the expression". Like so many things in law this problem of identification is not unique to legal studies. Think of the plot to a book or a film. The facts are clear, the storyline can be described; but if a group of people were asked to say what the film etc. was about then opinions would vary. Some might see the film as nothing more than, say, an adventure film; others might see a social or political message in it; others might think the director was clearly paying tribute to an earlier famous director. And even if the writer or director was asked to spell out the meaning, the purpose, of the film (equivalent to reading the judgment of a case) the onlooker's reply could still be: "You may have meant that, but you produced something different."
>
> Thus to the student who asks "how do I spot the ratio" Twining and Miers would respond:
>
> "Talk of finding the ratio decidendi of a case obscures the fact that the process of interpreting cases is not like a hunt for buried treasure, but typically involves an element of choice from a range of possibilities."
>
> It is unwise, therefore, to presume that there is one and only one possible ratio to a case . . .

---

[2] HOLLAND J. and WEBB, J. *Learning legal rules*, 6th edn, Oxford: Oxford University Press, 2006, pp.162.

Now, if we were to pick out what ideas Holland and Webb have had in this passage, the obvious one is the film metaphor. So, if we wanted to borrow that idea it would certainly have to be acknowledged. But they have two further ideas:

1. that what Cross has to say supports their general argument that there is no easy answer to the question "what is the ratio";
2. that what Twining and Miers have to say also supports this general point.

Therefore if you borrow *these* quotations to support your argument, then you must acknowledge where you found them, which is in *Learning Legal Rules*, rather than in the original texts. In this situation, Holland and Webb are author X, and Cross and Twining and Miers are all in the position of author Y.

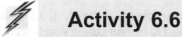 **Activity 6.6**

6–19   Have a look at the following passage. If this had been written by a student, which statements within it which would need to be referenced?

> Twining and Miers point out that the *ratio* isn't "buried treasure" and it is therefore simplistic to assume that there is only one possible formula for finding the *ratio*. The reason for this is that there will be a number of possible formulations for any given case, and therefore opinions might vary as to which of them is actually the *ratio* of the case. Holland and Webb liken this to the range of different opinions which might be given by a group of people who have just watched a film as to what the film's meaning was—and not even the director knows the "right" answer. In other words, expressing the *ratio* means selecting a possible *ratio* out of range of principles, any one of which is capable of being the *ratio*.

Compare your views:

This paragraph does three things which need referencing:

1. It summarises Twining and Miers's quotation including giving a direct quote of the words "buried treasure";
2. It borrows the "formula" idea from Cross, although without a direct quotation;
3. It paraphrases Holland and Webb's idea of comparing the *ratio* to saying what a film is about.

So, if the real source of all these three is the work of Holland and Webb quoted above, then as well as acknowledging the three "ideas" listed above, it would need to be made clear that this paragraph draws on the ideas of Holland and Webb for *all three* of these sources. This is done by acknowledging Author Y, and adding "cited by" or "quoted in" Author X, for example:

> TWINING, W. and MIERS, D. *How to do things with rules*, 4th edn, London: Butterworths (Law in Context) 1999, p.335, cited in HOLLAND, J. and WEBB, J. *Learning legal rules*, 6th edn, Oxford: Oxford University Press, 2006, p.162.

This demonstrates to your reader that this was a "source within a source" and acknowledges the work Holland and Webb did in tracking this quote down for you.

How do I deal with evidence which conflicts?

Once you have got the answers to your sub-questions, we know that you use these as the basis of your argument. However, it is extremely likely, as we acknowledged earlier, that your evidence may point in different directions. This is especially true in relation to an area of law which is not "settled"—and these areas of conflict are popular choices for assessment questions. **6–20**

To make a good argument, first of all you need to spot these conflicts when you are carrying out your research. Secondly, you have to evaluate the conflicting positions and work out which is the better view, which then forms your conclusion. To make a really good argument, you have to acknowledge the contrary evidence, and explain why, in spite of this, your conclusion is still correct.

If you can do this, then you are really developing your skills in argument. Dealing with a conflict in evidence is something which is especially important in legal study, because it is essentially what, in legal practice is involved in anticipating your opponent's case and stating why, despite the contrary arguments which your opponent may use in support of his or her client's case, your client's case is still the stronger one.

We're going to return to the previous football example to illustrate the point (and although earlier we speculated on a variety of possible sub-questions, to keep this illustration straightforward, let's stick to ones which have an objective, verifiable answer). So, supposing that in researching the question *Which is the best football team?* you had posed the following questions, and found out the following answers:

> **TIP**
>
> Try applying the following technique to your research:
>
> 1. In relation to each of your sub-questions, try to sum up in a nutshell what the position is of each of your sources in relation to that sub-question.
> 2. Compare these positions: which—broadly—complement (i.e. essentially agree with) each other, and which conflict with each other?
> 3. From the opposing positions, which is the better view?

Possible sub-questions	Answer
Who has won the most Premierships?	Manchester United
Who has won the most recent Premierships?	Chelsea
Who has won the most European Cups?	Liverpool (assuming we're concentrating on domestic sides)

The problem that we now have is that the research into our sub-questions has provided a conflict in evidence: depending on which sub-question you rely on, we have so far proved that the best football team is either Manchester United, Chelsea or Liverpool. So which of them is it? The answer would depend on further reasoning as to which of those sub-questions is the best indicator of footballing success.

The structure of the argument might be:

1. If consistency in the Premiership is the most important factor in rating football teams, then Manchester United are the best;
2. On the other hand, if a team is only as good as their most recent season, then success in recent Premierships is the most important, and Chelsea are the best;

3. Alternatively, if success against European teams marks a quality team then the domestic team with the best record is Liverpool.

Conclusion: success against European teams must be the best indicator of quality, therefore success in the European Cup is the key yardstick, and therefore Liverpool is the best football team.

Of course, the conclusion could equally well have been that either of the other sub-questions provided the best yardstick, and this would have produced an entirely different answer: the important element is that whatever position you take, you *justify* it with evidence.

Applying this to legal writing, there will frequently be competing positions in what you write, and this is fine. But what you need to do, in order to demonstrate that you understand your evidence and can make effective use of it, is to acknowledge these competing positions and tailor your argument accordingly. The best writing acknowledges, rather than attempts to hide, the opposite point of view, but demonstrates how this opposite point of view is weaker than the writer's position. In other words, you deal with conflicting evidence by essentially ranking and rating it.

In order to do this, you need to consider the weight and quality of your evidence. A classic example of failure to do this is when someone counters the huge weight of medical evidence that smoking is bad for you with a remark like "My uncle smoked 40 a day all his life and lived to be 90 so it can't be bad for you." Weighing up the evidence from this example would give us:

Smoking is bad for you	Smoking is not bad for you
Hundreds of objective medical studies (which if you were really pursuing this in an academic study you would have researched, of course)	One anecdotal example

From this example, we can see that the weight of evidence is strongly on the "smoking is bad for you" side. It can often be helpful to draw up a table in this way, and use it to list the arguments for and against a particular position. This will help you to judge where the weight of evidence lies. However, remember that you are not just looking for the longest list of "pros" in order to pick the winning argument. You must also bear in mind the *quality* of your evidence: if your table of conflicting evidence produces a *ratio* from the House of Lords on one side, but an *obiter* from the High Court on the other, the numbers are even—but clearly the House of Lords' *ratio* is stronger.

Dealing with conflicting evidence is a skill which is likely to be especially needed in legal writing when you are using cases as evidence. As well as ranking the cases according to which court they were decided in (in relation to the hierarchy of the courts) and whether the evidence you are relying on forms part of the *ratio* or is merely *obiter*, it will usually be appropriate to rank the relevance of the cases to the particular facts in your question. For example, a case with exactly the same material facts is more valuable evidence than a case with only some similar material facts.

You must also ensure that the way in which you deal with conflicting evidence is *logical*. This is explored in the following activity.

> **TIP**
>
> The point of giving the facts of cases is:
>
> 1. to demonstrate the relevance of a case to the point you are making;
> 2. to highlight similarities/differences between the facts under discussion and the case being discussed.
>
> Remember that case facts are simply descriptive, so limit their use to the above situations, and even then be as concise as you can.

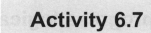

Activity 6.7

Returning to our question about which is the best football team, supposing a student argued as follows: **6–21**

> Liverpool FC are the best football team, because they have won the European Cup five times. However, Chelsea have won the Premiership twice in a row, which is even better.

What is wrong with this statement? If you find it difficult to put your finger on exactly what is wrong with it, then try identifying what the conclusion drawn by the author is, to see if this helps you pinpoint the problem with the statement, and then identify the reasons given to support this conclusion.

Compare your answer:

The main problem here is the lack of logic. At first, the conclusion appears to be that Liverpool is the best football team, and there is a reason given for this, namely that they have won five European Cups. This is fine so far, as it appears that the author has found a yardstick against which to measure what makes the best football team, namely success in the European Cup. However, the next supposed reason given relates to success in the Premiership, and the author states that this reason is even more important. Logically that must mean that Chelsea is the best football team, not Liverpool.

Of course we already know that you can have more than one "yardstick" to help you carry out an evaluation, and it is entirely appropriate to rank your yardsticks against each other. However, the problem here is that overall the statement is illogical: if Chelsea ranks best against the "better" yardstick, then the logical conclusion is that Chelsea is the better team, yet the statement starts by asserting that Liverpool is. In other words, the writer takes two positions:

1. Success in the European Cup is the best indicator of the best football team.
2. Winning the Premiership is a better indicator than this.

Clearly, these positions are not compatible with each other. There can be nothing better than the best. What the author should have done is acknowledge that both are important ways of rating the best football team but decided which yardstick was the best, in order to take one (concluding) position.

So for example:

> Chelsea is the best football team because they won the Premiership twice in a row, which demonstrates consistency. Liverpool have won the European Cup five times but this success can be achieved by a succession of lucky results in knock-out competitions.

There are again two competing arguments here, but the ultimate *position* taken ranks one (domestic consistency) above the other (success in the European Cup) and is therefore *logical*. Of course this doesn't necessarily mean that it is *right*, but remember that in your legal writing you will only rarely be dealing with issues which have a simplistic "right or wrong" answer, and so logical argument based on quality evidence should be your goal rather than a fruitless search for the "right" answer. There is more about the concept of a logical progression of ideas in the next section.

How can I make sure my arguments progress logically?

6–22   By now you should understand that the process of answering the sub-questions you have set yourself as part of your diagnosis will throw up conflicts, and you know that you need to rank these to work out which is the better view. You then need to make sure that you structure these appropriately.

If you have ever watched the TV show *Little Britain* then you will be familiar with the character of Vicky Pollard. If this means nothing to you, then for the purpose of this explanation all you need to know is that this character is famous for the catchphrase "Yeah . . . but no . . . but yeah . . . but no . . . but . . ." with which she begins more or less every answer to a question. Basically, your goal in logical progression of argument is to avoid being Vicky Pollard. In other words, if you have a number of conflicting arguments, then don't give a pro, then a con, then a pro, then a con, then a pro, then a con. This will produce the Vicky Pollard effect. It is usually much better to produce an essay which looks at all the pros and then all the cons before proceeding to your conclusion. In a problem answer, this pattern will vary according to the particular "formula" which may apply to tackling questions on particular topics.

The following example of a logical progression of argument is based on the question about democracy which we looked at as an example of diagnosis in Ch.4.

> "The voting system used at UK General Elections requires urgent reform to reflect the values of a liberal democracy". Discuss.

In order to understand how the arguments in this essay should progress logically, it may help to think of the essay title in abstract terms. In other words, this essay title can be represented as:

> Measured against standard X, which is better—model A or model B?

Standard X, in our example, is the values of a liberal democracy—our yardstick for this assignment. Model A is the current voting system; Model B comprises alternatives for reform. (Note that this "formula" can be modified to suit most *do we need reform* type questions.)

Breaking this down into our sub-questions, they could be as follows:

1. What is standard X?   DESCRIPTIVE
2. What is model A?   DESCRIPTIVE
3. What is model B?   DESCRIPTIVE
4. How does A rate against X?   EVALUATIVE
5. How does B rate against X?   EVALUATIVE
6. So, measured against X, which is better—A or B? CONCLUSION

Activity 6.8

6–23   How could the sub-questions listed above be organised into a logical progression of argument?

Compare your views:

Number 6 clearly goes last, because you need the answers to all five preceding questions to answer it— your conclusion must always go last. Similarly, it seems logical to start with number 1 because this sets out your "measure" or yardstick. Further, number 4 has to go after 1 and 2, because the explanation in 1 and 2 is needed before the evaluation in 4 can take place; on the same basis, 5 has to go after 1 and 3.

So therefore, our two possible structures are:

> 1 – 2 – 3 – 4 – 5 – 6

or

> 1 – 2 – 4 – 3 – 5 – 6

Looking back at the questions, you can see this is a choice between dealing with all areas of description first and then moving on to all areas of evaluation, or dealing with all issues to do with Model A both descriptive and evaluative, and then dealing with all issues to do with Model B both descriptive and evaluative. If it was you trying to understand it, which would you find most helpful? It is probably best to evaluate Model A while the facts about Model A are fresh in the mind, and then do the same for Model B.

This means that your progression of argument would be as follows:

1. The values of a liberal democracy are . . .
2. The current voting system is . . .
3. The strengths and weaknesses of the current voting system as compared to the values of liberal democracy are . . .
4. Alternatives to the current voting system are . . .
5. The strengths and weaknesses of the reform possibilities as compared to the values of liberal democracy are . . .
6. Conclusion.

Finally, as alluded to in the football example, a logical progression of argument needs a *conclusion*, and you need reasons to support this conclusion. Your reasons should lead logically to your conclusion. In academic writing, you are likely to make a number of conclusions, or sub-conclusions, which lead to your overall or main conclusion.

A common mistake in student writing is to confuse your final conclusion with a summary. A conclusion gives your final position on your arguments, having evaluated the conflicting evidence to decide which way is the way forward. Returning to our football example (for the final time), a student might finish their consideration of which is the best football team like this:

> So in conclusion, if the best way to judge a football team is by reference to the number of premierships won, then the best team is Manchester United, but if recent success is a better guide then the best team is Chelsea.

Does this tell you which is the best team? No—so this is not a conclusion at all! This is simply a rehash or repetition of the conflicting evidence which (presumably) has been given in the main body of the essay. To be an effective and logical conclusion, it must reach an overall position on which of these conflicting arguments is the better view. In a legal answer, the example above is the equivalent of something like "Therefore Fred may win if . . . but he may lose if . . ." You should have already made clear this conflict in your evidence in the main body of your work, so in your conclusion you need to say whether Fred is more likely to win or lose. Simply saying "in conclusion" at the beginning of your final paragraph is not enough to make it a conclusion: you must make your final position clear. There is much more help on how to write an effective conclusion in Ch.8.

We now need to return to the issues of plagiarism and referencing.

What is plagiarism?

6–24   Unfortunately, despite the emphasis placed on avoiding plagiarism and collusion by universities, there is no universally accepted definition of exactly what it is, other than that it is a form of dishonesty or *cheating*. Alison Bone's *Plagiarism: a guide for law lecturers*,[3] draws on the definition by Ryan[4] that plagiarism is "stealing someone's words or ideas and passing them off as your own". Your university may have its own definition of plagiarism or may class it together with collusion as "academic misconduct". It is vital that you check out your own institution's definition and penalties, which you will probably find in your assessment regulations or student handbook. If you cannot locate a definition, or any guidance which will help you avoid plagiarism, then **ask** where you can locate this information.

> **TIP**
>
> Find out your university's rules on plagiarism and/or other academic misconduct—don't be caught out by ignorance as it is unlikely to be a valid excuse.

A further area of confusion is whether plagiarism has to be intentional or whether it can be committed accidentally. Although most definitions do **not** require intention, it may be that your institution regards a first offence, or an offence early in your academic studies, as less serious on the basis that you might not have been fully aware of what plagiarism is. In other words, although plagiarism can be committed accidentally, it may be punished less harshly in this case than where it is deliberate. Again, this is something that you need to check in your own university's regulations. Of course the safest course of action is to ensure that you do not commit plagiarism at all, whether intentionally or accidentally.

The basic rule is that you must acknowledge where you have drawn on the words or ideas of others in your work, and give a reference to this material so that, if they wanted, the person reading your work could go and find the original source and read it for themselves. This will avoid any penalties being imposed (for example having your marks reduced or having to resubmit work). Additionally, Law Schools are obliged to report incidents of plagiarism to the Law Society and the Bar Council; understandably, they may not consider someone who has committed plagiarism suitable to become a solicitor or barrister, so it is particularly vital for law students to make sure they are clear on what needs to be referenced and how. However, the concept of plagiarism can be over-hyped: we have already explained how you need to give evidence as a matter of putting together a good argument—if you do this properly then you will avoid plagiarism as a matter of course, as well as improving your marks because of the high quality of your arguments.

There are a number of misconceptions about plagiarism, for example, that:

> Plagiarism can only be committed deliberately.

From what you've read already, you should be aware that plagiarism is plagiarism whether it is committed intentionally or accidentally, which is why it is your responsibility to make sure you understand what it is and how to avoid it.

> It isn't plagiarism to copy from a book as long as you put the book in your bibliography.

---

[3] BONE, A. *Plagiarism: a guide for law lecturers*. UK Centre for Legal Education, www.ukcle.ac.uk/resources/trns/plagiarism/index.html, accessed May 25, 2006.

[4] RYAN, J. *A guide to teaching international students*. Oxford: Oxford Centre for Staff and Learning Development, 2002.

This is false. You certainly need to put any books you have used in your bibliography, but that is not enough in itself. You have to make it clear throughout your work whenever you draw on someone else's ideas by referencing it at the appropriate point.

> Copying from the internet isn't plagiarism—plagiarism is only copying from books or journals.

This seems to be a common idea: as long as you can find something on the internet, then it is "ok" to cut and paste it into your work. However, plagiarism is copying from *anywhere* without acknowledging the source (and think how easy it is for your tutors to check up on quotes from the web).

> Tutors have too many assessments to mark to spot plagiarism.

Well, it is certainly likely that your tutors have a lot of assignments to mark, but this therefore means they are very experienced in spotting plagiarism. And in any case, remember that your tutors will want to reward effective arguments—i.e. those that are supported by evidence—so providing references is genuinely to your benefit.

It can be easy to focus on the penalties which attach to plagiarism, without stressing enough the benefits which come from good academic practice: if you use and cite your materials in the right way this will result in good marks. Remember that we've emphasised throughout this book that marks are not awarded for simply being able to replicate information: the marks are for what you do with the information. It follows that being able to show that

TIP

Use a highlighter pen to identify quotes or use quotation marks when copying a quote so that it stands out in your notes, but remember you need to acknowledge **ideas** as well as quotes.

you can use sources to develop your own reasoning and argument is the best way to improve your writing—and will have the added benefit that you avoid plagiarism!

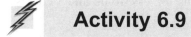

Activity 6.9

We are going to return to our quotation from Lord Denning's book, *The Discipline of Law*[5] which we looked at earlier in the chapter when we were looking at paraphrasing. Here is a reminder of Lord Denning's original: **6–25**

> In almost every case in which you have to advise you will have to interpret a statute. There are stacks and stacks of them. Far worse for you than for me. When I was called in 1923 there was one volume of 500 pages. Now in 1978 there are three volumes of more than 3,000 pages. Not a single page but it can give rise to argument. Not a single page but the client will turn to you and say: "What does it mean?" The trouble lies with our method of drafting. The principal object of the draftsman is to achieve certainty—a laudable object in itself. But in pursuit of it, he loses sight of the equally important object—clarity. The draftsman—or draftswoman—has conceived certainty: but has brought forth obscurity; sometimes even absurdity.

If a student wrote the following in an essay, would you consider it to be plagiarism?

[5] DENNING, *The discipline of law*. Butterworths, 1979, p.9.

Statutory interpretation has become much more significant with the rise in the number of reported cases from 500 pages in 1923 to more than 9,000 pages in 1978. Every page may have some issue of statutory interpretation on it, and although the principal object of the draftsman is to achieve certainty—a laudable object in itself—problems with the method of drafting may mean that this is at the expense of clarity.

Compare your views:

Remember that you are looking out for using someone else's words or ideas without proper credit. There are therefore two main problems with this example:

TIP

You need to cite all the following:

1. Direct quotations, whatever the source;
2. Paraphrasing of ideas from a source even where you don't quote directly;
3. Summarising of ideas from a source even where you don't quote directly;
4. "Borrowing" ideas, such as quotations or case ratios, from a secondary source—i.e. a source within a source.

1. It directly quotes the phrase "the principal object of the draftsman is to achieve certainty—a laudable object in itself" without acknowledgment.
2. The rest of the passage draws very heavily on Lord Denning's ideas, for example about the pages in the law reports, and certainty/clarity. This is therefore a paraphrase. Paraphrases as well as direct quotations must be referenced.

How should my legal writing be referenced?

6–26   In this section, we will demonstrate:

TIP

Keep in mind your goal in referencing is to acknowledge the use you have made of other people's words or ideas and to enable your readers to locate these works for themselves.

- how to write citations for primary sources of law;
- how to write citations for printed secondary sources;
- how to write citations for electronic and web-based sources.

However, to make things more complicated there are a number of different ways of doing this, which are explored below.

Different systems of referencing

6–27   There are two main systems for citing secondary material. The first is called the Numeric system (sometime also called the footnoting system) and the other is the Harvard or Author-Date system. You will probably already have seen both styles in academic books (although legal textbooks are more likely to use the Numeric system).

The Harvard or Author-Date system—the author's name and the year of publication are included in brackets within the text, for example:

Legal writing is a skill which can be learned (Smith, 2003, p.6).

The bibliography would then set out in full the reference for the work. The bibliography is an essential accompaniment to the essay because it shows the location of all the material cited (which in this case, we have invented).

The Numeric System—numbered footnotes (or endnotes) are used to provide the reader with the location of the material which has been referenced in the main text.

Legal writing is a skill which can be learned.[1]

1. SMITH, P. *Legal writing*. London: Sweet and Maxwell, 2003, p.6.

As well as the two major systems of referencing, there are also different *conventions* covering how to cite different types of material:

The most well-known are found in the following texts.

1. The British Standard, published by the British Standards Institution: *Recommendations for citing and referencing published material*. London: BSI, 1990. BS: 5605:1990, which can be accessed from the following website: www.bsonline.bsi-global.com/server/index.jsp. This does not give guidance specifically on the citation of primary legal materials but contains standards for secondary sources.
2. The Oxford Standard for Citation of Legal Authorities (OSCOLA), which can be downloaded from www.competition-law.ox.ac.uk/published/ oscola_v2_formatted.pdf. This gives advice and detailed rules on the citation of both primary and secondary legal sources.
3. Derek French's guide *How to cite legal authorities*. London: Blackstone Press, 1996. This contains exhaustive examples and alternatives of how to cite all kinds of legal materials.

> **TIP**
>
> If you use a word processor then it is likely to contain a mechanism for inserting footnotes (or endnotes) for you (in MS Word, it is located in the Insert menu), which makes life a lot easier. If you are unsure how to use this facility then seek guidance—mastering this will only take a couple of minutes and will save a lot of time later.

Guidance on how to reference

Your starting point should be whatever your institution recommends. Are you expected to use Harvard or footnotes? Are you expected to follow the British Standard or OSCOLA or does your Law School have its own system? Is there a guide to how you should cite material? If there is, get hold of it and use it.   **6–28**

> **TIP**
>
> Remember that all the following advice is suggested **only** if it does not conflict with specific conventions recommended by your own institution—if you've been given a guide by your Law School make sure you **use it**.

If your institution does not provide specific instructions, then the key is to be *consistent* in your referencing. The safest way to do this is to pick one of the systems mentioned above and stick to it. There are examples of how the alternative systems look later on in this chapter.

Citing statutes

6-29   Cite a *statute* by reference to its short title, including the calendar year, and, where needed, specific section number.

> Children Act 1989, s.1(1).

Citing cases

6-30   Cite a *case* by identifying the law report in which it is reported, and whereabouts within the law report it is. Usually this is very straightforward, because most cases are reported in annual volumes (in other words you can find the right volume if you know the year) like the All England Reports. The standard citation format is (in this order): case name in italics, year reported in square brackets, volume within that year (if any), abbreviated name of the law report, number of the page on which the report begins.

> *Law v National Greyhound Racing Club* [1983] 3 All ER 300
> *Birch v Birch* [1992] 1 FLR 564
> *Polkey v Dayton* [1988] ICR 147

The OSCOLA system suggests that you should also indicate the court in which the judgment was made after the citation, and provides further detail on variations, as does French.

The problem with the above citations is that the same case can be reported in a number of different law reports which can cause some difficulty over which one to cite. The alternative to this is a new system of *neutral citations*, which was introduced in January 2001 and gives each case one unique citation, based on the court in which the case was heard, which can be used to identify the case regardless of which law report(s) it appears in.

A neutral citation would look something like this:

> *Smith v Bloggs* [2002] EWCA Civ 15

Here, EWCA Civ indicates the England and Wales Court of Appeal Civil Division, and 15 indicates that it was the 15th case heard in 2002. Similar abbreviations exist to cover the other major courts—for example UKHL indicates the House of Lords and EWHC indicates the High Court.

> **TIP**
> Find out whether your institution allows/ prefers you to use neutral citations.

Citing secondary sources

6-31   If you use the Harvard system, then citing secondary sources is straightforward—use the author and date and then make a full reference in the bibliography. However, it is conventional in legal study for the footnoting system to be preferred. Again, the suggestions below—which are based on the British Standard and the OSCOLA systems—should only be used if your institution does not provide its own guidance on how to cite.

Books

When citing a *book*, indicate the following: who the author/editor is (if an editor, use (ed) after the name), what the title of the book is, the edition number unless it is the first edition, where it was published, which publisher published it, and when it was published, and (if appropriate) particular pages referred to. **6–32**

Under the British Standard, the author's surname followed by initial is given in UPPERCASE, and the title of the book is in italics, usually in sentence case (in other words only one capital letter at the beginning) except for any words which would have a capital letter anyway (names for example). After the title comes the place of publication, then a colon and the name of the publisher, and then a comma and the year of publication. If there are two authors give both, if three or more give the first followed by "et al".

AUTHOR, A. *Title of book*, 2nd edn, London: Sweet & Maxwell, 2006.

Under the OSCOLA system, the author's first name (or initials) and surname are followed by the title in italics in title case, and the information about edition number, publisher, place of publication and year in brackets, followed by any relevant page numbers. Up to three authors are named; more should be indicated by the first followed by "and others".

A Author *Title of Book* (2nd edn, Sweet & Maxwell, London, 2006).

Journal articles

When citing a journal article, again, the rule is to give the information the reader needs to locate the material, so you will need to give the author, and the title of the article, the journal where it is located including volume/edition and page and year where appropriate. **6–33**

Under the British Standard an article written by Rebecca Bailey-Harris called "Contact - challenging conventional wisdom?" which was published in the fourth issue of vol.13 of the journal *Child and Family Law Quarterly* in 2001 would be referenced like this:

BAILEY-HARRIS, R. Contact—challenging conventional wisdom? *Child and Family Law Quarterly*, 2001, 13 (4) pp.361–370.

Under the OSCOLA system, this would be referenced differently by giving the name of the author, title of the article in single quotation marks, year, volume number, journal title abbreviation and initial page, so:

Rebecca Bailey-Harris, 'Contact—challenging conventional wisdom?' (2001) 13 CFLQ 361.

For more information consult either the British Standard guide or the OSCOLA guide (whichever you are using: remember don't mix the two).

Web-based materials

You are likely to wish to utilise the wealth of legal information available on the web to support your arguments. If you have located cases or statutes on the web, then simply cite these in the normal way, as you would for printed sources. **6–34**

However, for secondary sources, you indicate that you found the documents on the web, and indicate when and where you located them. Again, there are different conventions for how to cite web-based material, but the key is to give as much information as possible about author and title and so on, as you would in citing printed sources, but indicate the date on which you accessed the information (because web material changes) and the URL (i.e. the web address) where you found the material.

TIP

Don't make the mistake of thinking that web-based material doesn't need to be cited.

As a note of caution about web sources, remember that the web obviously contains a mass of information of varying quality, so when you want to use websites to support your arguments you do need to be careful. Remember that if something is published in paper form, this usually (though not always) means that some publisher somewhere thought it was worth publishing. You might not agree but there will usually have been some kind of review process involved. Material from the internet could have been published by literally anyone with no review and no regard for accuracy.

Citing the same source on more than one occasion

6–35   It is very likely that in the course of your legal writing, you will want to refer to the same source more than once. Rather than giving the entire reference every time, it is acceptable to give the full reference the first time you cite it and then use some form of abbreviation on subsequent occasions, but there are many different ways of doing this. You may have read in your textbooks use of Latin phrases like *op. cit.*, *loc. cit.* and *ibid*. Generally it is best to avoid these as they are confusing, and neither the British Standard nor OSCOLA recommends them.
Don't reference again if:

- you are referring to the same source several times in a row (for example during the course of a paragraph).

However, **do** reference again if:

- there has been a gap in which you have referred to other sources or moved on to other issues. You must then reference the source again in abbreviated form by indicating the original citation;
- you have previously referred to the source but now need to provide a reference to a different page or section;
- not citing it again might cause confusion—if in doubt, cite again.

Where you are providing a subsequent reference, then the British Standard "running notes" system suggests the following:

1. On first reference, give the full citation.
2. On subsequent reference, where needed according to the suggestions above, give the author's name again and then reference the footnote in which the previous full reference is located. So for example, if you are referring to a work by Smith, previously cited in full in footnote 6, then a subsequent reference would read:

SMITH, ref 6.

Add specific pages if you are referring to a different part of Smith's work. If you are referring back to a case or statute, then simply give the footnote at which the previous full citation is located (as long as you included the name in the original reference: if not, give the name of the case, followed by the appropriate reference number).

The OSCOLA system follows the same principle but the format is slightly different, as it uses "n" rather than "ref". The above example would look like this:

> Smith (n 6).

One thing to be careful of is that you must not use this technique as you write, because at the draft stage, your footnotes are very likely to change. When you use the "insert footnote" facility, your word processor will helpfully keep the numbers of the footnotes straight for you. So, if you've got 10 foot notes, but then decide that you need an extra footnote somewhere between 4 and 5, when you insert it, it will appear as 5, and 5 will be renumbered as 6 automatically, 6 as 7 and so on. So far, so good. However, what the word processor *can't* do is keep track of what the *contents* of your footnotes say, so supposing footnote 10 said "SMITH, ref 6", you are now pointing your reader to the wrong material because the full citation for Smith is now at ref 7.

Therefore the best thing to do is insert your footnotes in full as you write (or alternatively using your own shorthand system throughout). Only when you are absolutely sure that your main text is the final copy should you then go through and sort out your subsequent references, so that you can be certain which footnote is the first reference to Smith. You can then abbreviate appropriately for all further references to Smith (or alternatively if you used your own shorthand system, insert the full reference for Smith on the first mention, and abbreviate appropriately for subsequent references). How to set out your bibliography is explained in Ch.9, and there is a sample bibliography in Appendix 6.

TIP

Sorting out your subsequent references should be the last thing you do before printing your final copy to hand in.

Summary of Chapter 6

- An academic argument consists of reasons supported by evidence which lead logically to a conclusion.   **6–36**
- Weigh up conflicting evidence to conclude which side of the overall argument is stronger.
- You should use a case or statute as evidence to support a proposition of law and a secondary source such as a book or journal to support other propositions, except those which are "common knowledge".
- You must acknowledge where you have used the words or ideas of others to avoid plagiarism.
- Your work must be correctly referenced according to your institution's requirements or other consistent method.

7 The writing phase of your assignment

What is the purpose of this chapter?

7–1   We have already shown that all legal academic courses will involve some kind of writing for assessment to a greater or lesser degree, and that the key to succeeding at this is good communication. So, we know that the starting point of planning any writing is to identify for what purpose you are writing; in other words, to diagnose the task. Diagnosing the task, or working out what is expected of you, is likely to be one of the criteria used to mark your work. In many respects much of the hard work is done if you get this stage right. We also know that this diagnosis forms the basis of the research which you carry out. However, once your research is completed, you need to move to the next stage, which is to begin to put your pen to paper—or, more likely, your fingers to the keyboard—and begin writing. This can be daunting, but once you know what is being asked of you through diagnosis and research, then there is not too big a leap to actually doing it. You need to take your diagnosis and research, and begin to plan your answer accordingly.

    By the end of this chapter you will:

- have developed an improved understanding of the importance of utilising a "good" structure in your writing;
- be aware of techniques for writing introductions and conclusions to your work;
- understand the importance of developing "flow" or logic in your writing.

What does "structure" mean in relation to academic writing?

7–2   A word often used by assessors when considering writing, particularly at university level, is "structure". We talked earlier about reflecting on your previous experiences of receiving feedback on your work; you might have seen feedback such as: "This work lacks a coherent, logical structure" or

"Excellent well-developed structure and line of argument" (or something in between). You may find that your institution uses "structure" as one of the criteria for assessing your written work. In fact, even if it is not an explicit assessment criteria you can still assume that it will be of importance, as it goes to the heart of good writing. A "good" structure lends an automatic air of credibility to your writing because it means you are communicating more effectively. This will produce a radical improvement in your work.

One of the most common uses of the word "structure" is when we talk about a building of some kind. Whilst we can all probably identify what is meant by the term "structure" in a building context, it is not as easy to define what is meant by "structure" in a writing context. It is one of those things that markers can recognise when it is done well but can find hard to describe in words. In this chapter we are going to try and identify what structure really means, what a good structure to a piece of writing looks like, and how you can develop the skills necessary to create a workable structure in your writing. Whilst the structure you adopt may differ according to the nature of the writing you are doing, the process of creating a structure on which to hang your writing will not.

Remember, before you even start considering your structure, you will already have done quite a lot of work towards your assignment. You will have examined the title or question and worked out what it is asking you to do through your diagnosis (see Ch.4). You will have thought about the sources you want to use, and you will have gathered together lots of useful information, from cases and statutes, books, journals, your lecture notes and other relevant sources, to answer the diagnostic questions you have posed (see Ch.5). You will have developed an idea of how you can utilise these sources logically (see Ch.6). Now you have reached the point when you must pull this together. Some writers find this hard, but if you have followed our advice, it should not be as difficult as you might anticipate.

The importance of writing a plan

There are a number of reasons why using a plan for your writing is helpful. First, if you find it difficult to order your thoughts when preparing to answer an assignment then a plan will be invaluable in helping to keep you on the right track as you negotiate the path towards completion and submission. Even if you have an ordered mind, a plan will still help you focus on your writing.

7–3

Planning the structure of your answer should not be rushed. Any time spent on planning will invariably be time well-spent because it means that when you start "writing up" you won't have to interrupt your creative flow to wonder if you are on the right track; your plan will tell you whether you are. This will make the writing of the assignment faster and easier.

Secondly, you will probably be using a personal computer ("PC") or Mac to write up your assignment, giving you the added bonus of being able to start writing wherever you like. When writing in longhand, before the advent of computerised word processing, it was usually necessary to start at the beginning and go on until you

> **TIP**
>
> Keep a copy of your plan stuck somewhere prominent while you are writing and keep referring to it to make sure your writing is going where it is supposed to.

> **TIP**
>
> The ease with which you can edit word processed work is a major advantage of learning to write by typing directly into a computer, and if you are not used to this method of working, resolve to make this something you adjust to now: it will pay dividends.

reached the end with any corrections being difficult to make and messy to look at. Now you can choose where in your answer you want to start. However, this makes it all the more important to have a clear plan to stick to.

How to write a plan

7–4   When you have completed your diagnosis, you will have worked out what the question is asking for and gone on to identify a series of sub-questions. In your research phase you will have identified the "answer" (as far as there is one) to each question you have posed as well as the relevant authority for each point you want to make in answer to these sub-questions. Next, and this may come out of your initial analysis of the question or out of your extended research, you will need to make decisions about the relevant weight, i.e. which of these points are major points at the heart of your argument and which are minor points which won't need to be covered in as much detail. In other words you will concern yourself with both coverage and depth. These decisions should be reflected in your plan. The last step is making decisions about the order in which your major and minor points will be made in your answer. Our students often identify "ordering" as one of the hardest parts of preparing a plan. How do you decide which point goes where? What we tell them is that this should grow from the diagnosis and research carried out.

We discussed various techniques for diagnosing essay questions and problem questions in Ch.4 and to a certain extent you will also need to develop different plans for answering essays and problems. With essay questions your plan, and therefore your structure, will be complete once you have diagnosed the task and made decisions on minor and major points. With a problem question it is the question itself which may well give clues as to the best approach to planning. Any plan needs to adopt a logical style and approach and the very nature of a problem question is that it offers these elements.

Once you have your plan you need to start the writing itself. Remember you don't have to start at the beginning. If it suits you to start at the end and work backwards do so. However, in whatever order you choose to approach your writing, you must remain clear on your goal of answering the question, and in order to do that, effective essays contain the following elements:

- an introduction, which identifies the issues you will discuss;
- a main body, which develops the issues into an argument;
- a conclusion, which gives your final position.

We now consider these elements in more detail, beginning with the concept of an introduction.

How do I write a successful introduction?

7–5   An introduction is a fundamental element of your answer. If your essay is an exploration of a central idea, or "thesis", this will need to be defined before it can be developed. Whatever is contained in the essay must relate to this main thesis and so that thesis must be introduced to the reader. The introduction is where you impress: you inform your reader about what is to come to encourage them to read further in a positive frame of mind. In a non-academic context a reader chooses whether to continue reading a particular piece of writing, and they will often decide on the basis of the introduction—in other words, the introduction should *invite* the reader to go further. Obviously, with assessed work you can assume it will be read whether the introduction is good or bad, but nevertheless this idea of an invitation is important: you must make a good impression. You do this by demonstrating in your introduction that you have identified the relevant issues (which arise from your diagnosis). The introduction sets the scene and context for the rest of the piece. Get this right and your work will be read by an interested marker looking forward to hearing what you are going to say in the rest of your answer.

Introductions are sometimes described by students as the hardest part of an assignment to write. Often what these students *really* mean is that the hardest part of writing an assignment is actually to *start* writing. There is no need to confuse writing the introduction with starting to write the answer —if you prefer to write the introduction last, you can. As long as your plan and structure are successful it does not matter in what order you tackle the different elements of your assignment. Of course, in an exam situation, you have less flexibility here: it is better to focus on writing your answer from start to finish rather than to mess about with where to start.

Another reason given by students for finding it hard to write introductions is that they can't see the *point* of an introduction. Why write down something in the introduction when you are planning to say it again in more detail in the next paragraph? This is missing the point of an introduction: it is your chance to specify the *issues* which are raised by the question. You then go on to *discuss* those issues in appropriate detail in the main body of the work.

The next activity will help you understand the importance of an introduction.

 ## Activity 7.1

Below are two example introductions, which both introduce the same question. Read them and see   7–6 if you can work out roughly what the subject matter of the assessment is, and the type of question which has been set.

Example 1:

> Contract law is a huge subject with lots of aspects to it like consideration, misrep., mistake and offer and acceptance. A contract needs to satisfy many elements in order to be held valid and we need to see if they have been complied with in order to answer this question.

Example 2:

> The negotiations between Peter and David over the sale of Peter's guitar seem to have reached some kind of settlement or agreement as they are both at some point willing to go through with the transaction at an agreed price. Whether this "agreement" can equal a contract will depend on a number factors. English contract law requires more than an "agreement" between Peter and David—we need a matching "offer" and "acceptance".

Compare your views:

Presumably you could see that both these examples concerned the same subject area (contract law), but you may have struggled to work out in any more detail than this what the subject matter of the question was from Example 1, which is vague and generalised. There is no indication in this introduction as to who needs advice about what. It is not until we read Example 2 that we can see clearly that the subject matter of the question is a problem which relates to the sale of a guitar from Peter to David, and whether the agreement they have made in relation to this forms a valid contract.

If you were marking these assignments (or indeed if you were seeking advice from a lawyer about the sale of a guitar) which of these introductions do you think does a better job of identifying the issues which need to be considered? By using the names of the parties and beginning to pinpoint the material facts, Example 2 is a much better introduction to a problem question. Example 1 gives no indication of the issues on which the parties require advice. Indeed, if we hadn't told you that these were introductions to the same question, you might have presumed that only Example 2 was the introduction to a problem, and that Example 1 was introducing an essay.

We will return to this later and in the next activity we give you the chance to develop your approach to preparing introductions, but this time using an essay question.

It almost goes without saying that your ability to write a good introduction, to a certain extent, relies on having completed the planning and preparation stages satisfactorily.

> **TIP**
>
> An introduction explains what the answer is going to do. So: reveal your diagnosis of task, set out the issues you will be examining in your essay and identify how you are going to go about doing that with each issue and in what order.

Your first few sentences need to set out the main issues that have been raised by the question. By carrying out the diagnosis of the task correctly you will have identified the "thesis" and you need to articulate this to the reader. Here we are not talking about discussing the minor issues—you need to highlight the key points or concepts or problems that are at the very heart of question.

Have a look at the following question, which is also based on contract law[1]:

In her *Textbook on Contract Law*, Jill Poole comments that:

"The doctrine of privity of contract states that a person may not enforce a contractual promise and obtain remedies for its breach, even when the promise was expressly made for his or her benefit, if he or she was not a party to the contract."

Consider the effects that the Contracts (Rights of Third Parties) Act 1999 has had on this traditional approach to the doctrine of privity.

Your introduction might look like this:

Historically, the doctrine of privity of contract has always been a central underpinning force in the law of contract ensuring that only the parties to a contract can be bound by it and can therefore enforce it. The coming into force of the Contracts (Rights of Third Parties) Act 1999 has radically altered this position. The new position is that people other than the original contracting parties may, in some circumstances, enforce the contract to which they were not parties, for their own benefit.

---

[1] The full reference for the textbook cited in the question below is: POOLE, J. *Contract Law*, 7th edn. Oxford: Oxford University Press, 2005.

This introduction identifies the main issue arising from the question (privity) and indicates the relevance and importance of the particular statute identified in the question part, in terms of its effect on the doctrine of privity of contract. This is setting the scene for the reader, which means you are showing that you know what you are talking about. This doesn't mean a repetition or rewriting of the question. Neither will your marker expect an historical treatise on the background to the subject area; both of these will tend to indicate a "write all you know" approach. "Setting the scene" means something different: showing you are familiar with the subject area, you have identified the issues to be discussed and what is expected of you in this assignment. The main body of your answer will then demonstrate that you can fulfil the expectations you have raised in the introduction.

> **TIP**
>
> Tips for writing a good introduction:
>
> - Consider using a "topic sentence" to indicate the main point to your answer.
> - Be concise (10 per cent of the total words allowed should be the maximum) and relevant—use your diagnosis as your guide.
> - Don't include background history unless it is directly relevant to the question.
> - Don't just rewrite the question in your own words.
> - Don't assume "knowledge" on the part of the reader.
> - Don't write a "conclusion" instead: you are setting out the issues here, not giving the answers to those issues.

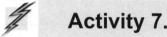 ## Activity 7.2

Read the four passages that follow and consider how well they introduce or set the scene for an essay on privity of contract. Use the following questions to help you evaluate the usefulness of the four introductions:

- Is the key issue identified?
- Is the passage clear and easy to understand?
- Is it obvious what the subject matter of the question is?
- Does it include authority to support any propositions of law?
- Does it encourage you to read on to find out more?
- Is it clear where the writer is going?

Example 1:

> The statement in the question refers to the traditional doctrine of privity of contract which is concerned with the question of who has rights and liabilities under a contract. The traditional doctrine, which became entrenched in the nineteenth century, made it clear that a third party could not sue on a contract to which he was not privy even if the sole purpose of the contract was to benefit the third party. Although there are many House of Lords' decisions supporting the rule (see for example *Dunlop Pneumatic Tyre Co Ltd v Selfridge & Co Ltd* [1915] A.C. 847 and *Woodar Investment Development Ltd v Wimpey Construction UK Ltd* [1980] 1 W.L.R. 277 where the House of Lords continued to comply whilst criticising the rule), the law was felt to be ripe for reform. The Law Commission published their provisional recommendations in 1991 (CP No.121), most of which were enacted in the Contracts (Rights of Third Parties) Act 1999 (CRTPA 1999). This essay will evaluate the original rule(s) on privity and continue by examining whether the law was indeed ripe for reform in 1999 and whether the CRTPA has resolved the issues with the old law.

7–7

Example 2:

> Privity is dead! The old ways have gone to be usurped by modern doctrines created by quasi-governmental organisations with their own protectionist stance. The Law Commission's proposals were clear—a complete rewriting and legislative continuity was needed. The final result, the Contracts (Rights of Third Parties) Act appears to be largely a skeletal structure which will need defining and refining before we can say for certain that the privity doctrine is dead and buried.

Example 3:

> The main issue with the doctrine is that it means that even where a contract exists solely to benefit a third party that third party cannot sue on it for non-compliance or breach. It often causes annoyance and, many attempts have been made to evade it. None of them have been totally successful and with the Contracts (Rights of Third Parties) Act 1999 being frequently excluded in commercial agreements, and not applying in contracts involving employment and carriage of goods, perhaps it is time for more reform in this area.

Example 4:

> Contract law covers many different concepts and situations such as offer and acceptance, consideration, mistake and misrepresentation. One area which is of interest is the idea of privity. This rule regarding contracts which are made for the benefit of third parties can be seen in operation in cases such as *Price v Easton* and *Tweddle v Atkinson*. It is clear that this rule needs serious reform as it just does not reflect modern life.

Compare your views:

OK, this was a bit of a trick. Bearing in mind what we've said so far about the introduction being where you have the opportunity to demonstrate your diagnosis, your first instinct should have been: *How can I judge which is the best introduction when I haven't seen the question?* In other words, in order to assess the quality of an introduction, you have work out whether it shows good diagnosis of the question. So, you need the question.

Here it is:

> The rule that a third party may not sue on a contract which is made for his or her benefit is outmoded. Discuss this statement with particular reference to the Contracts (Rights of Third Parties) Act 1999.

Now have another look at the passages. Remember that a well-written introduction should enable you to identify the gist of the question—does this help you evaluate them?

Compare your views:

Example 1 provides a clear introduction to the subject that an average reader with no specialist knowledge would be able to understand. The writer names, defines and explains the rule in the question title. The fact that there has been some reform in this area is identified making indirect reference to the suggestion in the question that the law is outmoded.

Example 2 is written in a somewhat "over the top" style and makes sweeping generalisations. There is no direct or indirect reference to the question, which makes it very difficult for a reader to identify the parameters of the answer. We know what the reader's position is but we don't really know where the argument is going to go.

Example 3 launches too quickly into the subject without sufficient attempt to "set the scene" or indeed settle the reader. We are given examples of when the rule is excluded or does not apply but we are not told what the rule itself is. **Example 4** makes some bald factual statements which it does attempt to support with some authority but as the relevance of these cases is not explained they are of little use. The last sentence is almost a conclusion and does not fit in an introduction "setting the scene".

> **TIP**
>
> Remember your goal in writing your introduction is to make your reader think: "Here's someone who knows what they are talking about, they have clearly done some research and they are going to answer the question that has been set and not one of their own making".

Before we go on to look at writing the main body of your answer, take some time to reflect on your own practice. Find something that you have written recently which has (or is supposed to have) an introduction. This might be from your current course or something you wrote before you enrolled. Look at the introduction and, bearing in mind what we have said above about what to avoid when writing an introduction, try to rate your own "introduction". How could you improve it? What would you do differently now if you had to write that same introduction again?   7–8

How do I structure the main text of my answer?

Between the introduction and the conclusion, the main text of your answer is where you develop your arguments. Creating and developing an argument have been explored more fully in Ch.6, so you should now have a clearer idea of how to put this together.   7–9

The main body is all about *demonstrating your knowledge and understanding* and may be seen as "easier" or "safer" to write than the introduction or conclusion. Essentially, the main part of your answer will consist of a series of paragraphs, each dealing with a different point in your argument (as identified in your plan) which will equate—broadly—to the questions raised in your diagnosis (appropriately ordered).

Each paragraph should be centred around an "organising idea" which gives meaning to that paragraph and is what you are attempting to persuade the reader to accept as true or valid. Without an "organising idea" or "thesis", the writing appears pointless (literally) to the reader. As a general guide, you should only deal with one organising idea per paragraph. It is vital that the opening sentence reflects what is in the rest of the paragraph. A good structure will not make markers search around the rest of your answer to find more points on that issue. Getting to grips with identifying an organising idea and how to support it effectively is one of the most important writing skills you can develop. Knowing how to express and sustain an organising idea is the building block of your writing and will lead to coherent and logical writing overall. You should draw these organising ideas from the sub-questions you have posed in your diagnosis.

To develop a point in your argument you should consider including the following elements in your paragraph:

- a sentence identifying the focus or theme of the paragraph;
- clarification of any issues which may be unclear;
- some kind of evaluation or analysis or examination or discussion of the point or issue covered by that paragraph supported by relevant evidence;
- reference to any implications of that point.

But it is the connections *between* these paragraphs that are the key to developing a good structure. So although your work will consist of a series of self-contained paragraphs, in order for your writing to reach its potential and achieve the best score possible, these paragraphs have to be connected in some way. You are looking to create a logical progression from one paragraph (and its organising idea) to the next, reflecting the "flow" of your argument.

How to make sure your writing "flows"

7–10 This is about linking your writing together. You may also have heard this aspect of structure in writing referred to as "transition". "Transition" in writing has the same general meaning as "transition" elsewhere, in other words "change" or "movement". So when we are talking about "transition" in your writing we mean that you need to pay attention to how the writing (and your argument) moves from sentence to sentence and from paragraph to paragraph. You are striving for a clear sense of direction in all of your writing so that a reader can follow your *sequence of ideas*. "Transitional" words or phrases can be used to link together sentences and paragraphs, ensure continuity in your writing and give signposts or clues to the reader about where you are going with your writing. Sometimes these words are referred to as "signal" words which help with the transition from one point to another, one sentence to another, or one paragraph to another.

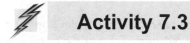

Activity 7.3

7–11 To explore the issue of transition more closely, look at the sample answers to a question on the Practice Statement in Appendix 5 and in particular look at Answers A and D. How would you rate the transition or progression of argument here?

Compare your views:

Answer A is a good example of a writer who has not taken the time to work on the transitions between paragraphs causing the answer to stop and start a number of times. Here we have a demonstration of how not to do it! For example, virtually every paragraph starts with "Another case where the House of Lords used the Practice Statement was . . ." leading to a list-like approach with no apparent connections between the points being made.

Now look at this extract from Answer D:

> A further example is the case of *Miliangos v George Frank Textiles* where the House was prepared to extinguish from the precedent books a ruling that sterling should be the only currency in which judgment can be awarded, a position which, as Lord Denning asserted in the court of appeal was more appropriate to the days of the empire than to modern global economies.
>
> If it were only in the interests of modernising and developing the law and the need for a legal system to maintain its grip on current affairs that the law lords were prepared to use the practice statement then we might justifiably conclude that the small loss to certainty would be a worthwhile price to pay in order to maintain a modern and vibrant legal system.

Don't consider the spelling, grammar and sentence construction at this stage; look only at the transition between these two paragraphs. The references to "modern" in the last sentence of the first paragraph and "modernising" in the second emphasises the connection between the two sentences and therefore paragraphs, and the writer's development of the argument. You should be able to see that this writer has a better understanding of the need to link or connect their ideas and paragraphs in order to best demonstrate their understanding.

> **TIP**
>
> If the writing flows and makes good use of paragraph transitions it should be possible to take the first sentence of each paragraph and put them together to get a reasonably clear idea of what the remainder of the argument will consist of. Try this with a piece of your own writing.

Making effective transitions

Transitions (or connections/links) can be used in a number of ways, and we can group them accord- **7–11** ing to what we may want to achieve. For example, you may use words or phrases such as: *but; however; on the other hand*; or *yet*, if you want to differentiate between two points or facts. If you are extending a point or an argument you may use words like: *in addition; moreover; furthermore; similarly; likewise*; or *correspondingly*. To conclude a topic or a section of an essay or even the whole essay words such as: *thus; as a result; therefore*; or *consequently* can be useful. So essentially, these kinds of words can tie sentences, paragraphs, and arguments together effectively and make interpretation easier for the reader. You may find it helpful to refer back to Activity 5.1 where we looked at reorganising these words.

As mentioned in the previous activity, the key transitions are those between paragraphs. You are looking to create a link between the last sentence of one paragraph and the first sentence of the next one.

For example:

> . . . So it is clear that in some cases the literal rule is not always the best means at our disposal when trying to establish Parliament's intention.
> *In addition*, a linked but alternative means that we may wish to consider is the golden rule . . .

This example also uses the technique of echoing a key word—*means*—which can be effective. However you do run the risk of repetition—a common mistake in student writing.

For example:

> . . . The other key element to the formation of a contract is acceptance.
> One of the most important elements of contract formation is the notion of acceptance . . .

Sometimes it is easier to write a transitional or linking *sentence*. This will not tell you what is coming next in the writing but will let the reader know that this paragraph is a reversal of the last one.

For example:

> . . . It would seem that the court put an end to arguments on this point.
> However, this was not always the case. In the time of . . .

Don't forget that sentences also need to follow each other in a logical manner, and so because your work must adopt a logical pattern you will be using transitions within and between paragraphs almost continuously.

Activity 7.4

7–12   Read the sentences below and insert the best of the three alternatives in the blank spaces provided. Remember to keep an eye on the relationship between the sentences or the constituent parts of the sentences given and also that punctuation will affect what you can use.

1. There are occasions when you might use extremely hot water but _____ 26 to 27 degrees celsius is adequate.

as a rule	otherwise	consequently

2. Student numbers have increased steadily over the past few years. _____ the numbers of staff employed to teach them has declined.

In contrast	Above all	Correspondingly

3. Courseworks must be handed in by the deadline, _____ they will not be marked.

obviously	as a result	otherwise

4. _____ it is a comparatively simple procedure, mistakes are always made.

Nevertheless	Because	Even though

5. The two Houses of Parliament, _____ the House of Lords and the House of Commons are located next door to each other on Parliament Square in London.

for example	namely	in particular

Compare your views:

As we noted earlier in the book on some occasions it is a matter of preference which transitional words you use, but here are the ones we suggest for the activity above:

1. as a rule
2. In contrast
3. otherwise
4. Even though
5. namely

Now, reflect on your own practice again. Using the same piece of writing as you did when reflecting on your introduction, look at your use of paragraphs and any connection or transitions between them.

*   First, have you used clearly defined paragraphs? It can be tempting when you are in the swing of writing to write in one long stream but this will make you writing harder to read and to mark, as your "organising ideas" will be lost. Stick to your plan, with a point per paragraph.

- Next, does each paragraph contribute to the argument? Does each one develop a point? Are they so short that you can usefully combine two or three without losing the flow? Are they too long? If so, consider splitting a paragraph in two wherever you introduce a new point.
- Have you actually connected the separate paragraphs to the ones that come before and after? Or does a reader come to an abrupt stop at the end of each paragraph?

This construction of a logical and flowing argument is not always as easy as it may appear and you may find it helpful to refer back to Ch.6.

To finish our consideration of structure we need to look at writing conclusions.

How do I write a successful conclusion?

As we mentioned earlier, along with writing an introduction, writing a conclusion is often considered to be the most difficult part of an assignment. Some of our students complain that they have "nothing left to say" having already written the assignment. Or they may feel writing a conclusion is "risky"—they may not want to come down on one side or another for fear of being "wrong". This demonstrates a misunderstanding of the purpose of a conclusion.   7–13

The aim of a conclusion

The introduction is where you set out the issues to be discussed, so the conclusion is where you provide "answers" or "solutions" to these issues. In other words, together with the introduction, a conclusion is the frame around the main body of the work. A conclusion lets your reader know that you've finished developing your ideas and shows them your final position. It is the last word on the points you have made in your writing. In addition, a good conclusion leaves the marker with a good final impression (just as they are about to allocate a mark to your efforts). Always end with a definite statement . . . as this concluding paragraph does.

> **TIP**   7–14
>
> Tips on writing a conclusion:
>
> - Do make it brief and to the point.
> - Do answer the core question arising from your diagnosis.
> - Do not introduce completely new ideas.
> - Do not conclude with a cliché.
> - Do not apologise for anything you have said.
> - Do not contradict yourself.
> - Do not merely summarise what has gone before: remember that a conclusion is not the same as a summary.

Activity 7.5

This complements Activity 7.2 on introductions. Imagine those same four students have also written conclusions to the same essay, as set out below. Bearing in mind the advice above, look at these attempts and evaluate them.   7–15

Example 1:

> I have attempted to show in this essay that the rule that a third party may not sue on a contract made for his/her benefit is indeed outmoded. Several cases have been analysed, although some were slightly out of date (i.e. from before the statute). This essay also examined whether the 1999 Act has made any difference at all. The question of the Act's impact on trusts was also discussed but we concluded that this was probably true although we are unable to say for sure.

Example 2:

> My essay has therefore looked at all the cases concerning privity from before the Act like *Beswick v Beswick* and *Jackson v Horizon Holidays* and all the cases since the Act came into force. It is clear that Mrs Beswick would now be able to sue her nephew directly. It is interesting to also consider the Act's impact in the area of Tort e.g. *Junior Books Ltd v Veitchi Co Ltd*. Whether the Act has such far-reaching consequences as was originally feared—only time will tell!

Example 3:

> I have looked at the nature and impact of the rule on privity of contract. To a large extent this may now be regarded as historical with the major development of the enactment of the Contracts (Rights of Third Parties) Act 1999. What is clear is that the operation of the Act is essentially governed by the choice of the parties to the contract. As such it is not the case that the rules on privity are outmoded as in reality many contracts expressly make it clear that there is no intention to create rights under the Act.

Example 4:

> The privity of contract rule is not outmoded and the Act doesn't really have much of an impact after all.

Compare your views:

Example 1: do you think this writer has much confidence in what they have written? Phrases such as "I have attempted", "slightly out of date" and "unable to say for sure" do not make us trust that this reader knows what they are talking about. It repeats what was in the essay (the Act's impact on trusts was also discussed) and indeed doesn't really finish properly. It just comes to an end as if the writer's pen ran out!

Example 2: this writer adopts the "repeat it again in the conclusion and it'll have more impact" approach to the writing of conclusions. However, there does seem to be some attempt at giving an overview and an attempt to set the points in a wider context.

Example 3: this conclusion is appropriate. It refers back to the main points of the title and makes a reasoned conclusion based on the question apparently having been answered. It ends positively and leaves us with a good impression.

Example 4: too brief and bland!

You have now considered the approach to take when creating and developing a good structure to your writing. You need to match this structure with a sound grasp of written English. This is considered in the following chapter.

Summary of Chapter 7

7–16

- Structuring your work with an introduction, main body and conclusion will help you to communicate your understanding to the reader.
- You must plan your writing carefully to achieve a coherent structure.
- The introduction should express your diagnosis of the task.
- The main body of your assignment should form a logical and linked progression.
- The conclusion should give your overall position.

8 Writing in good English

What is the purpose of this chapter?

8–1 We cannot repeat too often that the cornerstone of successful legal writing is good communication. In order to communicate well, it is necessary to use language which your reader can easily understand, which in the current context means English. Your tutors are likely to require you to do the following:

- use English grammar accurately including appropriate sentence construction;
- write in an appropriate academic style, including making accurate use of technical legal terms and phrases.

If you have any concerns about whether you are able to do these, then work through this chapter which contains a number of exercises and worked examples which we hope will help you to improve your written English. Although this is not a grammar textbook, and therefore we can discuss these issues only briefly, by the end of this chapter you should understand:

- the importance of writing in good English;
- the main principles of sentence construction;
- how to avoid common punctuation errors, such as misuse of apostrophes; and
- what constitutes good academic style for your writing.

To gauge your existing skills, try the following exercise:

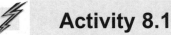 ## Activity 8.1

8–2 Have a look at the following paragraph and then consider the questions which follow:

> In 1966 the House of Lord's issued the Practice Statement, it's significance cannot be underrated. As it allowed the Law Lords' to depart from they're own previous decisions where they thought it was right to do so, this went against the authority of the London Tramways case, who's influence had lasted since 1898. The cases purpose was to ensure that the law would be consistent by making the Lord's decisions binding on themselves, however, it also meant that the law couldnt develop for modern times. Consequently, the Practice Statement reversed the position which gave potential for the Lords to make decisions appropriate for modern day's. But the Practice Statements main danger is that it could make the law uncertain if it's over-used and therefore its important to note that the Lord's have shown they will only use it sparingly.

How would you grade your reaction to this piece of writing?

A. I did not notice any mistakes.
B. I noticed a few mistakes but the meaning of the paragraph is still clear.
C. I thought the level of mistakes was irritating and interfered with my understanding of the paragraph.
D. I was so irritated by the mistakes that I stopped reading for content and started counting the mistakes.

Of course, there's no right answer to this question; the idea is to gauge your reaction which is personal to you. Your reaction will probably depend on a number of factors, including:

- whether you were "drilled" in English grammar at school (which in turn depends on where and when you went to school);
- whether you have dyslexia, which can make it more difficult to recognise spelling and grammar errors, and consequently more difficult to correct them;
- whether English is your first language (if it is not, this may help you because more attention may have been paid to grammar when you learned English, but can also make it more difficult if you do not have the same "instinct" for English that you have in your first language);
- whether you are reading this or listening to it through a screen reader which will have done what it can to make sense of the mistakes (but may not have made a very good job);
- how old you are (there have been trends in the teaching of grammar in state education in recent years).

Compare your views:

Answer A: If you did not notice any mistakes, then you are likely to need to put in some work on your own grammar, punctuation and spelling, as there are a large number of mistakes in this piece, which—to those who regard these matters as serious (a body of people which is likely to include the tutors marking your work as well as many of those to whom you might be applying for work in due course)—are seriously distracting from the author's message.

Answer B: You clearly have some idea about grammar and punctuation but do not regard these as seriously detrimental to effective communication. Again, as with answer A, you are going to have to put some work in to make sure that mistakes in something you don't regard as particularly important don't affect the rating of your work by those who do regard these matters as important.

Answers C and D: If you felt that the level of mistakes in this paragraph seriously interfered with your attention to the meaning of the paragraph, then you already understand why we are stressing the importance of good grammar and spelling as part of effective communication. And the fact that you were able to spot the mistakes is likely to mean that you already have a good standard of written English, so you may find that you are already familiar with the rules covered in this chapter.

If you answered either A or B to this exercise, were you surprised to be offered the choices in C and D? If you have not been schooled to regard accurate grammar, punctuation and/or spelling as fundamentally important, it can be difficult to realise the emphasis which is placed on them by others (and particularly the tutors marking your work).

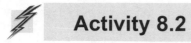

Activity 8.2

8–3   If you didn't count the mistakes, try doing so now (hint: look out for missing apostrophes, apostrophes used where they are not needed and commas in place of full stops).

Compare your views:

Now have a look at the following, where the basic grammar and punctuation errors have been highlighted. There is more information about this later:

In 1966 the House of Lord's issued the Practice Statement, it's significance cannot be underrated. As it allowed the Law Lords' to depart from they're own previous decisions where they thought it was right to do so, this went against the authority of the London Tramways case, who's influence had lasted since 1898. The cases purpose was to ensure that the law would be consistent by making the Lord's decisions binding on themselves, however, it also meant that the law couldnt develop for modern times. Consequently, the Practice Statement reversed the position which gave potential for the Lords to make decisions appropriate for modern day's. But the Practice Statements main danger is that it could make the law uncertain if it's over-used and therefore its important to note that the Lord's have shown they will only use it sparingly.

How many did you spot? We counted 17 mistakes, although many of these were the same mistake repeated on more than one occasion. We'll return to this example, and explore what the mistakes are in more detail later on in the chapter. The more you spotted, the easier it will be for you to understand how distracting it is to read material which contains a number of errors. This demonstrates the first reason why it is important to get matters of spelling and grammar right. It is a simple matter of communication: maximise the effect of your message by making sure it is easy for the person marking it to understand what you are saying. You might feel that the point of the message is more important than the presentation, but not only are you likely to be given specific marks for presentation in assignments (although your institution may be more flexible on these matters in exam situations), a poor level of communication will reduce your marks across the board because it is more difficult for the examiner or marker to follow what you are saying. (If someone sent you an expensive but delicate present in the post without packing it carefully, and it therefore arrived in pieces, the notion that it's the thought that counts isn't much consolation, is it?) Even if you only noticed one mistake, your attention was distracted from the writer's explanation and argument. The more mistakes you noticed, the more your attention was distracted. Your tutors are likely to regard such matters as important and therefore your work will lose impact. Even aside from any specific marks which may be allocated to reward good use of English in the assessment criteria, an answer which contains a distracting number of basic grammatical errors simply loses authority.

So, accurate grammar is important because it enables you to communicate effectively with whoever is marking your work. The reason why we place such importance on this is not solely because law lecturers are a bunch of sad people who have nothing better to do than sit around the staff room exchanging horror stories about misplaced commas. Grammar is especially important for a lawyer because he or she may have to draft complex documents, and grammar will provide essential signposts as to the meaning. You will already have begun to learn about the importance of *interpretation* as a legal skill, and the construction of grammar can be a vital part of that interpretation. Even a single error could make a vital difference. Finally, think about those job applications you'll be making later. Which do you think has a better chance of impressing an employer—a well-put together application with correct spelling and grammar, or an application with good content ruined by grammatical errors?

We'll return to the example in the activity shortly. Before we do, we're going to look briefly at a few issues about spelling and grammar which some of our students have raised in the past.

What if I'm really bad at grammar and spelling?

Being good at grammar and spelling has nothing to do with intelligence. Some people have more of an instinct for it than others, some have been better taught than others, some have genuine difficulties with it. However, *paying attention* to spelling and grammar *is* a matter of intelligence. The intelligent student reflects on his or her standard and if it isn't up to scratch, does something about it. Look at it this way: if your work is otherwise very good, poor spelling and grammar might cost you those few marks which could be the difference between a good mark and an excellent mark. On the other hand, if the rest of your work is satisfactory, you'd be crazy to risk tipping it down below the satisfactory level by ignoring your spelling and grammar. That said, you are studying law, not English and/or grammar. You will need to use (and if necessary learn) a satisfactory level of grammar so that the meaning of your message is clear. Work through this chapter and you should have an idea of the basics. **8–4**

Should I make use of spelling and grammar checkers?

If you are using a word processing package like Microsoft Word it will have a facility to check your grammar and spelling (in Word, which is the package in commonest use, these are found in the Tools menu). It is also likely to have an "autocorrect" facility. Opinions on the value of these tools differ. A spelling checker is a good way of spotting mis-spelled words and typographical errors and if you have one, then do make use of it. It is no substitute for a careful read through, however, because it can only identify spelling errors by means of highlighting words which are not recognised in its dictionary. Hence it couldn't pick up errors like *In the House of Lords, witch is the highest domestic caught* for *In the House of Lords, which is the highest domestic court* because "witch" and "caught" are both accurately spelled words used in the wrong context. **8–5**

If you commonly mis-spell (or mis-type) certain words then you can also use the automatic correction facility in your word processing program (in Word, it is called AutoCorrect). These days, it is common for a number of common mis-spellings to be pre-programmed into word processors (for example when I typed *dictionery* in the preceding paragraph, my PC helpfully changed it to *dictionary* for me without being asked because it guessed that was what I meant) but you can add further ones.

Grammar checkers are generally less reliable (perhaps because the rules of grammar are more difficult to apply than highlighting any words not found in the dictionary, which is essentially what the spelling checker is doing). Using a grammar check is therefore unfortunately no substitute for understanding the basic rules of grammar and being able to apply them in your writing.

I'm dyslexic—can I overcome this?

8–6 Dyslexia and other learning disabilities make effective writing, including grammar and spelling, more difficult. It does not mean however, that your institution can be more lenient: we've already seen how important accurate grammar is in the study and application of law and this applies equally to students with dyslexia. What your institution **can** do is to make sure you have the support you need to improve and attain a satisfactory standard. Seek advice from your tutors at an early stage as to how you can access specialist help, and if appropriate, assistive software. Other allowances such as additional time in exams may be appropriate. It is very important to realise that this support will be given to enable you to be assessed **on the same terms as everyone else**, so the responsibility is then on you to make sure that you use the support available to meet the right standard.

Does spelling, grammar and sentence construction really matter?

8–7 You may well be thinking "Surely the content is more important than a few old rules about sentences? Why are my tutor's perceptions of sentence construction any better than mine?" We have some sympathy for this point of view, but we've already explained that in terms of effective communication, it makes sense to make sure you follow the standard rules—so as to give your laboriously produced content the best showcase. If you want a further reason why it is important to pay attention to grammar and sentence construction, have a think about the following example.

There is a programme called *Dragons' Den* shown regularly on BBC2—you may have seen it— in which budding entrepreneurs appeal to a panel of millionaires (the "dragons") for funding for an invention or a business idea. If convinced, the dragons provide funding and bargain with the contestant for a suitable share of the business. If not convinced, the contestant leaves empty-handed. One of the panel consistently comments on the standard of dress of the contestants, as he believes that when appealing for funding for a business venture, business attire should be worn. Now, you might think, "surely the quality of the venture is what's important, rather than what people are wearing?" This is entirely a matter of debate (just as it is a matter of debate whether we should throw out the old rules of grammar and embrace text message style writing instead) but the crucial point, however you feel about formal dress, is that *the dragons are the ones with the money*. Therefore, knowing this particular dragon feels that business attire is important, anyone who goes into the "den" in casual clothes is automatically jeopardising his or her case.

The point here is that *your* views on grammar and spelling are important but they are not as important as your tutors'! This may sound harsh, and by all means make it your mission to become the Vice-Chancellor of a university and change the rules on the weight to be attached to matters of grammar and style. For the time being, however, bear in mind that a good degree will be of considerable use to you in this quest and therefore it would be wise to play the game for the time being. If it is any consolation, mastering only a few relatively straightforward rules is all that is needed to drastically improve the way your work comes across, if you currently have problems with grammar.

We're now going to return to the example in the earlier activity, which is reproduced again below.

Worked example

In 1966 the House of Lord's issued the Practice Statement, it's significance cannot be underrated. As it allowed the Law Lords' to depart from they're own previous decisions where they thought it was right to do so, this went against the authority of the London Tramways case, who's influence had lasted since 1898. The cases purpose was to ensure that the law would be consistent by making the Lord's decisions binding on themselves, however, it also meant that the law couldnt develop for modern times. Consequently, the Practice Statement reversed the position which gave potential for the Lords to make decisions appropriate for modern day's. But the Practice Statements main danger is that it could make the law uncertain if it's over-used and therefore its important to note that the Lord's have shown they will only use it sparingly.

These mistakes fall into the following categories:

- Misuse of apostrophes (using one when it is not needed or missing one which is needed).
- Confusion over when a comma is needed and when a full stop is needed, or to put it another way, not writing in complete sentences and/or getting confused about using "But" and "However".

Here is a more detailed explanation, taking it section by section:

In 1966 the House of Lord's issued the Practice Statement, it's significance cannot be underrated.

In this sentence, the first problem is with the apostrophes. *House of Lord's* does not need an apostrophe because it is simply the name of the court—it should read *House of Lords* (because *Lords* is the plural of *Lord*). *It's* does **not** need an apostrophe because it is a *possessive* (in other words, indicates that the "significance" is something which "belongs" to the Practice Statement: the use of *its* in this sentence is a shorter way of saying *the significance of the Practice Statement cannot be underrated*)— it should simply be *its*. If you didn't spot these, then look at the section on apostrophes below.

The second problem is with the sentence construction. What we have here are two statements:

1. In 1966 the House of Lords issued the Practice Statement
2. Its significance cannot be underrated.

The two statements are linked together with a comma, but both statements work independently as complete *clauses*, so it is **incorrect** to join them with a comma. Instead a full stop should be used to divide the statements, or a semicolon can be used where you want to retain the link between the statements (alternatively a word like "and" could be used to link the statements). Using a comma to join two separate independent clauses like this is called a "comma splice" and it is a very common mistake. If you didn't spot it, then make sure you read the section on comma splices later in this chapter, as you can improve your writing by learning to eliminate this one mistake.

As it allowed the Law Lords' to depart from they're own previous decisions where they thought it was right to do so, this went against the authority of the London Tramways case, who's influence had lasted since 1898.

We have three more apostrophe mistakes here. We already know *Law Lords'* doesn't need an apostrophe when it is used simply as a plural, so it should read *Law Lords*. There are two further apostrophe errors which have led to spelling mistakes: *they're* when *their* was meant (because the meaning is *the previous decisions belonging to them* rather than *they are*); *who's* when *whose* was meant (again this is a confusion between a *possessive* word and an apostrophe indicating *omission*). These are discussed in the section on apostrophes later in the chapter if you didn't spot them.

As well as the apostrophe errors, there is another problem with the sentence construction. *As it allowed* is not the right way to begin a sentence, although it would have been an acceptable way to continue the *previous* sentence (if a comma rather than a full stop had been used). On the other hand, before *this went against . . .* a full stop *is* needed, because a phrase like this indicates a new sentence is starting. *This went against the authority of the London Tramways case, whose influence had lasted since 1898* is a complete sentence statement in itself and therefore cannot be preceded by a comma. It is another example of a *comma splice*.

> The cases purpose was to ensure that the law would be consistent by making the Lord's decisions binding on themselves, however, it also meant that the law couldnt develop for modern times.

We've got three more apostrophe mistakes here. *The cases purpose* is an example of possession (it means the purpose of the case) so it should read *The case's purpose*. *The Lord's decisions* is also an example of possession, so it is correct to use an apostrophe, but it has been put in the wrong place because there is more than one Lord—it should be *The Lords' decision* (decision of the Lords). How to deal with possessive apostrophes is covered later in the chapter. You will probably have spotted the missing apostrophe in *couldnt*, which needs an apostrophe to indicate the omission of the *o* in *could not*. Generally in formal academic writing it is better to use *could not* rather than *couldn't* in any case (there is more on academic style towards the end of the chapter).

There is also a further example of comma splice in this example. If you look at what the sentence is saying there are two statements:

1. The case's purpose was to ensure that the law would be consistent by making the Lords' decisions binding on themselves
2. however, it also meant that the law couldn't develop for modern times

Both these statements are complete in themselves, so should be linked by a semi colon or separated by a full stop. Alternatively, the word *however* could be replaced with *but*. As the word *but* cannot be used to begin a sentence, this would mean statement 2 is not complete in itself anymore, and therefore the comma would be appropriate. It is a good tip to remember that *however* should follow a full stop and *but* should follow a comma. Follow this up in the sentence construction section later if you need to.

> Consequently, the Practice Statement reversed the position which gave potential for the Lords to make decisions appropriate for modern day's.

Arguably this sentence could be improved with a comma after *position* to make it easier to read, but this can be classed as a matter of taste. The only real error here is another apostrophe where none is needed in the word *day's* which is simply a plural (more than one day), and which should therefore be written *days*.

> But the Practice Statements main danger is that it could make the law uncertain if it's over-used and therefore its important to note that the Lord's have shown they will only use it sparingly.

You already know that *But* should not be used to open a sentence (you often see it used at the beginning of a sentence, as this particular rule is one which is frequently broken as a matter of style —we have done this ourselves—but it is better to stick to the rules in academic work). Having checked that this is a complete statement in itself, then the *But* should be replaced with *However*, to correct the sentence. The paragraph should therefore read:

> In 1966 the House of Lords issued the Practice Statement. Its significance cannot be underrated, as it allowed the Law Lords to depart from their own previous decisions where they thought it was right to do so. This went against the authority of the London Tramways case, whose influence had lasted since 1898. The case's purpose was to ensure that the law would be consistent by making the Lord's decisions binding on themselves, but it also meant that the law could not develop for modern times. Consequently, the Practice Statement reversed the position, which gave potential for the Lords to make decisions appropriate for modern days. However, the Practice Statement's main danger is that it could make the law uncertain if it is over-used and therefore it is important to note that the Lords have shown they will only use it sparingly.

Next, we're going to follow up the main errors which featured in this example; first, we will explore sentence construction, including use of appropriate grammar and joining words, and secondly, we will look in more detail at the correct use of apostrophes.

How can I improve my sentence construction?

Although this is not a grammar lesson, a basic understanding of some of the principles of   **8–8** grammar will help you to improve your writing. These days, thanks to the best-selling book by Lynne Truss, a commonly known example of the difference in meaning which a misplaced comma can make is the story about the panda who has a meal and then commits a massacre before departing, because he "eats, shoots and leaves" (instead of "eats shoots and leaves" which would indicate, as intended, the favoured food choices of the panda). Truss's book (it is actually called *Eats, Shoots & Leaves*, if you haven't heard of it)[1] is a humorous but meticulous account of various rules on spelling and grammar and is highly recommended if you really want to get to grips with the subject.

As Truss points out, many matters relating to placement of commas and other punctuation are a matter of taste. However, there are some basic rules and an understanding of these basic principles will improve your writing. One error which has already been mentioned, and which causes annoyance, is the matter of the *comma splice*—using a comma where a full stop or semi-colon is needed. This is caused by a basic misunderstanding about what forms a complete sentence—which also leads to misuse of full-stops and words like *however*. The ability to write in complete sentences is an important element of expressing yourself clearly and will help your reader (i.e. the marker) to understand your argument more easily.

---

[1] TRUSS, L. *Ears, Shoots & Leaves*. London: Profile books, 2003.

What makes up a sentence?

8–9   Here is a basic summary of the principles of sentence construction:

- A sentence is made up of one or more *clauses*.
- Clauses may be *independent*—also referred to as *main* clauses—which means (as is pretty self-explanatory) that they may stand alone as complete sentences, or alternatively *dependent* (also called *subordinate*) in which case they must be joined to an independent clause and cannot stand alone as a sentence.
- An independent or main clause which stands alone as a complete sentence is called a *simple* sentence. However, more than one independent clause can be linked together to make a *compound* sentence. A dependent clause **must** be joined to an independent one to form a *complex* sentence. We explain this later in the chapter.
- To be independent, a clause must contain a verb (essentially, an action) and a subject (someone or something doing the action). The verb must be in a finite form (in other words, not in the infinitive form like *to be* or *to go* but with a tense, for example past, present or future).

Simple and compound sentences

> **The students** *handed in* their coursework last week. **It** *is being marked* at the moment. **The tutors** *will return* the feedback in a few days' time.

8–10   Here we have three statements. Each has a subject (highlighted in bold) and a verb in finite form (in italics)—the first sentence uses the past tense, the second the present tense, and the third sentence the future tense. Therefore each statement is an independent clause so it is quite correct to separate them out into three simple sentences using full stops. Note that a sentence always begins with a capital letter and ends with a full stop (or a question mark or an exclamation mark, if more appropriate to the context).

As an alternative form of punctuation, semi-colons or colons could be used *instead of* full stops. Semi-colons can be used in the same places as full stops and have the effect of separating the clauses but not as completely as a full stop: the clauses have more of a link. Colons are used between independent clauses to indicate, loosely, that one is the consequence of the previous one, although both are matters of style:

> The students handed in their coursework last week; it is being marked at the moment: the tutors will return the feedback in a few days' time.

Note that this is now one (compound) sentence, so it still begins with a capital letter and ends with a full stop, but after a colon or semicolon a lower case letter is used (unless there is another reason to have a capital letter, for example someone's name).

Avoiding a comma splice

It is important to grasp that although it is fine to substitute a colon or a semi-colon for a full stop, **8–11** where appropriate to your meaning, it is **not** acceptable to use commas in place of full stops. Therefore the following is wrong:

> The students handed in their coursework last week, it is being marked at the moment, the tutors will return the feedback in a few days' time.

This is an example of a *comma splice*, which simply means a comma being used (incorrectly) to join (i.e. splice) two independent clauses together.

Conjunctions

A further correct way of handling these three independent clauses would be to link them together **8–12** using a *conjunction*. This would also make a compound sentence. Conjunctions are "joining words", for example:

- *and*—where the independent clauses express a linked idea or a continuation of a theme;
- *but*—where the independent clauses express opposite or contrasting positions;
- *or*—where the independent clauses are alternatives;
- *so*—where the position in one independent clause leads to the next one.

Which do you think would be appropriate in relation to our three statements? You should spot that these statements are linked and continuing, rather than contrasting or alternatives, so *and* is the appropriate link here (arguably *so* could also be used). However, if we try that, it comes out like this:

> The students handed in their coursework last week and it is being marked at the moment and the tutors will return the feedback in a few days' time.

Although *and* is the right conjunction to use here, using it twice like this sounds childish. When using conjunctions to link clauses into compound sentences you need to take care not to overdo it—the following is better:

> The students handed in their coursework last week; it is being marked at the moment and the tutors will return the feedback in a few days' time.

Where the two clauses express opposing or contrasting positions, then the appropriate conjunction is *but*. For example:

> The House of Lords can use the Practice Statement 1966 "when it is right to do so", but in practice it is used rarely.

Here the two statements are:

1. **The House of Lords** *can use* the Practice Statement 1966 "when it is right to do so"
2. but in practice **it** *is* used rarely.

These are both independent clauses (both have a **subject** and a *finite verb*) but the statements are contrasting: on the one hand the House of Lords has a free hand to use its Practice Statement power; on the other hand in practice this power is not used very much. Therefore *but* is the right conjunction here.

Could you substitute *however* instead of *but*? The answer here is definitely "no"—although this is a very common (and irritating) practice. *However* is not a conjunction and therefore **must not** be used to *join* two independent clauses. It can be used only as *part* of an independent clause—usually at the beginning followed by a comma, but also potentially elsewhere (which sometimes has the unfortunate appearance of being used as a conjunction—we'll show you what we mean by this shortly).

Therefore:

> The House of Lords can use the Practice Statement 1966 "when it is right to do so", but in practice it is used rarely.

is correct (two independent clauses joined with the conjunction *but*), and

> The House of Lords can use the Practice Statement 1966 "when it is right to do so". However, in practice it is used rarely.

is also correct (two simple sentences—*however* is an appropriate beginning for a sentence). Therefore

> The House of Lords can use the Practice Statement 1966 "when it is right to do so"; however, in practice it is used rarely.

is also correct (because the semi-colon is an appropriate substitute for the full stop to divide the independent clauses less completely than the full stop would do—and to remind us that the separation is less distinct. The word *however* loses its capital letter).

But—and this is an important *but*—the following example is wrong:

> The House of Lords can use the Practice Statement 1966 "when it is right to do so", however, in practice it is used rarely.

As *however* is not a conjunction but rather, part of an independent clause, this is also an example of a comma splice (because the two independent clauses are only separated by the comma). This is a common mistake which might lead to feedback like "you don't always write in complete sentences".

Unfortunately there is no easy trick to help you remember this rule. The basic gist is that *however* should only follow a full stop, colon or semicolon, and never a comma, but this is only true where the *however* is at the beginning of its clause. It is fine to re-order the clause so that the "however" comes at the end, in which case it would look like this:

> The House of Lords can use the Practice Statement 1966 "when it is right to do so". In practice it is used rarely, however.

This means that the rule "However mustn't follow a comma" is not always true. Hopefully you can see that even with the *however* at the end, the distinction between these two independent clauses has been appropriately marked with a full stop. This is something you will simply have to look out for.

Another common mistake is to misuse *this* in the same way. For example:

> In 1966 the House of Lords issued the Practice Statement, this gave the Lords power to overrule their previous rulings.

The use of *this* makes the second clause here an independent one. Therefore these should be separated with a full stop or linked with a semi-colon.

Choosing how to join or separate your clauses

It is not always necessary to use conjunctions to join independent clauses at all. Returning to our previous example of the coursework marking, the original three simple sentences work well, but as a matter of style using simple sentences continually throughout an essay tends to give it rather a simplistic feeling. For example:

8–13

> Negligence is a tort. It has several elements. The first element is duty of care. The claimant must show they are owed a duty in law and a duty in fact. Duty in law means it falls within the categories of negligence.

Too much of this and your readers will start to feel they are being addressed by a Dalek. It would be better to create more compound sentences, for example:

> Negligence is a tort and it has several elements. The first element is duty of care: the claimant must show they are owed a duty in law and a duty in fact. Duty in law means it falls within the categories of negligence.

On the other hand, it is possible to go too far and leave a reader mentally gasping for breath:

> Negligence is a tort and it has several elements; the first element is duty of care: the claimant must show they are owed a duty in law and a duty in fact; duty in law means it falls within the categories of negligence.

Generally, for the sake of clarity, it is a good rule to limit your sentences to 20–25 words or so. Putting in a full stop gives your reader a bit of breather. Combining the use of simple and compound sentences can be an effective style tool, and we'll consider that later on in the chapter.

One final note about these conjunctions is that technically they should be used *only* to join independent clauses to turn a simple sentence into a compound one. This is the source of the "rule" that you should not begin a sentence with *and, but, or* or *so*. However, as already discussed, this is a rule which it is generally seen as acceptable to break occasionally as a matter of style. Nevertheless, you would be wise to adhere to it most of the time: breaking it frequently will tend to make your writing sound too informal (you will note that we've done it quite frequently, because the tone is meant to be less formal). To help you avoid too much use of *but* and *and* at the beginning of your sentences, here are some suggested alternatives to use to begin an independent clause which opens a sentence (you should put a comma after them in this situation):

and	As well as, Additionally,
but	However,
or	Instead, Alternatively,
so	In consequence, Therefore,

It is worth noting that the rule in relation to *however* discussed above (i.e. it cannot be used to join two independent clauses) applies equally to most of the words in the second column but as a matter of style it is the misuse of *however* which is the commonest and most grating error.

Dependent or subordinate clauses and complex sentences

8–14   If the clause does not contain the necessary elements of subject and finite verb, then it will be a dependent clause. A dependent clause cannot be a sentence on its own but must be joined appropriately to an independent clause to make a complex sentence.

Have a look at the following example:

> The tort of negligence contains a number of elements which are essential to a successful claim.

The two statements here are:

- The tort of negligence contains a number of elements
- which are essential to a successful claim.

Do you consider these statements to be dependent or independent? If you are unsure, try to identify the subject and the finite verb. If you can spot these then you must be looking at an independent or main clause.

On this basis, you should be able to identify the first statement as an independent clause. It contains a subject (*the tort of negligence*) and a finite verb (*contains*—here in the present tense). You may find, instinctively, that the second statement "doesn't feel like a sentence" rather than being able to immediately identify why. If so, that's fine—you are correct, and the instinct you have about what makes a sentence and what does not will help you punctuate your sentences appropriately. If the second statement does not feel instinctively wrong then try applying the rules instead: does the clause have a finite verb? Yes, it does—*are* (present tense plural form of the verb *to be*). Does it have a subject? No, it doesn't. All it has is *which*, which is not a subject. Therefore this is a dependent (or subordinate) clause.

The vital rule to remember with **dependent clauses** is that they **cannot stand alone as a sentence**. Therefore it would be wrong to write:

> The tort of negligence contains a number of elements. Which are essential to a successful claim.

Instead, the dependent clause must be joined to an independent or main clause, using a subordinate conjunction. The one in the example is *which*. Other common ones include *when, where, while, until, unless, although, because* (or similar words like *as* or *since*). All of these essentially indicate the "relationship" between the dependent clause and the independent clause to which it is attached. In legal reasoning, it is important to use these appropriately, and understanding these will also help your reading of texts. There is more on this in Ch.6.

Making sure your sentence is consistent

Your subject and verb should match each other in terms of being singular or plural. In most cases this is extremely straightforward; you are extremely unlikely to write *The law on this point are discriminatory* instead of *is discriminatory*, or *The Law Lords comes from a narrow social background* instead of *come from*, because both of these examples look and sound so odd.   **8–15**

However, the rule about matching the subject and the verb can be more difficult in certain situations, for example with subjects where the line between plural and singular seems blurred (words like Parliament and jury, which can be viewed as a single body or a number of different people). In cases like this, you can treat the body as singular or plural—*it* or *they*—but you do need to be consistent.

A further word which causes difficulty is *none*. Here there is no room for flexibility: although it is common in spoken English in particular to regard *none* as a plural (*None of us are going*) that is wrong, and it must be treated as a singular. Therefore:

None of the precedents **is** binding is correct, as the singular *none* matches the singular form *is*.

So, in summary:

> **TIP**
>
> The trick to getting this right is to remember that *none* equals *not one*—try mentally substituting *not one* in sentences where you want to use *none* and you will never make a mistake as to the form of the verb.

Independent clause = simple sentence.
Independent clause + independent clause = compound sentence (join with a conjunction, a colon or a semicolon; NOT a comma).
Independent clause + dependent clause = complex sentence (join with a subordinate conjunction).
Each sentence needs a capital letter and a full stop (or question/exclamation mark).
Your subjects and verbs must match each other as to singular and plural forms.

We've touched on common punctuation in discussing sentence structure but we're now going to return to the punctuation mark which seems to cause more problems than all the rest put together: the apostrophe.

What's all the fuss about apostrophes?

Misuse of apostrophes (using one when it isn't needed, missing out one when it is needed, using one when needed but putting it in the wrong place) probably accounts for more of the grammatical errors commonly made than any other single mistake. If you can get this right, then you will be well on the way to making sure your work is of an appropriate standard in grammatical terms.   **8–16**

The most common mistakes to avoid are:

- using apostrophes for plurals;
- mixing up it's and its;
- mixing up other possessives with omissions;
- putting unnecessary apostrophes in possessive pronouns;
- putting apostrophes in unnecessary places.

Mistake 1: Using apostrophes for plurals

8–17   No apostrophe is needed for plurals.

Example:

✗The court's have indicated that . . .
✔The courts have indicated that . . .

Mistake 2: Mixing up *it's* and *its*

8–18   These have different and separate meanings: **It's** means *it is* or *it has*, while **its** means *of it* or *belonging to it*:

✗ Its important to acknowledge it's influence . . .
✔ It's important to acknowledge its influence . . .

The apostrophe is needed to indicate omission but not (in this case) for possession (because *its* is a possessive pronoun and the possession is therefore already built in to the word).

Mistake 3: Mixing up other *possessives* with *omissions* (whose and who's, theirs and there's, your and you're)

8–19   ✗ Lord Reid was a very influential judge who's opinions have a very high precedent value . . .
✔ Lord Reid was a very influential judge whose opinions have a very high precedent value . . .

Mistake 4: Putting unnecessary apostrophes in possessive pronouns (his, hers, theirs, ours, yours)

8–20   ✗ Her's was the best argument in terms of presentation, but ours' had the legal authority.
✔ Hers was the best argument in terms of presentation, but ours had the legal authority.

Mistake 5: Putting apostrophes in the wrong places

8–21   ✗ The judge's opinions were inconsistent (which makes it sound like there was only one judge who was inconsistent with himself or herself—not entirely impossible but the alternative below is more likely).
✔ The judges' opinions were inconsistent (this indicates there were several judges whose opinions were inconsistent with each other).

> **TIP**
>
> If you don't feel very confident about when and where to use an apostrophe, then the next few pages of this section explain in more detail. If you already feel quite confident that you can avoid the mistakes listed above, then just skim through the next few pages or move to the next section.

When should I use an apostrophe?

The two most important uses of the apostrophe are the following: **8–22**

1. to indicate a *possessive* (something which "belongs" to something or someone or is "of" someone or something)

> The judge's opinion (one judge)
> The judges' opinion (more than one judge)
> The woman's defence
> The women's defence

2. to indicate omission (letters missed out)

> It's important to note
> This isn't a valid argument
> The facts don't raise any issue of negligence
> There's a problem with this reasoning
> Who's going to win this case?

There are further examples of these on the following pages. In formal academic writing, it is best to be sparing with the latter, which has the advantage that if you don't use them, you can't make a mistake with them.

In contrast, you do NOT use apostrophes for:

1. simple plurals

> The courts are busy
> These cases can be criticised

2. possessive pronouns (*his*, *hers*, *yours*, *its*, *ours*, *theirs*) as the "possession" is already built into the word.

There are further examples of when **not** to use an apostrophe later in the chapter.

More on possessive apostrophes

Remember possessive apostrophes indicate something which "belongs to" someone or something or   **8–23**
is "of" someone or something:

> The barrister's arguments failed to sway the judge

Test whether you need an apostrophe by turning the phrase round into "the arguments of the barrister". This way you can see that the arguments "belong to" the barrister so the apostrophe is needed. On the other hand "The barristers argued before the judge for three hours" would turn round into "The argued of the barristers", which is obviously nonsense. This indicates that barristers in this sense is a simple plural and needs no apostrophe.

Indicating "joint" ownership

For example:

8–24

> The women's defence

Here, although you are talking about the defence of more than one woman, the plural "women" accounts for this already, so you treat it in exactly the same way as if it was only *one* woman's defence.

On the other hand, if you want to indicate the arguments of more than one barrister, you are talking about the arguments of the barrister**s**, which turns into:

> The barristers' arguments (no extra *s* is needed after the apostrophe)

This shows that turning the phrase round also helps you work out where to place the apostrophe when you are dealing with plurals.

> The judge's reasoning = the reasoning of the judge
> The judges' reasoning = the reasoning of the judges

Singulars which end in *s*

8–25   This can cause confusion, and there are varying opinions. Truss explores these and suggests that the modern approach (which is also the most straightforward way, and we'd therefore advise you to follow it) is to treat singulars the same whether or not they end in *s*. In other words: *Lord Simonds's speech* not *Lord Simonds' speech*. The latter is the more traditional approach, and if that is what you have been taught, have been used to or simply prefer, then of course it is perfectly acceptable.

Note: whatever you do, don't remove the *s* on the end of someone's name just because it seems to resolve the issue more easily: *Lord Simond's speech* is certainly wrong. Lord Simonds would not be impressed! Similarly, a name ending in a double *s* always needs an apostrophe and an *s*, not just an apostrophe, for example, *Lynn Truss's book*.

So, in summary:

> Singular, not ending in *s* - use *'s* : The claimant's action (just one claimant)
> Singular, ending in s - use *'s* : Lord Justice James's judgment
> Plural, not ending in s: use *'s* : The children's wishes and feelings
> Plural, ending in *s*: use *'* : The defendants' counter-claim (more than one defendant)

Exceptions to the possessive apostrophe

Just when we thought we had a rule sorted out, we have to note an exception to it (it's always the way). **8–26**
The "turning it round" trick doesn't work with what are called "possessive determiners" (which
simply means words like *my*, *your*, *his*, *her*, *our*, *their*, *its*) because if you try to turn the sentence round
they turn themselves into possessive pronouns such as *mine*, *ours*, *yours*, *his*, *hers*, *theirs*, *its* and ruin
everything. Don't panic—the thing to remember here, as noted earlier, is that the possession is already
"built in" to these words and therefore no apostrophe is needed. Similarly reflexive pronouns like
myself, *herself*, *yourselves* and *ourselves* need no apostrophe. In practice, as long as you remember that
there are no such words as *your's, their's, her's* or *our's*, the only one which is likely to cause any
difficulty is *its* (because, annoyingly, there is of course such a word as *it's*, although it means something different).

So:

> *The argument's logic can be faulted* does need an apostrophe (the logic of the argument).

But:

> *Its logic can be faulted* does NOT need an apostrophe (because although it sounds like it turns round into
> *The logic of it*, it is really *The logic of **its*** and the possession is already denoted).

This, unfortunately, leads to something we know from experience a lot of students have problems
with: telling the difference between *it's* and *its*.

The difference between *it's* and *its*

Truss has the following to say (at pp.43–44) about mixing up *it's* and *its*: **8–27**

> "The confusion of the possessive 'its' (no apostrophe) with the constractive 'it's' (with
> apostrophe) is an unequivocal signal of illiteracy and sets off a simple Pavlovian 'kill' response
> in the average stickler [for 'stickler' in this context, read 'law lecturer']. The rule is: the word
> 'it's' (with apostrophe) stands for 'it is' or 'it has'. If the word does not stand for 'it is' or 'it
> has' then what you require is 'its'. This is extremely easy to grasp. Getting your itses mixed up is
> the greatest solecism in the world of punctuation. No matter that you have a PhD and have
> read all of Henry James twice. If you still persist in writing 'Good food at it's best', you deserve
> to be struck by lightning, hacked up on the spot and buried in an unmarked grave."

Admittedly, that particular fate is unlikely to be specified
in your institution's assessment regulations, but you can
imagine that if that is how such a mistake makes the
person marking your work feel, it is not going to have a
positive effect on your results.

Never use an apostrophe in *it's* unless it makes sense
to say *it is* or *it has* instead.

For example:

> **TIP**
>
> The test is as simple as Truss suggests: if in
> doubt, try substituting *it is* or *it has* in
> your sentence instead of the *its*. If it
> makes sense, you need an "it's". If it
> sounds ridiculous, you need an "its".

> When you write an essay, its not that hard to get its grammar right, and its silly not to check it because its
> effect on your marks could be important.

Try changing every *its* to *it is*:

> When you write an essay, *it is* not that hard to get *it is* grammar right, and *it is* silly not to check it because *it is* effect on your marks could be important.

TIP

Generally in writing an academic essay it is usually preferable to say *it is* rather than *it's*. You can therefore avoid confusion by resolving always to use *it is* in full in your essay writing, never *it's*. This has the simple solution of meaning that your use of *its* will **always** be the possession kind and you will never need an apostrophe.

From this, it should be pretty easy to spot that the first and third uses of *its* can be changed to *it is* and the sentence still makes sense. This means that the *it's* needs an apostrophe to demonstrate the omission. On the other hand, the second and fourth uses of *its* make no sense when *it is* is substituted—this is *its* in the *of it* sense (get the grammar of it right, the effect of it on your marks), and no apostrophe should be used.

The correct version is therefore:

> When you write an essay, it's not that hard to get its grammar right, and it's silly not to check it because its effect on your marks could be important.

More omission apostrophes

8–28   *It's*, which we now know without exception to indicate *it is* or *it has* is the most common use of the omission apostrophe. Other commons ones are:

> isn't = is not
> doesn't = does not
> couldn't = could not
> wouldn't = would not
> shouldn't = should not

These are all pretty straightforward; the only note of caution is that the more you use the shortened versions, the less formal your writing will become, and you do not want to become too informal: use them sparingly, or avoid them altogether.

TIP

With these, use the substitution test as you would for *it's*: *who's* can only be short for *who is*, so if substituting that makes no sense, *whose* must be correct instead. The same is true of *you're* and *there's*. It's trickier with *they're* as if you reject *they are* it could be *their* or *there* but remember that *their* denotes possession which may help.

Some other common ones create more problems because there are other words which sound confusingly similar and can easily be mixed up with them:

They're = *they are*, not to be confused with *their* (belonging to them or of theirs) nor with *there* (denoting a situation or place).

There's = *there is*, not to be confused with *theirs* (a variation on ownership by them).

Who's = *who is*, not to be confused with *whose* (of whom/which).

You're = *you are*, not to be confused with *your* (belonging to you or of you).

Using an apostrophe to indicate a length of time

This can potentially cause problems. An apostrophe is needed in the following examples: **8–29**

> In one week's time, the matter will be considered by the Court of Appeal.
>
> Twelve years' adverse possession will suffice to create legal rights.

The different placement of the apostrophe in the above examples is because one week is singular but twelve years is plural.

But remember, no apostrophe where it is a simple plural:

> The statute was repealed six years ago.

Titles/Names

Dealing with names and titles can cause some difficulty as to whether you need an apostrophe. There is no set rule about these—the only rule is that normal rules do not apply. In other words, for names and titles, you have to adopt the "official" version regardless of whether that complies with grammar.   **8–30**

For example, the House of Lords sounds like it might, somehow, need an apostrophe (in the same way that this hat of Jason's would need an apostrophe) but it doesn't (just as Kingdom of Leather doesn't need one, or indeed Court of Appeal)—this is simply what it is called.

When this does get confusing is if you have to combine such names with possessives. For example:

> In the House of Lords's opinion . . .

In the above examples the trick is to understand that despite the fact that the House of Lords sounds like a plural, it must be treated as singular: it is one court (albeit one made up of a number of judges). When you drop the reference to the court itself, and refer to the judges (the Law Lords or the Lords of Appeal) then of course this is plural:

> In the Law Lords' opinion

TIP

If in doubt, try one of the following strategies:

1. Try and find the phrase in a textbook where it should (hopefully) be punctuated correctly.
2. Try substituting a similar phrase to help you work out how to treat it: The Court of Appeal's opinion doesn't sound so difficult does it? (Then obviously switch back—don't pretend a different court decided the case in the final version!)
3. If you are really stuck, turn the phrase round and leave it like that—*In the opinion of the House of Lords* is fine!

How can I improve my spelling?

8–31   We've already strongly recommended the use of spell-check software to help you improve your spelling if you find that you have trouble with spelling. Of course this facility is not usually going to be available to you in an exam, where it is still the norm to expect students to write long-hand, in the absence of extenuating circumstances. However, although we certainly don't want to encourage you to be careless, you are likely to find that the tutors marking your exam work are far more understanding of spelling errors in an exam situation than they would be when marking a coursework assignment where there was substantial opportunity for review and correction.

Further, as we explained, the spell checker is not really checking your spelling but simply looking for the word you have used in its dictionary. If it isn't there, it assumes it is a spelling error and offers you alternatives. Therefore you have to be on the lookout for words which are only mis-spelled because of the context in which they are placed, as a spellchecker will not identify these as errors.

Common words which you are likely to use in legal writing and which are open to confusion include:

Principle This is the spelling for the noun meaning rule or standard— *the legal principle in this case*.	**Principal** This is the spelling for the adjective denoting the main or primary item—*the principal argument*. (Confusingly it can also be a noun denoting a headteacher—like Principal Skinner—but you are less likely to use this sense in your legal writing.)
Practise Spelt with an *s*, this is the verb form: *I intend to practise as a solicitor* or *I am practising my essay skills*. There is no such word as practicing.	**Practice** Spelt with a *c*, this is a noun: *In practice, this is not an issue*, or *Legal Practice Course*.
Advise Like the previous example, the *s* denotes the verb: *Advise Jim in respect of his criminal liabilities*.	**Advice** Like the previous example, the *c* indicates the noun: *I received excellent legal advice from this firm*.

What other matters do I need to know?

8–32   There are a few other points which may be of use to you in your writing:

Referring to judges

8–33   Additionally, some law-related plurals (especially those involving legal Latin) are confusingly constructed: the abbreviation for Lord or Lady Justice is LJ for example, but remember that the plural of this is LJJ rather than LJs. You can use LJs in your own notes if you like but never in formal legal writing, and then only use the abbreviation as part of the name of the judges: Smith and Jones LJJ agreed that . . . but NOT The LJJ were unanimous in their verdict—in that situation, you should write The Lords Justice were unanimous or The Lords and Lady Justice were unanimous or whatever (although *The appeal judges were unanimous* does the job just as well and avoids the whole tricky problem).

Referring to judgments

In normal English usage, the words *judgement* and *judgment* are interchangeable; inclusion of the middle *e* is simply a matter of preference. However, there is a convention in legal writing that the judgment of a court is always spelt without an *e*. It is therefore common for lawyers to omit the *e* all the time, whatever the context, and it would be a good idea for you to follow this practice so that you never have to think about whether to include the *e*.   **8–34**

Ordering your points

When enumerating points, you may wish to denote the order of your arguments by using "First, second, third" and so on (these are called ordinal numerals). If you do so, note that while you can use *second* and *secondly* (and subsequent numbers) interchangeably, you should avoid the use of *firstly*: simply use *first*. (It is perfectly correct to use *first*, followed by *secondly* and *thirdly*.)   **8–35**

Citing numbers within your text

There is some debate over the correct way to cite numbers in your work. There is general agreement that for lower numbers, the number should be spelt in *words* rather than given in figures (i.e. you should say *seven* rather than *7*). An exception to this general rule is where the figures are part of a case citation or other reference where it is correct to use the figures. With higher numbers, it is appropriate to use *figures*, rather than words (*99* rather than *ninety-nine*). Again you will have spotted that we have not followed this rule ourselves because we are not aiming for a formal academic style in this text.   **8–36**

The moot point is where the line should be drawn between low numbers which you spell out and high numbers which you don't. Twenty is the conventional place to draw the line, and this is logical because this is the point beyond which the full written forms of the numbers become more unwieldy. However, although this is a useful guide which you may wish to adopt, it is not a universal rule; some people suggest ten or twelve.

Citing percentages

When referring to percentages in written work, you should avoid the use of the symbol %. Instead, use the full words *per cent* (remember that this is two words, not one).   **8–37**

All right not alright

There is no such word as alright, despite the fact that it appears to be in common usage. The correct form is *all right*.   **8–38**

Different *from* not different *to*

8–39   The heading pretty much sums up the rule. Avoid the phrase *different to* as it is both sloppy and illogical (if A and B are different then they go away from each other not towards each other). You should always use *different from* instead.

Finally, in this chapter on the practical elements of writing, we are going to look briefly at issues around style in formal legal writing.

How do I write in an academic style?

8–40   For some reason, it seems to be a common mistake to equate "academic argument" with writing in a pompous tone, or that being "learned" is indicated by the length of the words and sentences used. This is not the case. What you should be aiming for is to write in clear and straightforward sentences and language. We've seen that you should not write in simple sentences all the time but should aim to use a mixture of simple, compound and complex sentences. That said, writing is not a science. We aren't expecting you to think "oh, I've used two simple sentences in a row—I'd better throw a compound one in next". Writing is a more instinctive process than this and you will already have a style of writing which is based essentially on your "habit" in writing. You need to reflect on whether your current style is appropriate to take you through your university studies. What makes this difficult is that because your style is based on habit/instinct, it is hard to rate it yourself. Look at feedback on previous work; get someone to read through something written in your "normal" essay style; ask a tutor to look through something you have written to advise on whether your style is appropriate. It is also a good tip that the more reading you do, the more you will get a feeling for an appropriate academic style.

Writing objectively

8–41   Depending on what you have studied in the past, you may have been used to writing in the first person, which means presenting the work from a personal standpoint—"I think", "in my opinion". Generally this is not seen as appropriate in most legal academic writing, although there may be certain reflective exercises or progress logs you are asked to do which do require you to write in the first person: your tutors are likely to advise you if this is the case. Further, as you progress into writing on the professional courses, you will be expected to use appropriate drafting techniques for advice notes and letters to clients, and this will involve use of the first person (because by this time, you are the expert, so your personal opinion is what you are going to be paid for as a professional). At undergraduate or graduate diploma level, however, you will usually be expected to write in the third person.

You will note that we've written in the first person throughout this book, but that is because we're aiming for a much less formal style than you will need to adopt for your assignments: essentially we're trying to achieve a conversation with you, so that it is easier for you to engage with what we're saying. You are not expected to have a conversation with your tutor in this way: as you know from Ch.6, you are expected to present **conclusions** on the basis of **evidence**.

It can be a fine line to draw, because we've encouraged you to critically evaluate the materials you draw on, and this involved forming your own opinions about them. The trick is to realise that phrases like "I think . . ." make your views sounds unsubstantiated, whereas a critical evaluation provides the evidence for the conclusion you have drawn. You therefore don't need to present this as opinion (even though to some extent it still is). Think to yourself when tempted to write "I think . . .": "*why* do I think this?" and you should be able to come up with an answer starting with "because . . .". This "because" statement is the evidence for the view.

A further difficulty with writing objectively is that it tends to involve writing in a more "passive" style of writing; for example "this argument can be criticised" rather than "I am criticising this argument" (the latter is described as "active" rather than passive). Generally, writers are advised that active writing is clearer and more direct than passive writing, but passive writing has been traditional in academic legal writing (although active writing is becoming more preferred). This is likely to be a matter of preference amongst your tutors and therefore we'd advise you to ask for guidance.

Writing formally

In academic writing, a certain level of formality is expected. As we've already mentioned, we are not following our own advice because we're deliberately aiming at a less formal style, and therefore we've made more use of informal language and contractions like *don't*, *shouldn't*, *can't*. You should avoid these in your writing, and use the full *do not* and so on.   **8–42**

The real mistake to avoid is an assumption that formal writing requires the use of phrases like "it is submitted that" or even "it is respectfully submitted that", both of which will tend to make your writing unnecessarily pompous. Writing in normal, formal English is all you need to do. The style of a quality newspaper or the BBC news website is probably the right kind of tone to aim for.

Writing in a gender neutral style

Whilst it is generally accepted that academic writing must be gender neutral (in other words do not write "men" when you mean "people") there are differing views on the best way of achieving this. Particular problems occur when assigning *he* to denote a member of a group who could be male or female. Alternative methods for handling this include: **8–43**

- using "he or she" and "his or her";
- using "she" and "her" in a straight swap;
- using the artificial creation "s/he";
- using "them/their" instead—i.e. pluralising things.

All of these methods have advantages and disadvantages and different tutors may have different preferences (as do we as authors!); check whether there is a preferred way of handling this. If there isn't, find your own preferred way and stick to it, rather than switching throughout an essay—in other words, be consistent.

Summary of Chapter 8

8–44
- Academic writing requires you to follow normal conventions of grammar and spelling.
- A good standard of English and an appropriate style is part of communicating effectively.
- Spelling and grammar checkers may help you to spot errors but are no substitute for understanding the "rules" and checking your work.
- Key errors to avoid are misuse of apostrophes, incomplete sentences and spelling mistakes.
- Academic style should be clear and concise.

9 Finishing your work and utilising feedback

What is the purpose of this chapter?

Once you have actually completed a piece of writing (maybe with very little time to spare) it is tempting to heave a sigh of relief, print it off, hand it in and forget all about it. By now you may be sick of the sight of it, but before you can hand it in, knowing you've done your best, you need to do more.

Imagine attending a Black Tie event like a student Law Ball. Just as you probably wouldn't go out without checking that you had your tickets, your bow tie was on straight or that you had your handbag, so with your writing you need to check that it is submitted with everything asked for by the question setter and looking its best. You have worked hard on this piece of writing and want to make sure that this is fully recognised and rewarded—good presentation and a polished submission will help you. This chapter will help you with the finishing touches you need to consider before submitting your work. *Then* you can relax (and start work on your next assignment). But even after you've handed in your assignment, it won't stop there. Once your work has been marked by your tutors you are likely to receive feedback on it. The nature of this feedback may vary—in some cases you may get only the mark or grade, and in others more extensive comments will be provided; you may get your piece of work returned with specific guidance on it. Any feedback, however brief, can be of help in improving your writing for the next assignment you need to do. So the purpose of this chapter is to help you with these two aspects of successful legal writing—finishing your work and learning from your feedback.

By the end of this chapter you will:

• have a better understanding of the elements involved in "finishing" your work; and
• be able to use your feedback to reflect on your performance and make changes to your future practice.

What does reviewing and editing mean in academic writing?

9–2   Once you've finished the first draft of your assignment, the next step is to review your work. This stage refers to the positive reflective process which you should adopt with every piece of writing, by looking back over your work again before submission *but* in a different frame of mind.

There are different kinds of reviewing/editing:

1. Revision: whether on a large or small scale, this involves examining the entire assignment closely for structure, argument and any weaknesses or gaps or lack of authority that may be apparent.
2. Editing: here we are more concerned with minor problems that can be fixed by deleting or adding a word or two. Put yourself in the reader's position. Will he or she find your writing clear?
3. Proof-reading: where you are overtly looking for mistakes in your writing, particularly, for example, with punctuation, spelling, sentence structure and apostrophes. This needs to be done carefully—you must consciously slow your reading down to spot mistakes in work which is now very familiar.

If you word process your work, you will already be doing some kind of editing or reviewing as you write. Every time you cut and paste, delete something, or move a paragraph around in your document you are editing. However, the reviewing process we are talking about here may require more extensive changes.

All writing, whether it is an assignment, a dissertation or even this book chapter needs to be edited/reviewed. Things may need to be added or deleted, points changed and/or paragraphs re-organised. (Obviously this is not necessarily practical with exam answers and we look further at that later issue in this chapter). Doing this well can turn an average essay into a very good one, so it is not a step you can afford to skip no matter how tempting it may be. Make sure you have left enough time.

The key is to remember that your role as reviewer/editor is different from your role as writer. The main focus of this book has been to help you to develop your skills as a successful legal academic writer. You have already worked hard on the process of writing and diagnosing your writing task, addressed the structure of your writing and considered how to write in good legal English. Now you need to slip into another persona—that of your own critical friend. You need to put yourself in the position of the marker who will be making a final judgment on your work. To do this effectively you will need to adopt a somewhat dispassionate eye. This is very hard to do—especially because you are the very person who knows exactly what you meant to say when you wrote particular sentences or paragraphs. By this stage you will be very familiar (if not bored!) with your piece of writing. But this process requires you to be objective. Keeping the roles of writer and reviewer/editor separate will allow you to maintain a relaxed and creative approach to your legal writing, secure in the knowledge that you will be revising/editing later on in the process with weak areas/aspects being identified and fixed at that later stage.

How should I review and edit my work?

9–3   You would be wise to leave starting this revision stage of the writing process for a few days after you have finished your draft if your timescale allows. (If it doesn't, then build this in for the next time.)

Finish the first draft and put it aside. Do something else. Don't think consciously about your work. Taking a day or two in between finishing your work and reviewing it helps give some distance which can help you develop objectivity.

To help you with this process, we have put together a checklist which essentially combines all three aspects mentioned above. Some of these will be hard for you to do personally and you may need to enlist the help of a friend or family member. We will go on to explore some of these areas in more detail later on in this chapter.

Final checklist

- Go back to your diagnosis of the task and begin by reading the whole assignment again. Have you answered the question? Have you said what you intended to say? What are the strengths and weaknesses of your assignment?
- Check the assessment criteria for this piece of work. Have you addressed these (do not ignore the very aspects, i.e. criteria your markers *told* you they would be looking for)?
- Have you met any specific requirements for this assignment in terms of word length, bibliography and so on? (See below for further suggestions on these aspects.)
- Run the opening sentences of each paragraph together—does that provide a coherent structure which addresses the question?
- Look at your introduction—could someone reading *just* this part of your answer make an educated guess as to what the question you've been asked was?
- Now skip to your conclusion—does it contain an answer to, or your position on, the core question?
- Is every assertion or proposition of law supported by relevant authority or evidence?
- Do your sentences work? Do they make sense? Have you written in complete sentences?
- Consider your structure. Does it seem clear and logical? Is each point relevant and adequately developed? Does your work "flow"?
- What does the work look like? Is it presented in a typed format in a readable font type and size, with adequate margins and footnotes/endnotes if required?
- Does your use of grammar, including apostrophes and sentence construction comply with the rules in Ch.8?
- Have you spell-checked? Be aware of your individual pattern of errors. If you are prone to making certain mistakes over and over again, note them down and check for these particularly carefully. If you know there are words that you commonly mistype you could use the find and replace facility in your word processing package to sort these out.

Practice the process of finishing with reference to Answer B of the four sample essay questions on the Practice Statement which can be found in Appendix 5. Put yourself in the position of the writer of that answer and use the checklist above to conduct a "finishing" process on that answer (you may find it easier to imagine yourself as the marker instead of the writer). It is easier to spot the mistakes made by others than the ones you have made yourself.

Here are some suggestions for making the process easier:

TIP

- Give yourself plenty of time to review/edit.
- When checking your spelling you may find it helpful to start from the end of the document and work backwards to prevent accidental skim-reading.
- Use a hard copy of your work to review/edit as you can miss problems if reading from a computer screen.
- Read your work out loud.
- Use a second reader.
- Be someone else's second reader!

- Reading your work out loud to see how it sounds can be very helpful. You should be aiming for it to sound like (reasonably formal) speech. Reading aloud is a good way to tackle the problem of over familiarity we referred to earlier. Reading aloud helps to adopt a more objective approach when reviewing/editing (and can help with spotting punctuation errors).
- Asking a friend for help is useful too. They don't need to be expert writers or even law students (although that can help). This can help you to check your own "subjective" assessment with someone else's more objective assessment. You can read your work out loud to them or ask them to read it out loud to you. How does your work sound when being spoken by someone who has never read it before? Do your sentences work when spoken? Does the structure still seem clear and logical? Can it be read fluently and with ease? Does your friend understand the gist of what you are trying to say or are there gaps in your argument?

Make sure you meet the word limit

9–5   Effective reviewing also helps when meeting the word-limit for your assignment. It is fairly common to exceed the limit on a first draft, and if it happens to you, you must cut some words to meet the requirements of the assignment. Students sometimes complain about word limits and query their purpose: as markers, we appreciate that being told that you are being tested on your ability to write concisely may be frustrating. Nevertheless, your tutors think that the question can be answered effectively within the word limit they have set. So if you have gone over it this indicates that you need to make changes.

> **TIP**
>
> By keeping the question and your diagnosis of task in front of you, you should be able to check that you have only included relevant material.

When "trimming" for word count purposes you must be careful not to cut your core arguments. Instead, look to out descriptive explanation or marginal detail that is just not needed to follow the main lines of argument. Perhaps you have included a little too much descriptive material (facts of cases, for example). Similarly there can be a tendency to draw out historical background discussion. Check that only relevant information has been included. Check for repetition—you may have said the same thing in a number of different ways without realising it. As you read through your work during the reviewing/editing process try to justify your inclusion of all points/sentences/cases, etc.—if you can't then ditch them!

Conversely, you may find your work is short of the word limit. Although this may be a less likely occurrence (particularly having worked through the earlier chapters in this book) it nonetheless needs to be addressed if you are to achieve the best mark possible for your assignment. It is not good enough to say to yourself, "Well, I put in everything they wanted and it just didn't take that many words". You need to be more reflective than that. Your tutors have set this word limit for a reason: so if you are well short, it is extremely likely that you have made an error in your diagnosis—either you have missed an issue out, or you have wrongly labelled as a minor point something which needs much more detail as a major point. You need to go back to your diagnosis—and ask yourself whether you have fully answered the question(s). Do you need to include more information or analysis in answering any of the sub-questions? (It is more likely to be the latter as opposed to increased description being needed.) Do you need to do some more focussed research?

Finishing in an exam situation

Of course you will need to adopt a different strategy for this final checking-over process in an exam. Here, there will be less emphasis on presentation but you do still need to leave time to check through your answers for any obvious mistakes or any other errors which would make it harder for your marker to understand what you mean.

> **TIP** 9–6
>
> You may find you need to add clarification, in which case use asterisks and arrows to direct the marker's attention to any additions. However, bear in mind the need to do this too often is indicative of a lack of planning, so reflect on this for future exams.

What is "good" presentation?

In the context of "finishing" your work prior to submission, looks do count to some extent. If you 9–7 were a marker, would you prefer to read a document which is well presented or one which is sloppy with spelling and typing errors and has the pages in the wrong order? Remember that your goal is clear communication. Students often confuse the idea of "good presentation" with the need to provide elaborate title pages, or submit their work in fancy folders. Generally, simplicity is best. If you have been given specific submission guidelines, then follow them. If not, the following is a general list of suggestions to improve the appearance of your work:

- Use white paper.
- Typing is always preferable and usually required. If you have to handwrite, use lined paper.
- Use only one side of the paper.
- Double-space, so the marker can both read and comment on your work easily.
- Leave margins of at least one inch at the top, bottom and sides of the page.
- Page numbers should normally be placed at the bottom of each page. Make sure that all pages are numbered. Title pages are not numbered. Page 1 is the first page of the essay proper, and must be numbered.
- Ensure that the correct means of identifying the work as belonging to you is used on every page, for example, your name (unless your work is to be marked anonymously) and/or student registration number.
- Do not hand in loose pages; always bind them together. Simply stapling is best, but alternatively use a folder or plastic wallet. Make sure that the whole of the written text is clearly visible. Do not put each individual page into a separate plastic sleeve.
- Always keep a hard copy and an electronic copy of your work. Set up a system for storing copies in both formats.

How do I write a bibliography?

A further aspect of finishing your work is that you will—almost certainly—be expected to submit a correctly formatted bibliography. Your bibliography is a list of books, articles, reports, cases and statutory

> **TIP** 9–8
>
> There are examples of how a bibliography might look in Appendix 6 and you will find reference books on this in your library.

provisions which are referred to or cited in the text. To find out how to set out your bibliography, your first step should be to check whether your Law School specifies a format. If there is any guidance available, then of course you should follow it. You may be required to put only secondary sources in a bibliography, for example (although the guidance we've suggested below includes primary sources as well). Another possible variant is whether you have to cite material you have looked at but not referred to directly (although if you follow our advice above, then any material you have looked at will have been cited, even if only in general terms, but again, your institution may have a different policy).

If you are not given a specific format to follow, then you may wish to adopt the following:

1. list legislation referred to in alphabetical order;
2. list cases referred to in alphabetical order;
3. list secondary sources in one single list in alphabetical order of author. This will look slightly different depending on whether you adopted the Harvard or the Numerical system (see Ch.6 for more on referencing).

When is my work ready to hand in?

9–9   This is something which you must decide for yourself, with reference to the advice we've provided in this chapter. You come to a point when you must decide that the assignment is complete and ready to be handed in. This can be a hard decision. It is tempting to keep writing to improve the piece *ad nauseam*. Resist this temptation. Remember you have worked hard on this. The potential benefits to be gained from further reworking are not sufficient enough to risk submitting late, or to delay starting your next assignment.

One way of helping yourself to move on (and actually submit) is to make some notes for yourself on the process you have just been through. Ask yourself:

*   What did I do well in this piece of writing/assignment?
*   What aspect could I have improved on?
*   What would I like to do better next time?

These notes will help you to "finish" the assignment and also help you to develop an action plan for the next assignment you must complete. In addition to this post-assignment self-reflection you should also, eventually, have access to another source of help, namely feedback on your work.

What can I learn from feedback on my work?

9–10   You are likely to receive some kind of feedback on your work. As we stated earlier in this chapter, it is the amount and the detail of any feedback you receive which may vary—in some cases you may just learn the mark or grade allocated to your work, and on other occasions more extensive comments with suggestions on how to improve next time will be provided. Whatever the feedback you receive, you can learn from it.

Your tutors will be genuinely interested in what you have to say and their feedback has been designed to help you to understand why you were awarded the mark given and also as a tool to improve for the future. It is therefore really important to take time to interpret what the feedback means, and make a plan to act on it. You should resist the temptation to look only at the mark.

TIP

With the best will in the world it is sometimes impossible for your tutors to return work as fast as you—and they—would like. If the assignment feels remote by the time you receive the feedback, then get your copy out so as to make the most of the feedback you get on it. Don't just look at the mark!

If you do not take the time to read and then act on your tutor's feedback you are denying yourself a real opportunity for improvement. Comments from your tutor are a valuable resource at your disposal. Taking these comments on board means that not only are you working hard but you will be "working smart".

Whether the mark is as you expected, not as high as you would have liked or indeed exceeds your expectation, learning what you have scored may arouse strong feelings. To get the most out of feedback you need time to let these feelings settle before trying to "learn" for the future from this piece of writing. So it is really important to learn the skill of dealing objectively with feedback. Unless you are exceptionally able, you will from time to time receive marks and feedback which are disappointing to you, especially in the light of the amount of time you spent working on any particular assignment. We've all been there, and it can be tempting to assume that the marker is at fault rather than your own work. Unfortunately, as we've made clear, the length of time spent on a piece of work does not necessarily equate to the mark awarded. This is frustrating, but it is why we encourage you to focus on *all* aspects of the writing cycle.

TIP

Putting the feedback away for a few days and then coming back to it can help with getting the most out of it.

The only evidence the marker has of the amount of work you have put in is the work you have submitted.

Once you are ready to look at your feedback objectively ask yourself:

- Do I understand the comments?
- Can I identify what they are specifically referring to?
- Do I agree with the comments? If not, why? (remember "but I worked really hard" is not adequate evidence)
- What do I need to do to improve my performance?

From these questions, start to plan what you will do differently next time.

Understanding your feedback

Feedback will vary from tutor to tutor. Naturally, this can make understanding your feedback confusing, particularly when you may be getting feedback from many different tutors and subjects. "Translating" comments from tutors is a skill. Understanding what has been written is vital for your next piece of work so you will need to spend some time acquiring the necessary skills to

9–11

TIP

Your tutors should always be happy to explain their feedback if you are having trouble "translating" what they mean or even actually reading their comments. Go and see your tutor and ask for their help.

do this in order to benefit from any feedback you are given. Tutor comments can address a range of issues, e.g. grammar, structure and layout, referencing, content, errors, and can be positive or be more negative and critical. In order to learn from your feedback, essentially you need to practise the skills in reflection we identified in Ch.1.

So, if you are wondering what to do with all those tutor comments on your work, first read them carefully. Then, see if you can determine what kind of comments have been made by the marker and then use the following table for suggestions as to what you can do.

If the comments are . . .	Then you should . . .
Positive reinforcement	Feel good and accept any critical comments there are. If this refers to something in particular see if you can incorporate it into your next assignment.
Related to the bibliography	Be sure you are fully aware of any programme, institutional or discipline standard on this and use it!
Related to the range of sources	Try expanding and developing your research strategy. Either you have not read widely enough or you have just not created a sense of detailed understanding of the topic in your writing.
Related to structure/layout	Follow the comments. If you are not sure what is expected, check your lecture/tutorial notes when information may have been given and look back at Ch.7 for further guidance.
Grammar/spelling/sentence structure problems	Read these comments carefully and try to work out where the problems are. Re-read the early part of this chapter and Ch.8 and leave yourself enough time to proof-read carefully before you submit your next assignment.
Related to errors of law	Learn your material and how to apply it. It is clear that if your work does have a lot of errors on the law, your tutor will not be best pleased no matter how well it is written.
Related to content	See what general lessons can be learnt from it. This is harder to categorise as these comments will be subject specific, but, for example, if the marker suggests that there is something s/he particularly liked in your assignment look at it carefully and try to work out if a similar strategy would work with other assignments.
Related to your referencing	Revisit Ch.6. This tends to involve a discipline or department specific norm or method and you need to learn what it is in your institution very early on in your legal academic career.
Indicating a lack of analysis	Work on developing the evaluative or analytical parts of your argument. This is a hard one to understand. Essentially it means that you have been too descriptive and have not adopted a style which challenges and evaluates the law on this matter. You need to adopt an improved questioning approach to your next assignment, so look again at Ch.6.
Related to presentation	Work out what is wrong and fix it—this is easily done and as with referencing there is no excuse for poor presentation.

If the comments are . . .	Then you should . . .
Fails to answer the question	Reconsider how you diagnose your task. Read Ch.4 again to get some tips on how to do exactly what it says on the tin!
Related to a lack of authority	Remember every statement or assertion or proposition of law you make needs to be supported by authority or evidence, i.e. primary or secondary sources.

 ## Activity 9.1

Go back to the notes you made earlier when you undertook the "finishing before submission" of Answer B on the Practice Statement in Appendix 5. For this activity you are going to extend that exercise by providing feedback on the answer as if you had marked it. To do this, you will need to consider the matters discussed above. For example: Content (to include errors in law and use of authority); Structure (to include style); Grammar (to include spelling and sentence structure); Referencing (to include bibliography and sources); and Analysis/evaluation. You are *not* trying to allocate a mark, but considering the comments that might be made by a marker to give advice to the writer of this work that will help them with future assignments.   **9–13**

Try using this template to help you:

Subject of comment	Comment
Content	
Structure	
Grammar	
Referencing	
Analysis/evaluation	

TIP

Remember your tutors are not your only source of feedback. You can adopt a reflective attitude to your own performance as well as asking your fellow students how they did—if a colleague got a better mark then you, and they are willing to show you their assignment, then carry out this same critical evaluation comparing their work to yours.

Compare your views:

Our suggested comments are as follows: *Content:* Evidence of sound knowledge and arguments show understanding, covers most issues. Tackles important problems connected with the use of the Statement although you could extend this by providing a better insight into the actual *use* of the Statement.

Structure: Logical sequence adopted and your paragraphs are linked. Some of your sentences are confusingly long and tortuous: you need to try and make your good points more accessible in short, succinct paragraphs.

Grammar: Your grammar, spelling and use of apostrophes are poor—e.g. principal, its/it's. This is something you really need to work on. You can seek help from legal writing books in the library and should perhaps consider seeing if your tutor can make any suggestions.

Referencing: Secondary sources used (Alan Paterson) and quoted but where are the relevant cases? *Miller v Jackson* is the only case used and that was not even about the Practice Statement!

Analysis/evaluation: You do describe some arguments but offer few judgments on these although you do make some effort at an assessment of the advantages/ disadvantages linked to the Statement. Your answer is quite good on the issues but has ignored the instruction to illustrate from case law—some attempt at critical analysis.

If there were a lot of dissimilarities between your comments and our suggested comments, then you need to go back to the earlier chapters in the book and check your understanding of the various aspects that comprise successful legal writing.

Connected to the issue of learning from feedback is the question of the provision of model answers by your tutors and learning from your exams.

Learning from model answers

9–14   In our experience, students are often very keen to receive model answers to questions, and while they can be something of a "security blanket", there are a number of problems associated with them. The temptation with a model answer is to stick in the comfortable "knowledge transfer" domain instead of moving into the more challenging "transformative" or "process" domain. That is: it is not so much what you *know* but what you *do* with your knowledge and material that impresses us. Therefore, a model answer should only ever be indicative of a *process*. One thing which is certain with a model answer is that the same question will definitely not be coming up in your exam or coursework so the exact circumstances of any answer are valueless.

However, model answers have other benefits—they are not just the answers to a particular question in terms of the law. They also give a clear insight into tutor expectations as far as structure and approach for questions on that particular topic. In other words it is the *technique* used by your tutors in the model answers, to answer these types of question which is more important than what the actual answer was.

How to answer a question, in terms of structure, style and approach, in addition to coverage of the material is what needs to be taken from these model answers. These elements are transferable from question to question on the same topic and, in an even more general way, to similar types of questions such as other problem questions.

> **TIP**
>
> Remember to use any model answer in two ways: as an indicator of the material needed to answer a question on that topic again and as an indicator of the approach to be adopted when answering questions of that type.

Learning from exams

9–15   The nature and extent of the feedback provided on exam performance varies from institution to institution. You may be provided with individual feedback, generic comments on performance or you may receive your mark and nothing else. It may be that feedback is only provided to those who have failed in order to help them assess where they went wrong and to improve their performance next time. Alternatively feedback may be available on request rather than automatically. You may want to consider asking your tutor for feedback. The scope and depth of any feedback they can provide will usually be up to them but if they have time and are able to, most tutors are willing to help.

Finally, remember that if you have carried out all the steps we have suggested, you should be in a position to produce a successful piece of writing. If your feedback indicates that you have fallen short of this, then consider which chapter you need to revisit to improve.

Summary of Chapter 9

9–16

- It is vital to "finish" your work by revising, editing and proof-reading it before handing it in.
- Techniques which may help you "finish" your work include reading it out loud and asking a friend to look through it.
- You must make sure you comply with any guidance on format and submission.
- When you receive feedback on your work, you should use this to inform your future writing.
- Use your feedback to establish which part(s) of the writing cycle you need to work on to improve your performance.

Appendix 1: Sample Assessment Grade Descriptors

These grade descriptors taken from the law conversion course ("CPE") at Manchester Metropolitan University provide an example of different levels of attainment in respect of each of the assessment criteria.

	100 – 80 per cent	79 – 70 per cent	69 – 60 per cent	59 – 50 per cent	49 – 40 per cent	39 – 35 per cent	34 – 25 per cent	24 – 0 per cent
Diagnosis of task — 10 Marks	Identifies all major and minor points and distinguishes or ranks them. Shows outstanding perception in identification /discussion of hidden issues. Includes no irrelevant material. 10–8	Identifies all major and minor points, and distinguishes or ranks them. Shows perception in identification of hidden issues. Includes little or no irrelevant material. 7	Clearly identifies all major points and most minor points but may not necessarily rank them correctly. May show some perception in identification of hidden issues. Includes little irrelevant material. 6	Clearly identifies all or almost all major points and some minor points. Too little distinguishing or ranking of points made, or ranking contains some errors. Unlikely to identify hidden issues. May include some irrelevant material. 5	Identifies many major points and may identify a few minor points, but there are significant omissions. Little or no attention is paid to ranking of points, or ranking contains several errors. Includes some irrelevant material. 4	Fails to identify most major and minor points but does identify a few of the major points. Little or no attention is paid to the ranking of points, or ranking is completely or almost completely faulty or arbitrary. 3.5	Identifies very few major and minor points. Indicates only a few arbitrary points. A significant proportion of the work addresses irrelevant or wrong issues. 3	Identifies none or almost none of the major and minor points. Work addresses entirely or almost entirely irrelevant or wrong issues. 2 – 0
Relevant knowledge & understanding — 20 Marks	Displays complete and detailed knowledge of relevant law (and /or other required material). Gives full, pertinent & accurate explanations, examples & interpretations. Shows an outstanding grasp of the topic's wider context. 20–16	Displays comprehensive and detailed knowledge of relevant law (and /or other required material). Gives full, pertinent and almost entirely accurate explanations, examples & interpretations. Shows a firm grasp of the topic's wider context. 15–14	Displays broad and mainly detailed knowledge of relevant law (and /or other relevant material). Pertinent and generally accurate examples, explanations & interpretations. Shows a sound grasp of the topic's wider context. 13–12	Displays a secure knowledge of the main points of relevant law (and/ or other relevant material). Generally relevant examples, explanations & interpretations but includes some errors and/or omissions. Shows an awareness of the topic's wider context. 11–10	Displays some knowledge of relevant law (and/ or other relevant material). Provides few examples, explanations, interpretations and those offered may contain significant errors and/or omissions. Shows little awareness of the topic's wider context. 9–8	Displays incomplete and unsatisfactory knowledge of relevant law (and/ or other relevant material). Offers few examples, explanations & interpretations and those offered contain major flaws. Some generalised knowledge may be shown, but little or no awareness of its wider context. 7	Displays little understanding of the relevant law (and/ or other material). Offers no or almost no examples, explanations & interpretations and/or those offered are vague and incomplete contain major flaws or are mainly irrelevant. No understanding of the topic's wider context shown. 6–5	Displays no or almost no understanding of the relevant law (and/or other material). Any explanations, examples or interpretations offered are completely irrelevant or contain fatal flaws and/or omissions. No understanding of the topic's wider context. 4–0

Application & handling of knowledge							
Exceptional use of knowledge in addressing task requirements completely and concisely. Demonstrates outstanding ability in problem-solving or interpretation of knowledge, offering sustained, clear conclusions and alternative conclusions. Completely coherent, applying existing knowledge to new situations and/or unresolved debates logically and convincingly to the highest standard.	Excellent use of knowledge in addressing task requirements completely and concisely. Demonstrates comprehensive ability in problem-solving or interpretation of knowledge, offering sustained clear conclusions and often alternative conclusions. Completely coherent, applying existing knowledge to new situations and/or unresolved debates logically and convincingly.	Very good use of knowledge in addressing all or almost all task requirements. Demonstrates excellent ability in problem-solving or interpretation of knowledge, offering clear conclusions. May offer some alternative conclusions. Generally coherent, relating knowledge in most applicable areas to new situations and/or unresolved debates, perhaps with minor flaws in logic.	Sound use of knowledge in addressing most task requirements, but with some (few/minor) errors and/or omissions. Demonstrates solid ability in problem-solving or interpretation of knowledge but with some flaws in the conclusions drawn. Coherent, but little application to new situations and/or unresolved debates, or application offered contains significant flaws in logic.	Competent but often limited use of knowledge in addressing many task requirements, with some significant errors and/or omissions. Demonstrates only patchy ability in problem-solving or interpretation of knowledge; some conclusions drawn are plausible while others contain significant flaws. Some coherence but rarely tackles subtler issues or tackles them illogically.	Generally incompetent or limited use of knowledge which fails to address major task requirements, or addresses them with significant errors and/or omissions. Demonstrates patchy ability in problem-solving or interpretation of knowledge; few conclusions drawn are plausible and many contain significant flaws. Some limited coherence but generally lacking in logic.	Little use of knowledge in addressing task requirements; major errors and/or omissions are made. Very little ability in problem-solving or interpretation of knowledge shown; some attempt to address the issues may be made but these are insufficiently explored and contain significant flaws. Little coherence or logic shown; answer is inconsistent and unconvincing.	Almost no use of knowledge in addressing task requirements; many major errors and/or omissions are made. Little or no ability in problem-solving or interpretation of knowledge shown; little attempt to address the issues, these are insufficiently explored and contain fundamental flaws. Little or no coherence or logic shown; answer is almost completely inconsistent and unconvincing.
20–16	15–14	13–12	11–10	9–8	7	6–5	4–0
100 – 80 per cent	79 – 70 per cent	69 – 60 per cent	59 – 50 per cent	49 – 40 per cent	39 – 35 per cent	34 – 25 per cent	24 – 0 per cent

20 Marks

	100 – 80 per cent	79 – 70 per cent	69 – 60 per cent	59 – 50 per cent	49 – 40 per cent	39 – 35 per cent	34 – 25 per cent	24 – 0 per cent
Use of source material (10 Marks)	Outstanding evidence of independent research. Utilises a comprehensive range of quality sources. Use of sources is sustained, integrated and accurately referenced. **10–8**	Substantial evidence of independent research. Utilises a comprehensive range of quality sources. Use of sources is sustained, integrated and accurately referenced. **7**	Some evidence of independent research. Utilises a wide range of quality sources. Use of sources is usually integrated and accurately referenced. **6**	Limited evidence of independent research. Utilises a narrow range of sources and/or sources lack quality. Mostly accurate referencing but may contain occasional unsupported assertions. **5**	Little evidence of wider reading. Sources are limited. Makes unsupported assertions. May misuse sources by failure to reference sufficiently and/or indiscriminate use of quotations or paraphrasing. **4**	No evidence of wider reading. Sources are very limited. Makes many unsupported assertions. Misuses sources by failure to reference adequately and/or indiscriminate use of quotations or paraphrasing. **3.5**	Little if any evidence of any reading. Assertions are almost entirely unsupported by evidence. Seriously misuses sources by failure to reference and/ or overuse of quotations or paraphrasing. **3**	No evidence of research or reading. Fails to utilise any quality sources or completely misuses them with over-quotation or paraphrasing. Completely lacking in referencing. **2–0**
Evaluation (20 Marks)	Makes impressive judgments by fully identifying gaps/flaws/ inconsistencies in the material under discussion. Balances & ranks all arguments & counter-arguments, and reaches an entirely reasoned position. Offers an outstanding critique containing several original points. Explicitly separates evidence from opinion. **20–16**	Makes excellent judgments by identifying all or almost all gaps/ flaws/ inconsistencies in the material under discussion. Balances & ranks many arguments & counter-arguments, and reaches a reasoned position. Offers full critique which often contains some original points. Explicitly separates evidence from opinion. **15–14**	Makes very good judgments by identifying main gaps/flaws/ inconsistencies in the material under discussion. Balances most arguments and reaches a generally reasoned position, perhaps with occasional inconsistency. Offers sound critique which may contain some original points. Separates evidence from opinion. **13–12**	Attempts to make judgments by identifying only some gaps/flaws/ inconsistencies in the material under discussion. Notes main arguments but position is not sufficiently reasoned. Offers more description than critique but may contain some limited insights. Does not clearly separate evidence from opinion. **11–10**	Limited attempt to make judgments; few gaps/flaws/ inconsistencies in the material under discussion are made. Some reference to main arguments made but position is often incoherent and/or unsubstantiated. Offers mainly description and little critique. Barely separates evidence from opinion. **9–8**	Insufficient attempt to make judgments and those which are made are usually weak or unsubstantiated. Little critique of the material under discussion is offered and there is little coherent argument. Offers almost entirely descriptive assertions and does not separate evidence from opinion. **7**	Few if any judgments are made. No or almost no critique of the material is offered. No coherent argument. Commentary consists of descriptive or haphazard assertions. **6–5**	No judgments are made. No critique of the material is offered. No coherent argument. What commentary there is, if any, consists of entirely descriptive assertions. **4–0**

	100–80 per cent	79–70 per cent	69–60 per cent	59–50 per cent	49–40 per cent	39–35 per cent	34–25 per cent	24–0 per cent
Structure 10 Marks	Effective, thorough introduction and conclusion. Sustained logical flow of argument. Explicit links between discussion points. Effective signposting. **10–8**	Thorough introduction and conclusion. Logical flow of argument. Explicit links between discussion points. Effective signposting. **7**	Good introduction and conclusion. Logical ordering of appropriate content. Appropriate links between discussion points. Effective signposting. **6**	Generally functional introduction and conclusion. The content is presented in a generally logical order. Some links between points. Issues are signposted. **5**	Some attempt at an introduction and conclusion. Content may be presented haphazardly. Little signposting, or links between points. **4**	Little if any introduction or conclusion. Disorganised discussion. No or weak signposting of points. **3.5**	No introduction or conclusion. Little discernible organisation of material. Work jumps between topics in an incoherent way. **3**	No introduction or conclusion. No organisation of material. No help with identifying which point is being discussed. Completely incoherent. **2–0**
Presentation 10 Marks	Excellent use of English and sophisticated writing style. No spelling or grammar errors. Competent word-processing with no formatting errors. Citation and bibliography follow recommended format throughout. **10–8**	Excellent use of English and pleasing writing style. No spelling or grammar errors. Competent word-processing with no formatting errors. Citation and bibliography follow recommended format throughout. **7**	Very good use of English and a good writing style. Almost no spelling or grammar errors. Competent use of word-processing with virtually no formatting flaws. Citation and bibliography usually follow recommended format. **6**	Good use of English and competent writing style. A few spelling or grammar errors. Mainly competent use of word-processing with few formatting flaws. Citation and bibliography do not always follow recommended format. **5**	Use of English is only competent and writing style is weak. Some spelling and grammar errors. Mainly satisfactory word-processing but with some formatting flaws. Citation and bibliographical errors. **4**	Poor use of English and writing style is unsatisfactory. A number of spelling and grammar errors. Word-processing contains major formatting flaws. Serious citation and bibliographical errors. **3.5**	Very poor use of English and writing style is unacceptable. Serious spelling and grammar errors. Word-processing is very poor. Citing and bibliography are seriously flawed or may be missing. **3**	Use of English raises serious concerns. Littered with spelling and grammar errors. Word processing is very poor. Citing and bibliography are missing or completely inaccurate. **2–0**

Appendix 2: Assessment Grid Pro Forma

Following the reflective exercise in Ch.2 you may wish to copy this pro forma to help you manage your own assessments successfully.

Subject	Weighting (i.e. how much this assessment counts for as part of the whole grade in this subject)	Type of assignment	Group or individual	Word limit	Deadline

Appendix 3: Planning Log

In this appendix there is a pro forma which you may want to use to help you diagnose your task and plan your research. There are two versions provided—one is blank for you to copy and use yourself if you wish, the other contains ideas for how you would complete each section.

Planning Log with guidance

Essay title	Insert the essay title given

Diagnose your task See Ch.4 for further advice	Write what you really think the question is asking for, i.e. identify the topic under consideration and specific angles or elements required by the question. It may help to try the following: • Imagine why the examiner set this particular question in this particular way. • Put the question round another way: if it is a statement, put it as a question and then break it into further questions.

Key words	Identify the key words—i.e. the words which define the subject and scope of your assignment

Instruction words	Identify the instruction words—i.e. the words which tell you what to do with your material

Materials review See Ch.5 for further advice	Note down what materials you already have on this topic, for example lecture notes, tutorial preparation notes, notes from your textbook(s), suggested reading lists, etc.

Search for relevant primary materials See Ch.5 for further advice	Remember that by primary sources, we mean cases and statutes. Note down: (a) which database(s) you searched and why you chose this database; (b) the search terms you used; (c) with reference to the results generated evaluate whether the search was effective in helping you address the question set (Did it generate too few results? Too many results? Results which were not relevant to the question?); and (d) if your initial search was not effective, describe what changes/refinements you made for your next search (Did you change your search terms? Search within results? Narrow your search to only particular sources? Narrow your search by date? Use a different database altogether?).

Search for relevant secondary materials See Ch.5 for further advice	Remember that by secondary sources we mean commentary on the law rather than the law itself (e.g. books, articles, etc.) Note down: (a) which database(s) you searched and why you chose this database; (b) the search terms you used; (c) with reference to the results generated evaluate whether the search was effective in helping you address the question set (Did it generate too few results? Too many results? Results which were not relevant to the question?); and (d) if your initial search was not effective, describe what changes/refinements you made for your next search (Did you change your search terms? Search within results? Narrow your search to only particular sources? Narrow your search by date? Use a different database altogether?).

Blank Planning Log for Your Own Use

Essay title	

Diagnose your task	

Key words	

Instruction words	

Materials review	

Search for relevant primary materials	

Search for relevant secondary materials	

Appendix 4: Research Record Pro Forma

You can use this pro forma to help you organise and record the sources you find during your research. This will help you organise your referencing later. Depending on the source you may not use every category for every source.

Record of Sources Found

Type of source	
Author/Editor	
Title	
Journal title and pages (if applicable)	
Publisher (if applicable)	
Year of publication	
Place of publication	
Date accessed if online	
Main topics	
Other topics it refers to	
What points help address the question	
Relevant pages	

Appendix 5: Sample answers on the Practice Statement question

Here are four sample answers to a question on the Practice Statement.

Question: Critically assess the effect of the Practice Statement 1966 on the doctrine of precedent, illustrating your answer with case examples.

Answer A: The Practice Statement 1966 was passed in 1966 by the House of Lords and had a big impact on the way the doctrine of precedent operates. The doctrine of precedent or stare decisis as it is more properly known is the system that is used in English law to determine how cases in the legal system are influenced by previous cases, this will depend on three important elements, a system of law reporting, a hierarchy of courts and a concept of ratio. Ratio is the principle of law which decides the case in the context of or in the light of the material facts.

   The purpose of the doctrine of precedent is to create certainty, this is essential for us to have confidence in the idea of justice. There is an argument that we need flexibility to make sure each case can be decided fairly, but I think that it is more important for people to be certain about what the law is. Otherwise solicitors and barristers will not be able to advise their clients properly, this will increase costs and cause unfairness.

   An example of a case where the House of Lords used the Practice Statement is the case of *Miliangos v George Frank Textiles*. This was a case about whether judgment could be made in sterling or not. Lord Denning in the court of appeal had stated that it could be made in any currency, which was contrary to the position in the case of Havana Railways, this had said that judgment must be given in sterling. Bristow J said that it had to be given in sterling in the High Court. When the case got to the House of Lords, their lordships decided that Lord Denning had been wrong to disobey the previous case of Havana because it should have been binding (this was in another case called *Schorsh Meier v Hennin*). However, the House of Lords also decided that Lord Denning had been right about whether to give judgment in sterling. This meant they used the Practice Statement to depart from their own previous decision and changed the law. Havana Railways was no longer "good law" after this.

   Another case where the House of Lords used the Practice Statement was in *R v Shivpuri*, the issue they had to decide was whether it is possible to be convicted of a criminal attempt if it was impossible to do the crime. Mr Shivpuri had handled a suitcase full of harmless powder thinking it was drugs. This was the same as the previous case of *Anderton v Ryan*, the defendant in this case had handled a video recorder which she must of known was stolen, because it was suspiciously cheap. She admitted to the police officers that she had suspected that it was stolen because of the cheap price she paid for it however the police did not prove that it was actually stolen. This meant that she could only be convicted of attempting the impossible, but the House of Lords interpreted the Criminal Attempts Act 1981 to decide that she was not guilty. Lots of legal academics decided that this was plainly wrong, so the House of Lords used the Practice Statement to overrule *Anderton v Ryan* in the case of *Shivpuri*. This was the first time the House of Lords had decided to use the Practice Statement in a criminal case, which shows how serious it was. Previously they had said it would be better to keep hanging people than create uncertainty.

Another case where the House of Lords used the Practice Statement was *Murphy v Brentwood*, this was to overrule the case of *Anns v Merton Borough Council*. The reason they did this was because interpretation of the case of *Donoghue v Stevenson* was getting out of hand. *Donoghue v Stevenson* was the famous case about the snail in the ginger beer bottle (although actually it was never proved whether there was a snail in the bottle because Mr Stevenson died and his executors settled the case out of court). In *Grant v Australian Knitting Mills* they widened this ratio to include any product which might injure your neighbour (in this case, the goods in question were long underpants which had given him dermatitis). By the time of the Anns case, this had been extended to include pure economic loss. The House of Lords used the Practice Statement to depart from this decision because they felt that the law would be unworkable otherwise because the "floodgates would open".

This shows that whenever the House of Lords decides to use the Practice Statement 1966 to depart from their own previous decisions, it has serious implications for the doctrine of precedent because it creates uncertainty. However, we must always remember that the House of Lords will only use this power rarely.

Answer B: The Practice Statement 1966 was a Practice Direction issued by the House of Lords in which they indicated that they would no longer consider themselves bound by their own previous decisions but would be free to depart under certain circumstances. This was in itself a departure from the pervious position which had stated that the House of Lords would be bound by it's own previous decisions, in the interests of certainty, because if the House of Lords was free to depart from it's own previous precedents then no legal issue would ever be decided finally, which would create serious issues for precedent and the legal system. The Practice Statement did not specify what circumstances would need to apply in order to justify departure, but stated that the House of Lords could do so when they thought it was right to do so, so this therefore had the potential to return the legal system to the position of no case ever being decided finally and whether or not this actually happened was to be in the hands of the Law Lords. In this essay I shall examine whether this happened or not.

There are a number of reasons why certainty is thought to be beneficial for the legal system. First of all, the idea of certainty corresponds with usual notions of justice and fairness, which state it should be possible for people to be able to predict whether or not it is worth pursuing a case by reference to previous cases which have been decided as this is the whole point of the principal of stare decisis, which literally means "stand by what has been decided", which is the central feature of our common law legal system in contrast to the alternative European 'Code' system. A further point in relation to this is that it would not seem very fair if someone could pursue a case and get a particular result, and then another person pusuing a very similar case later should get a different result, as this would result in a lack of confidence in the legal system in the eyes of the general public, because the legal system would appear to be subjective rather than objective. An example of this is the case of *Miller v Jackson*, where Lord Denning's judgment appeared to indicate that he was deciding the case contrary to precedents which should have been binding on him on the basis that he liked cricket! Certainty is also important because legal relationships are formed on the basis of the law existing at the time they are made, so if the House of Lords was prepared to overrule it's previous decisions frequently this would have implications for contracts which might have been formed which could potentially be worth millions of pounds, so the House of Lords must always bear this in mind. A final benefit of certainty within legal system is that it provides a basis upon which lawyers can advise their client's, and thus reduce litigation, because if the House of Lords was prepared to reopen areas of settled law frequently it would always be worth pushing a case to the House of Lords, even if the authority's suggest the contrary, on the basis that previous precedents could be overruled, and this would increase the costs involved and lead to more cases than the legal system could cope with.

It is therefore reassuring to note that the House of Lords has only exercised their discretion to overturn existing precedents by using the Practice Statement 1966 on rare occasions. However there are certain circumstances under which the House of Lords has felt that it is necessary to use the Practice Statement, and the power that it has to do so can be used to combat some of the problems which exist within the doctrine of stare decisis. The first of these is that the doctrine of precedent is rigid. From the point of view of certainty, this is a good thing because it leads to the benefits I have discussed earlier in this essay, but it also has its drawbacks, for example the fact the law is prevented from developing to meet a modern societies needs, and that bad decisions are perpetuated. Therefore circumstances in which according to Alan Paterson in The Law Lords (1982) the House of Lords might be prepared to use the Practice Statement include to modernise old legal decisions, and to correct serious errors of law, although the House of Lords has also indicated that it would not use the Practice Statement to overrule a previous decision on the grounds that it was 'merely wrong' but only where both the reasoning and the decision were wrong and there is a public interest in correcting the law.

In conclusion therefore it seems that the House of Lords has got the balance right in choosing whether to exercise it's discretion to use the Practice Statement. They will do so in order modernise the law and prevent the legal system becoming stifled, but generally pay heed to the vital need for certainty in the legal system and so use the power only rarely.

Answer C: The Practice Statement 1966 indicated a radical departure from the traditionally conservative position adopted by the most senior judges in the kingdom, namely the Lords of Appeal in Ordinary, that the needs of certainty within our legal system outweigh other considerations and indeed their own desire for judicial creativity. The classic embodiment of this conservative position was the statement in the *London Tramways* case in 1898, in which the (then) Lord Chancellor, declared that it would be a "disastrous inconvenience" if the House of Lords could review each previous decisions because it would mean "...having each question subject to being re-argued and the dealings of mankind rendered doubtful by reason of different decisions, so that in truth and in fact there would be no final court of appeal." In this essay the writer proposes to consider the effect on the doctrine of precedent of this "disastrous inconvenience" which was rendered possible by the Practice Statement.

The Practice Statement opened the doors on the potential to revisit and rejudge each legal issue afresh; nevertheless their lordships house has demonstrated their unwillingness to walk through these doors on more than a handful of occasions. A notable early exception to this unwillingness is the case of *British Railways Board v Herrington* in which the court reconsidered the rules on liability to child trespassers in the light of modern attitudes to the issue. This, then, is a typical example of why the House of Lords was prepared to offer itself the very freedom afforded by the Practice Statement, namely that "too rigid adherence to precedent may lead to injustice in a particular case and also unduly restrict the proper development of the law..." as the wording of the Practice Statement itself states. A further example is the case of *Miliangos v George Frank Textiles* where the House were prepared to extinguish from the precedent books a ruling that sterling should be the only currency in which judgment can be awarded, a position which, as Lord Denning asserted in the court of appeal was appropriate to the days of the empire than to modern global economies.

If it were only in the interests of modernising and developing the law and the need for a legal system to maintain its grip on current affairs that the law lords were prepared to use the practice statement then we might justifiably conclude that the small loss to certainty would be a worthwhile price to pay in order to maintain a modern and vibrant legal system. However this writer submits that the House of Lords has created confusion by its attempts to impose rules upon its own use of the Practice Statement, and then its departure from these rules in arbitrary cases. The epitome of the House's confusion over appropriate use of the practice statement is the case of R v Shippuri, in which the House took the opportunity to overrule its own very recent decision in Anderton v Ryan. In doing so, they appeared to show a reckless disregard for principles which previous incarnations of the House had declared to be applicable in deciding whether use of the Practice Statement would be appropriate. The first of these considerations was that the House should be especially cautious in using the Practice Statement in criminal cases, because of the "especial need for certainty" in criminal cases (as stated within the text of the Practice Statement itself). The second was that they should not use the Practice Statement to overrule a decision relating to statutory interpretation since this would constitute an infringement of the fundamental constitutional cornerstone that it is for Parliament to amend its statutes not the judiciary. Finally the house appeared to succumb to pressure to change a decision because it was 'merely wrong'. The academic furore which had resulted from the *Anderton* case had proved embarrassing and the House of Lords felt compelled to admit that they had got it wrong.

Thus we can conclude that for the main part, the House of Lords has maintained a conservative position to the use of the Practice Statement and has shunned the radical opportunities it offers. Nevertheless we cannot state this with absolute certainty because of the examples which conflict with this position. Hence it seems that the ultimate effect of the Practice Statement has been to create uncertainty and thus attack the notions of justice upon which our legal system is based Yet although we cannot predict when the House of Lords will use the Practice Statement this writer submits that there use of it has generally been too rare for the contention that there is now a lack of certainty in the legal system to realistically be sustained.

Answer D: The Practise Statement 1966 gave the House of Lords the oportunity to depart from there own previous decisions. Previously these had been binding on them under the principle of the *London Tramways* case decided in 1898. The justification for the old position was that it would cause uncertainty if the House of Lords changed it's mind all the time, and certainty is often equated with notions of justice, fairness and equality, as Holland and Webb point out in Learning Legal Rules, page 122. By 1966 the House of Lords had realised that if they always adhered rigidly to precedent they would be stuck with decisions which might be out of date and inappropriate for modern circumstances. So the Practise Statement gave the House of Lords a certain amount of freedom. In order to assess the affect of the Practise Statement, it is necessary to look at examples of how they have used this freedom, to conclude whether this has been at the expense of certainty.

It is impossible to draw firm conclusions about when the House of Lords will or won't use the Practise Statement, because it is a matter for there discretion in each case. However, educated guesses can be made. Alan Paterson in The Law Lords in 1982 suggested that the House would consider use of the Practise Statement in order to modernise the law. Two examples of this are the cases of British Railways Bord v Herrington and Miliangos v George Frank Textiles. The former changed the law on liability to children who trespass and harm themselves which previously had been based on Victorian liassez faire morality. In Miliangos, the question was over whether judgement should be given in sterling or in any currency. The more modern view was that sterling was no longer the gold standard it was in the previous case of Havana Railways, and that therefore the House of Lords should over-rule its previous decision.

However, the House of Lords can also use the Practise Statement to restrict the law, as well as develop it. An example of this is Murphy v Brentwood where limitations were imposed on the liability for pure economic loss by overruling the case of Anns v London Borough of Merton. Here, the House of Lords appeared to realise that liability for negligence under Donoghue v Stevenson had been taken too far and therefore narrowed it down again.

The House of Lords has given guidance in some cases about when they might use the Practise Statement, for example the statement itself says they would be more cautious in criminal cases because of the "especially need for certainty", and this is shown by their refusal to overrule the criticised decision of DPP v Shaw in R v Knuller. They also stated in Jones v DHSS that they would not use it in cases of statutory interpretation because this was a constitutional issue for Parliament rather than the judges to correct. They also stated that they would not use it simply to correct errors (although it might be argued they did this in Murphy v Brentwood). A case which seems to break all these rules is R v Shivpuri. This overruled Anderton v Ryan on the interpretation of the Criminal Attempts Act 1981. The issue was whether someone could be convicted of attempting to do something which was actually impossible, and there had been widespread critisism of the ruling. So the House of Lords ignored all their own guidelines and overruled it.

By looking at the way in which the House of Lords has used the Practise Statement, it seems that they do pay a lot of attention to the fact that the more they use it the less certain the law will be. If the House of Lords changes it's mind often, then there will be more litigation because people will not have confidence in the system of precedent and lawyers will not be able to advice there clients. It will also be difficult for people to form contracts with confidence based on the existing state of the law. The House of Lords has to remember that people rely on the certainly of the law. So they only use it rarely. However, it is going too far to say that they only use it in particular defined circumstances, because it is a matter for their discretion. In any case, the nature of the Practise Statement means the House of Lords cannot set binding rules for themselves because they could use overrule any rules a previous House had set. It seems that the most likely case where they would use it is to modernise the law, if they thought this would not have too many ramifications on people who had relied on the old law, and according to the terms of the statement itself, this is probably the most appropriate circumstance for them to use it, as long as this is done sparingly.

Appendix 6: Sample bibliographies

Here there are two sample bibliographies. One is what your bibliography will look like if you have adopted the Harvard system of referencing. The other shows what a bibliography would look like if you have used the numerical (footnoting) system. In both cases the British Standard has been used for the citing of secondary sources. Remember you should only rely on these if your institution does not provide you with a specified layout for a bibliography. All the sources referred to are fictional.

Harvard System; British Standard Bibliography

Statutes

Student Rights Act 1998
Punishment of Young Adults Act 2001
Study for Students (Higher Education) Act 1989

Cases

Higgins v Tatham (2001) 24 BLT 675
R. v Higham [2000] 2 All ER 356

Bibliography

DEPARTMENT FOR EDUCTION AND SKILLS, 2006. *Sleep patterns on the LLB programme.* [online] [accessed September 1, 2006] London: HMSO, http://www.dfes.gov.uk/highereducation/sleep.pdf
HIGGINS, E. and TATHAM, L., 2006. *The minds of law students*, 2nd edn, Manchester: Manchester Metropolitan University Press.
MEAN-PERSON, A. *et al.*, 2005. *Whip your students into shape.* 2005, 24 (4) *Journal of Lecturing* pp. 672–675.

Numerical System; British Standard Bibliography

Statutes

Student Rights Act 1998
Punishment of Young Adults Act 2001
Study for Students (Higher Education) Act 1989

Cases

Higgins v Tatham (2001) 24 BLT 675
R. v Higham [2000] 2 All ER 356

Bibliography

DEPARTMENT FOR EDUCTION AND SKILLS, 2006. *Sleep patterns on the LLB programme.* [online] [accessed September 1, 2006] London: HMSO, http://www.dfes.gov.uk/highereducation/sleep.pdf

HIGGINS, E. and TATHAM, L. 2006. *The minds of law students*, 2nd edn, Manchester: Manchester Metropolitan University Press.

MEAN-PERSON, A. *et al.*, 2005. *Whip your students into shape.* 24 (4) *Journal of Lecturing* pp. 672–675.

Index

STRODE'S COLLEGE
LIBRARY